AF594473

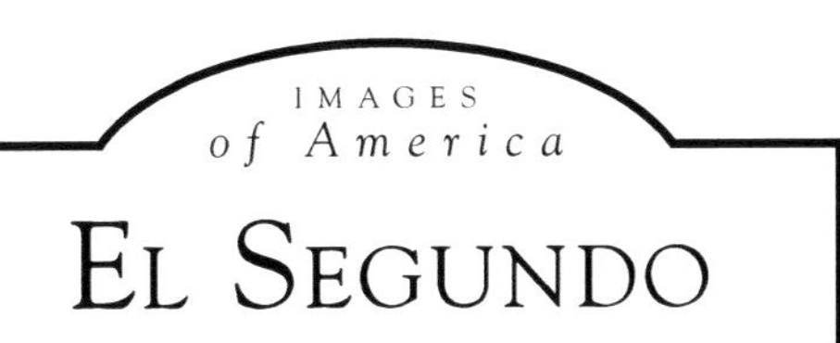
IMAGES
of America
EL SEGUNDO

On the Cover: In 1912, running on sand dunes, this Red Car on the Pacific Electric Railway line brought workers from Los Angeles to the Standard Oil Refinery in El Segundo. Then, it continued south to nearby beach cities. Although the young girl is unidentified, the banner reads "Direct to El Segundo the Standard Oil Payroll City." After they ceased operation in the 1940s, some of the Red Cars were used to create artificial underwater reefs about a half mile off the shores of the South Bay. (El Segundo Public Library History Room.)

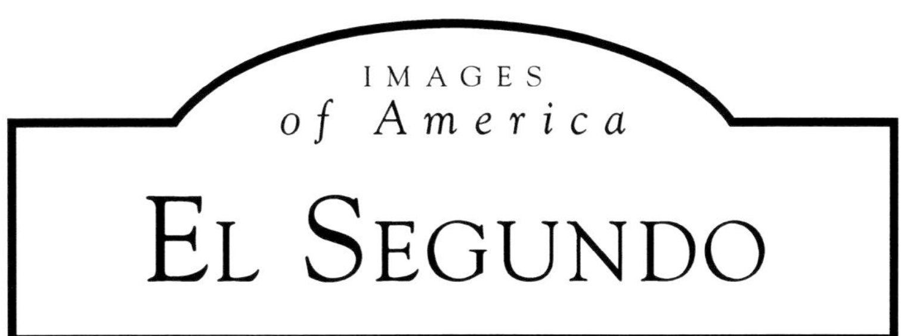

Debra Brighton

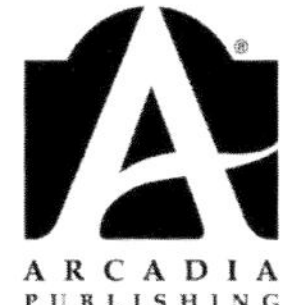

ISBN 978-1-4671-1589-6

Published by Arcadia Publishing
Charleston, South Carolina

Printed in the United States of America

Library of Congress Control Number: 2016941009

For all general information, please contact Arcadia Publishing:
Telephone 843-853-2070
Fax 843-853-0044
E-mail sales@arcadiapublishing.com
For customer service and orders:
Toll-Free 1-888-313-2665

Visit us on the Internet at www.arcadiapublishing.com

The photographs collected here, which span almost 11 decades of El Segundo history, are highly selective and represent only a very small fraction of what has been collected in the El Segundo Public Library History Room. Even the complete archives of close to 10,000 items, including photographs, yearbooks, maps, scrapbooks, multiple cabinet files, and collected memorabilia, could never tell the complete story of all the early pioneers of this town and how they left an indelible mark for future generations. Many of their families continue to live here. This book of images is dedicated to them. It is for all those who came before and worked hard to establish this very special town called El Segundo. It is also for those who live and work here now and who would like to better understand how this unique area of 5.5 square miles became the wonderful city it is today.

Contents

Acknowledgments

All photographs used for this work are with full permission of the Friends of the El Segundo Public Library, who own the archival collection. Special mention must be given to Sue Carter, former president of the Friends, and her 25 years of work to make the History Room in the El Segundo Public Library a special place for community research. Sue heads a history committee, and credit must also be given to the core group—Kerry King, Mark and Marcia Marion, Marie Milner, Howard Treloar, and Sharon Williams—for their service in committing time to gather and organize the materials and assist library users who visit the History Room.

A huge compilation of photographs and text called *El Segundo Seventy-Five Years: A Pictorial History of El Segundo, California* was published in 1991 by Eileen Curry Hunter. I will be forever in her debt and wish someday to thank her personally for all the assistance she gave me in identifying photographs and providing background material in her work.

I must also thank Lily Craig, who was the project manager for another historical work, called *Chevron El Segundo Refinery: Energizing California for 100 Years.* She was also instrumental in arranging access for the aerial shots in chapter 6 when I and a crew from the local cable TV station, Dan O'Toole and Robert Cetl, took many photographs one clear morning on top of the tallest building in the South Bay.

I am extremely thankful that Sari Brann, current president of the Friends, has taken over the reins of the History Room. She has spent countless hours making copies of the local newspaper, the *El Segundo Herald*, and organizing them into easily accessible files, maps, and scrapbooks.

Mark Herbert, senior librarian, has faithfully scanned all the photographs found in the archives for me and sent them to the publisher. My executive assistant, Jessie LeMay, deserves recognition for taking such excellent photographs of the newest developments in town, which are also in chapter 6.

Also, retired detective Craig Cleary generously donated photographs and related his personal involvement with the double homicide of officers Richard A. Phillips and Milton G. Curtis, the investigation, and the final arrest of Gerald F. Mason 46 years later.

This project could not have been completed without the approval of the El Segundo City Council and the city manager, Greg Carpenter, as part of the city's centennial celebration.

Introduction

The year was 1910, and the demand for crude oil was rapidly increasing due to booming automobile sales throughout California and across much of the nation. The Standard Oil Company of California began looking for a site in Southern California, since the refinery in Richmond was at maximum capacity and 600 miles away. R.J. Hanna was hired to look for sufficient acreage to construct a refinery for processing oil and housing a tank for storage. On June 11, 1911, Standard Oil purchased 842 acres near a clump of sand dunes where a farmer, Frank Bennett, was growing melons and lima beans. Hanna's wife is credited with naming the site El Segundo, Spanish for "the second," since the Richmond facility was "the first" in California.

The early decades were a time of tremendous development and formation of the city of El Segundo, not only at the local refinery but also on the 1,470 acres of land surrounding the plant. The promotion of El Segundo as Standard Oil's "payroll city" is heavily advertised in surviving postcards from that era, a banner on the Red Car that stopped on the sand dunes near town, and in the *El Segundo Herald*, which issued its first copy in the fall of 1911. The area on Richmond Street between Ballona Avenue (now El Segundo Boulevard) and Franklin Avenue, closest to the refinery, experienced the first and largest construction effort. A string of small retail shops, craftsmen stores, a hotel, and an apartment complex were built, along with a growing number of civic structures to administer them and keep them protected. This expansion grew farther southeast in the late 1920s and 1930s when Grand Avenue was also populated with grocery stores like Jensen's Market and Piggly Wiggly, a post office, and a Ford dealership. Finally, the first high school and grammar schools were built even farther out on Main Street and Mariposa Avenue.

Even before World War II began, Douglas Aircraft and North American Aviation were firmly established on the east side of town. Douglas was known for its World Cruiser biplanes, and North American built the popular B-25 series during the war. As production plants across America switched gears to the mass production of artillery for the war effort, so did El Segundo. However, this activity did not stunt the continuing expansion of the downtown area. From the photographs of this period, the community clearly desired a strong recreation program, its own public library, a plunge, parades, sports teams, dances, and a drive-in hangout called Patmar's. It pursued all those social structures and activities that hold a city together during times of great tragedy and sorrow.

More civic development projects were carried through in the 1950s and 1960s than at any other period before or since. A new city hall complex, including council chambers and a police department and fire department next door, were completed by the mid-1950s.

The construction of Recreation Park, including the George E. Gordon Clubhouse in 1956 and the Joslyn Center a decade later, took up an immense area of town to accommodate all the outdoor and indoor activities. Even the public library spread out into Library Park's southeastern quadrant as a new wing was built to accommodate more shelving to keep up with the growing demand for children's and adult materials. All this community pride makes the three tragic incidents and major losses during this time even more catastrophic. A downtown fire, a plane crash, and the brutal killing of two police officers will never be forgotten by many who lived through them. And, for the families that suffered the loss of the two young men in their prime, it will be carried in their personal life histories forever.

The last decades of the 20th century saw the east side of town flourish into multistory towers along the Sepulveda Boulevard corridor. Near the end of the 105 Freeway in El Segundo, corporate aerospace and satellite designers manufactured high-technology defense mechanisms to support the nation's military efforts and the local Los Angles Air Force Base. Other Fortune 500 companies in El Segundo, such as Mattel, also sprang up near Grand Avenue, plus several hotels in various locations, including Embassy Suites, the Hacienda, and Doubletree. The Metro Green Line was also completed in the mid-1990s, which provided an additional transportation option to mediate heavy auto traffic coming into the area. Back across Sepulveda Boulevard to the downtown area, an expanded library in 1992 brought information services into the modern era with an online catalog, more seating, and a remodeled children's room, History Room, and several small and large meeting rooms. A residential senior apartment complex called Park Vista was constructed. Several fire safety events and a K-9 program for the police department were started and became established traditions.

Now, we arrive at our centennial celebration with the local economy looking stronger than it has in many years, and many new developments in El Segundo are just beginning or nearing completion. Three large retail projects have been finished, called the El Segundo Plaza, the Edge and the Point. More hotel construction is under way, including the Hyatt Place, the Cambria Suites, Hampton Inn, and a remodeled Hacienda (to be two hotels, an Aloft and a Fairfield Inn). Several more highly anticipated developments on the horizon are the expansion of the Raytheon Campus, the Top Golf Project, and a new Los Angeles Lakers training center and sports arena.

In conclusion, it has been a wild ride. Although difficult to sum up in just a few words, the small-town atmosphere residents have come to know and love has survived a hundred years of massive growth and development; it has held on tight to deep social connections and community pride during the war and later, when more deep losses occurred; and finally, the city has found its way to becoming a mecca for big businesses and the aerospace industry, which heavily supports all the benefits of living and working in this amazing place called El Segundo.

One

Laying the Foundation 1910–1920

El Segundo Land and Improvement Company purchased 1,470 acres of townsite property on July 1, 1911, from J.S. Vosberg, who originally bought the land from Daniel Freeman in the 1880s. On October 12, 1911, the *El Segundo Herald*'s first issue reported that the city was "one that must be built, and built quickly to provide for the army of well-paid and highly skilled workmen that will pour out daily from the refining plant of the Standard Oil Company." By that time, according to Eileen Hunter's book *El Segundo: Seventy-Five Years*, the town already had "a meat market, two cigar stores, two barber shops, three rooming houses, two restaurants, one hotel, a plumbing shop, two lumber yards, a sign painter, a grocery store, and a general merchandise store." By February 1912, the first elementary class had 13 pupils enrolled. Interestingly, the school was located next door to a candy store.

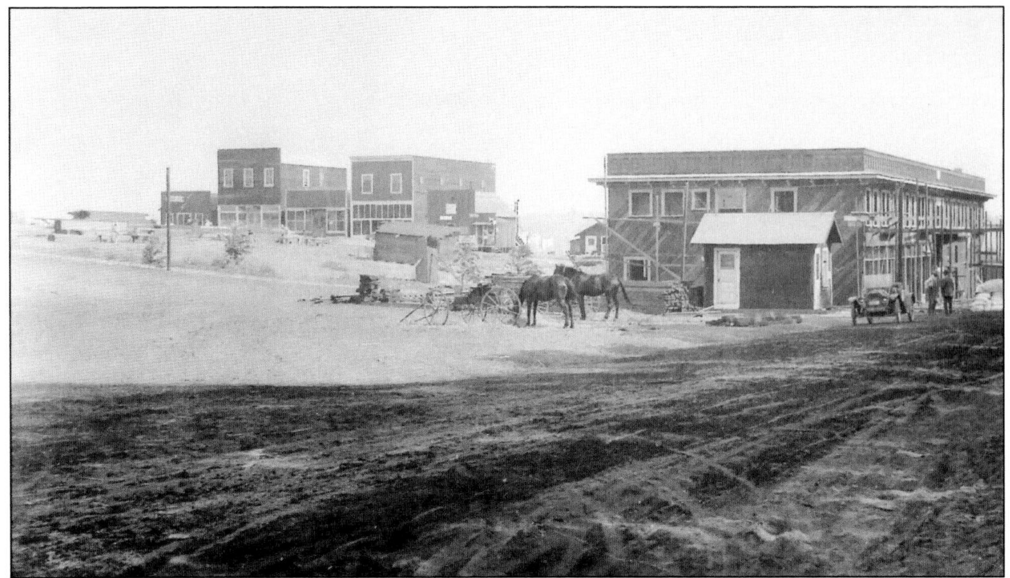

First Shops along Ballona Avenue (now El Segundo Boulevard) and Richmond Street, 1910. The formation of El Segundo as a town began along Ballona Avenue and Richmond Street in 1910. In this view looking east on Ballona Avenue, the early storefronts along Richmond Street are in the background. The El Segundo Hotel was being constructed in the right foreground facing Richmond Street. A drugstore, grocery, and café were soon to be open for business along the Ballona Avenue street-level side in the hotel.

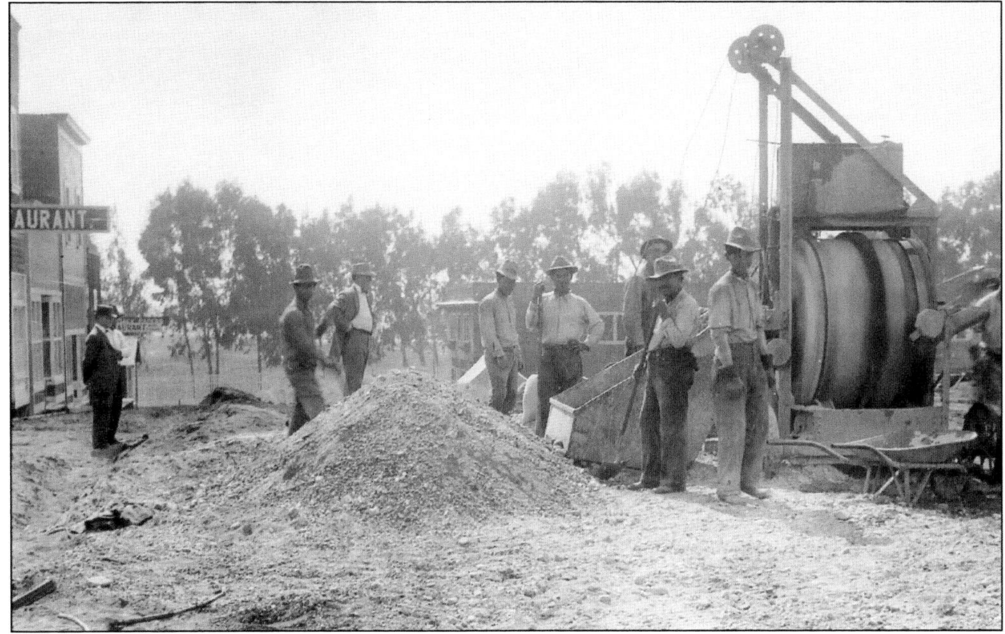

Richmond Street Construction, 1915. This is a postcard image of workers laying down the roadwork for early Richmond Street and Ballona Avenue in the background. Their machinery, storefronts, and the El Segundo Hotel (right back) are seen in a view looking south towards trees bordering the Standard Oil Refinery. The earliest known origin of the street name *Ballona* is from Rancho La Ballona, a land grant given to the Machado family in the 1820s.

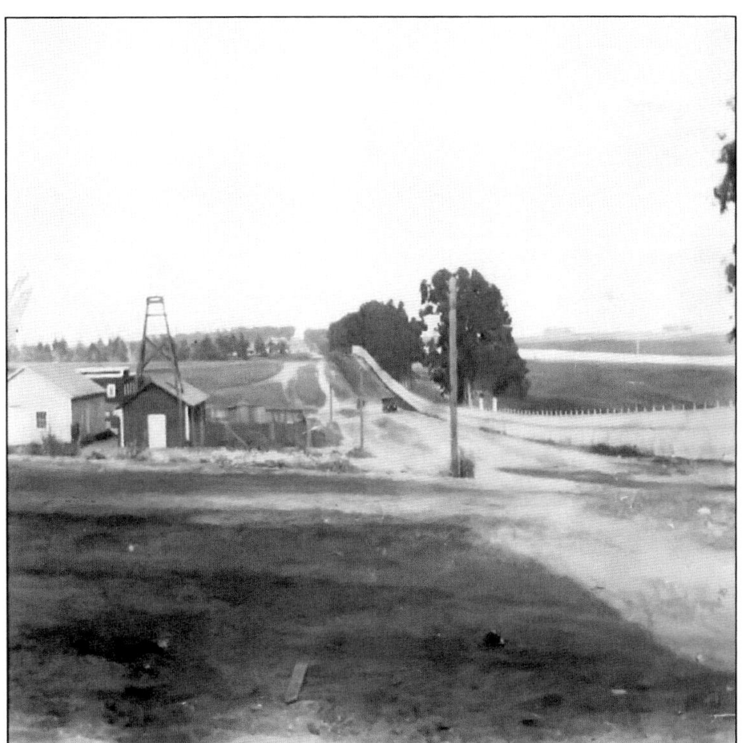

Main Street and Ballona Avenue as Dirt Roads, 1912. This view at the intersection of Ballona Avenue and Main Street is facing east, with a solid fence bordering the property of the Standard Oil Refinery. In the distance on the refinery side are two oil tanks, and traveling up the dusty Ballona Avenue is a lone driver maneuvering along the dirt lane.

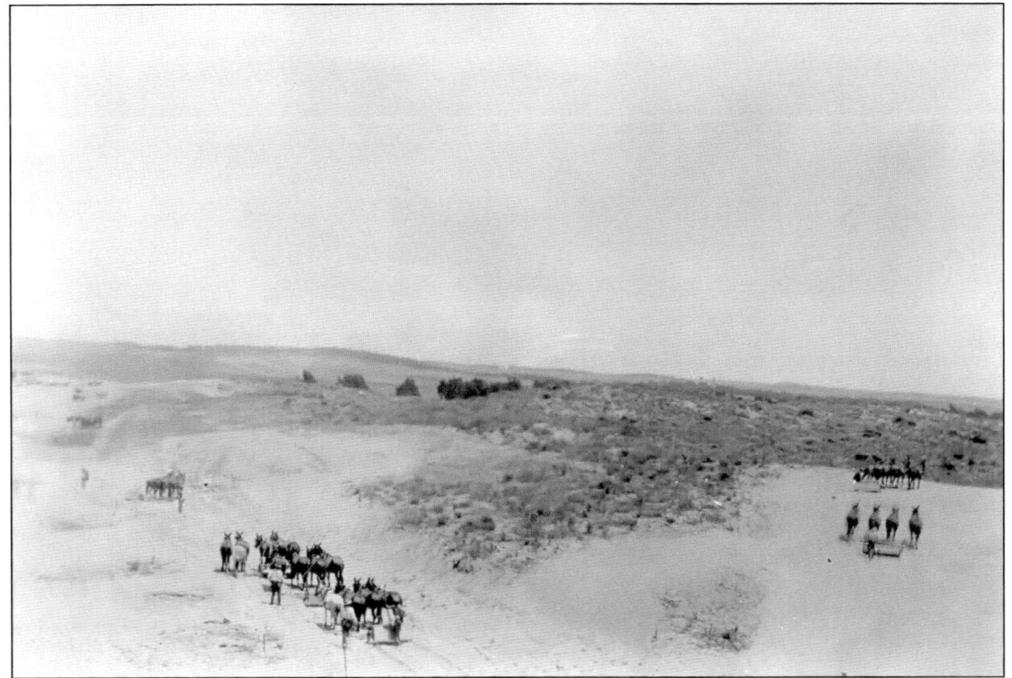

Standard Oil Refinery Site Preparation, 1911. Over 500 mules were used to level the sand dunes in preparation for the refinery. This is one of the earliest aerial views before the town and refinery were developed. It was taken looking westward from what is now the current area of Sepulveda Boulevard at the eastern boundary of the refinery.

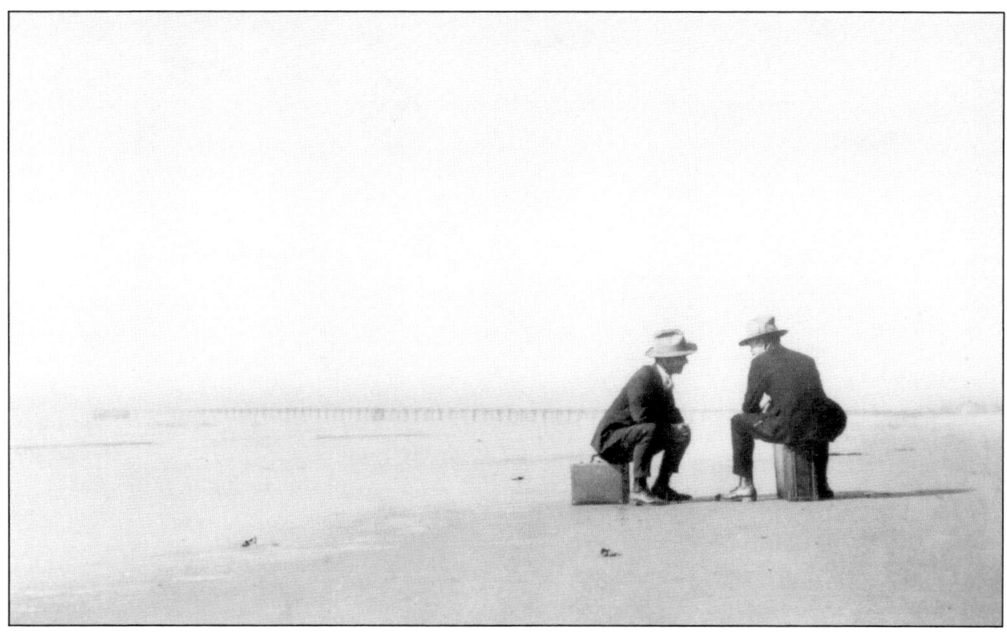

TAKING A MEETING, 1912: DAVID W. PETERSON (LEFT) AND RICHARD J. HANNA. Fifty-year-old R.J. Hanna was assigned the task of building and managing the new refinery. The Peterson family is still very prominent in the community and is involved with a number of civic organizations and charitable events.

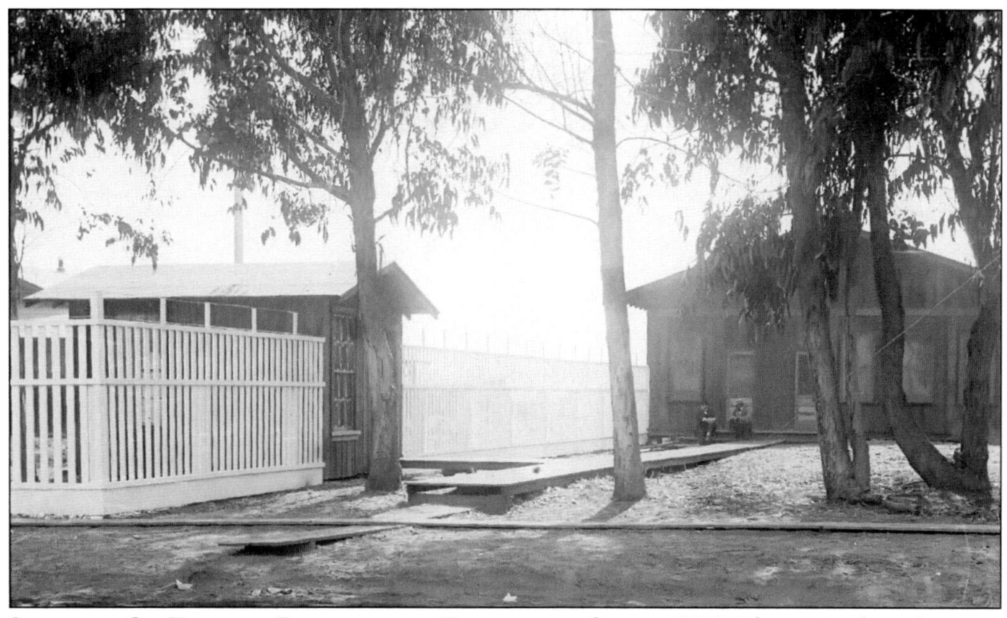

STANDARD OIL EMPLOYEE ENTRANCE AND EMPLOYMENT OFFICE, 1911. The original employment office of Standard Oil is on the right. The entrance to the refinery is the building on the left.

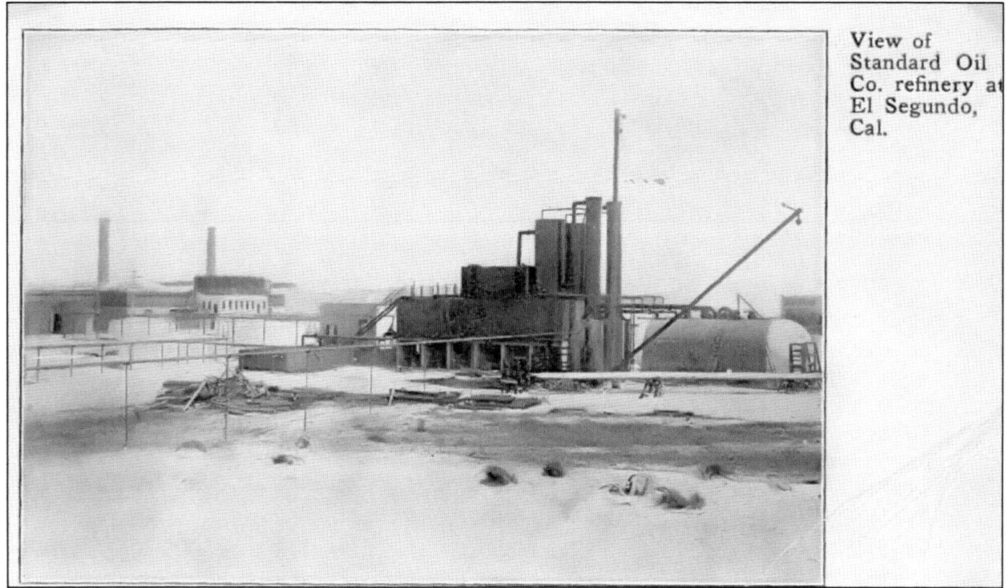

Postcard of the Early Standard Oil Refinery, 1912. The front of the postcard is shown above and its reverse below. Postcards were published by the Neuner Company of Los Angeles to encourage land investors to buy in El Segundo. The description of the town on the back mentions the "mammoth refinery" with a "growing payroll." The card also states that the town has 75 residences, a bank, a newspaper, hotels, churches, a school, and electric lights.

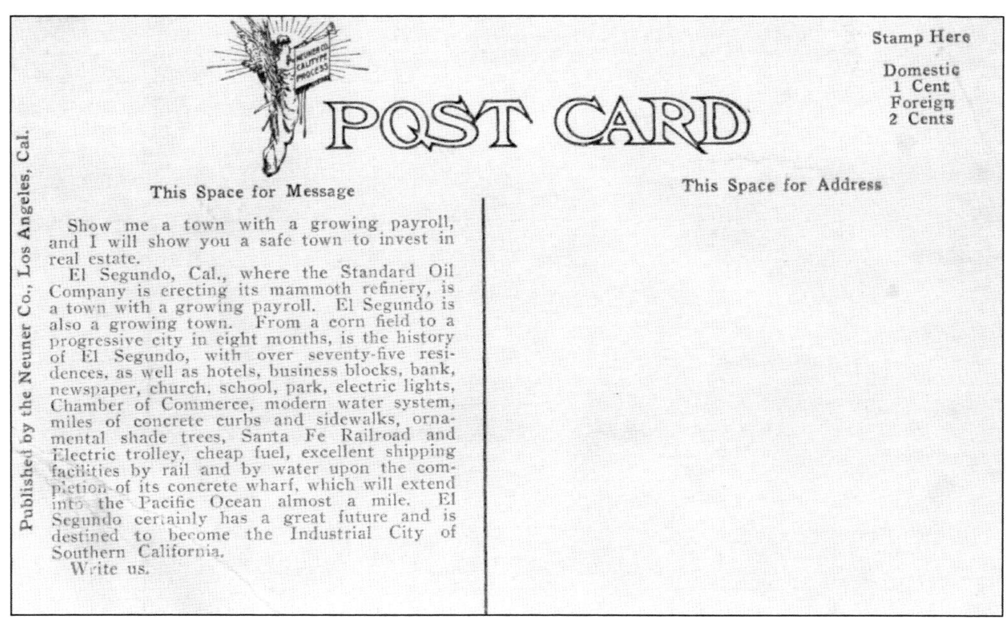
POST CARD

Stamp Here

Domestic
1 Cent
Foreign
2 Cents

Published by the Neuner Co., Los Angeles, Cal.

This Space for Message

Show me a town with a growing payroll, and I will show you a safe town to invest in real estate.

El Segundo, Cal., where the Standard Oil Company is erecting its mammoth refinery, is a town with a growing payroll. El Segundo is also a growing town. From a corn field to a progressive city in eight months, is the history of El Segundo, with over seventy-five residences, as well as hotels, business blocks, bank, newspaper, church, school, park, electric lights, Chamber of Commerce, modern water system, miles of concrete curbs and sidewalks, ornamental shade trees, Santa Fe Railroad and Electric trolley, cheap fuel, excellent shipping facilities by rail and by water upon the completion of its concrete wharf, which will extend into the Pacific Ocean almost a mile. El Segundo certainly has a great future and is destined to become the Industrial City of Southern California.

Write us.

This Space for Address

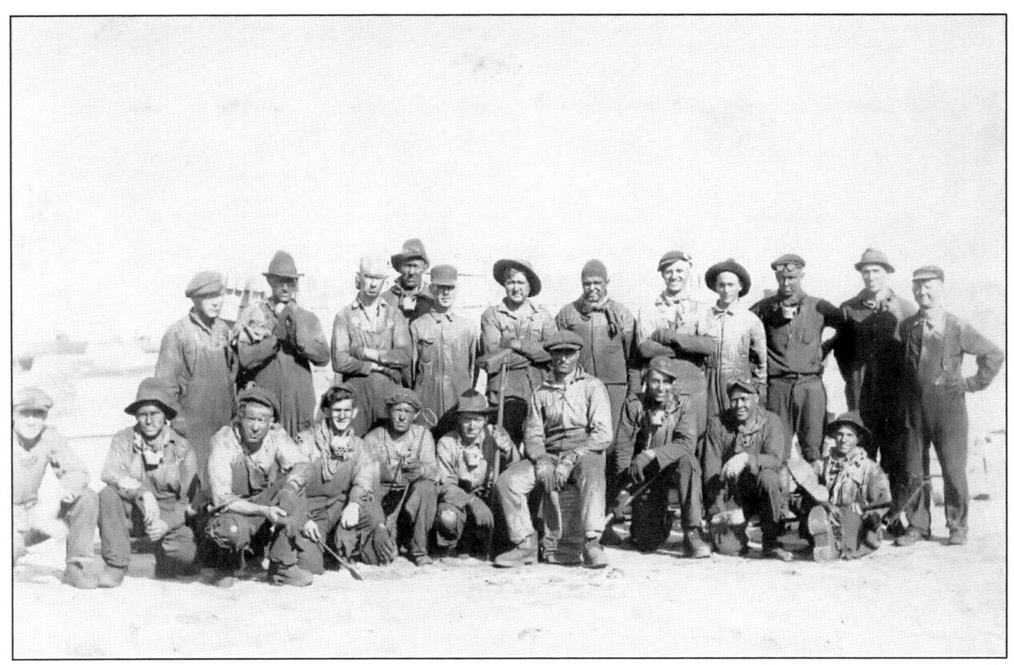

STANDARD OIL STEEL CLEANERS, 1911. These men were also known as "chimney sweeps." People came from all over the country to work at the new refinery.

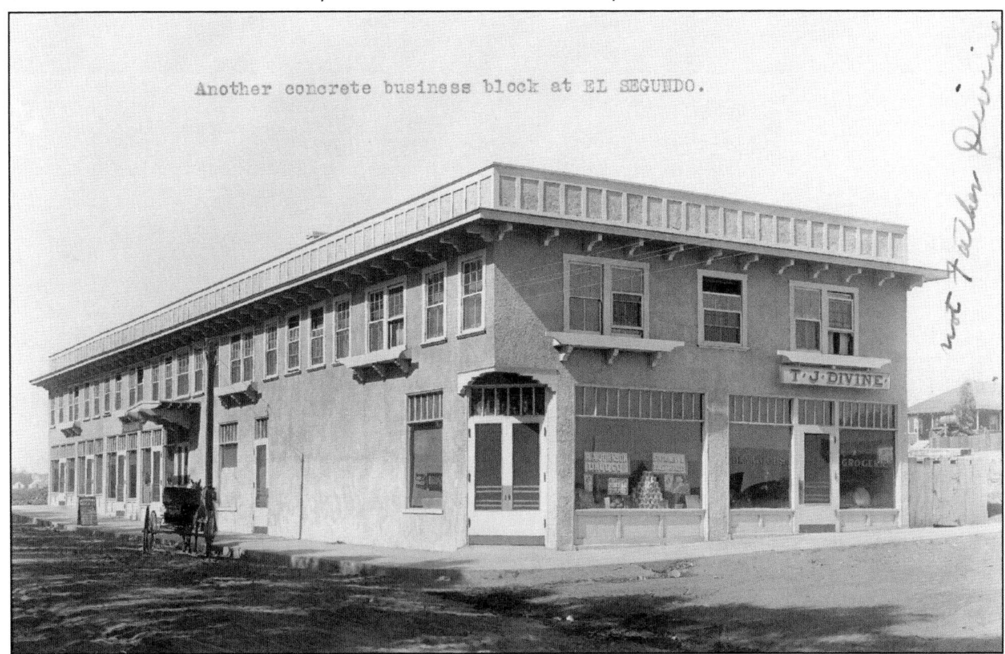

THE FIRST HOTEL, THE EL SEGUNDO HOTEL, 1910. The newly built El Segundo Hotel was located at the northwest corner of Richmond Street and Ballona Avenue. The first floor facing south on Ballona had two proprietors—R.A. Johnson Drug Company and T.J. Divine Groceries. Located along the Richmond side facing west was Mrs. J.G. Davis' Café. Her menu board on the sidewalk reads: "Restaurant Meals 25," which most likely means the offerings were 25¢. Later, this was the site of the first library.

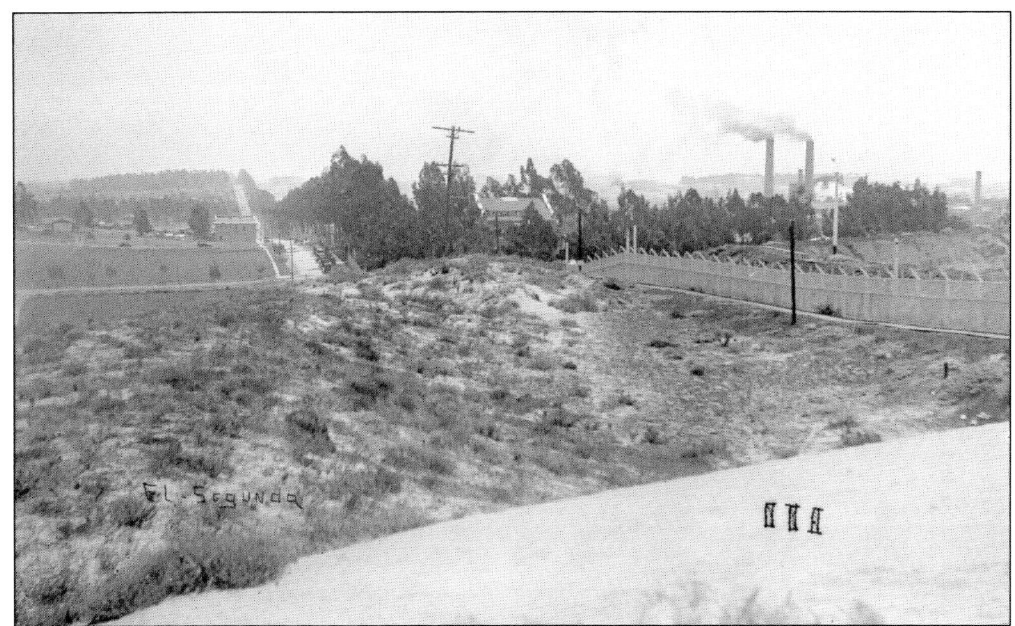

VIEW FROM THE SAND DUNES, 1911. This is another early postcard depicting the start of the sand dunes west of Ballona Avenue with a southeastern view of the developing town. The smokestacks of Standard Oil on the right show the refinery already in production. The back of the card reads: "J. Griffin, gift, B. Longworth."

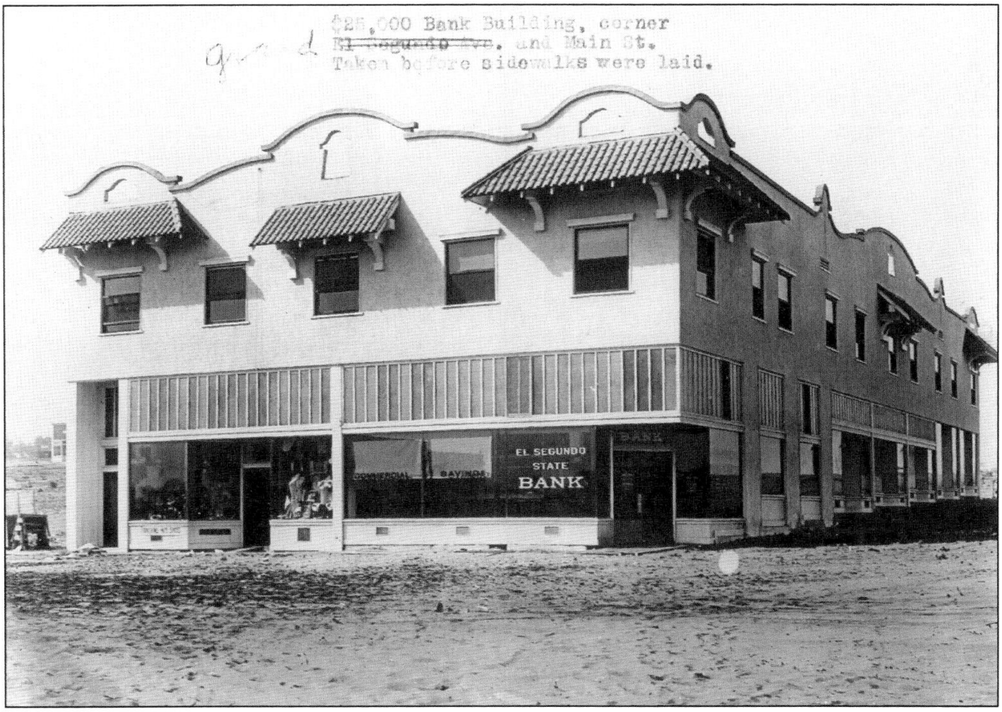

EL SEGUNDO STATE BANK, 1910. The El Segundo State Bank was located at the corner of Grand Avenue and Main Street. Text on the photograph reads: "$25,000 Bank Building . . . Taken before sidewalks were laid."

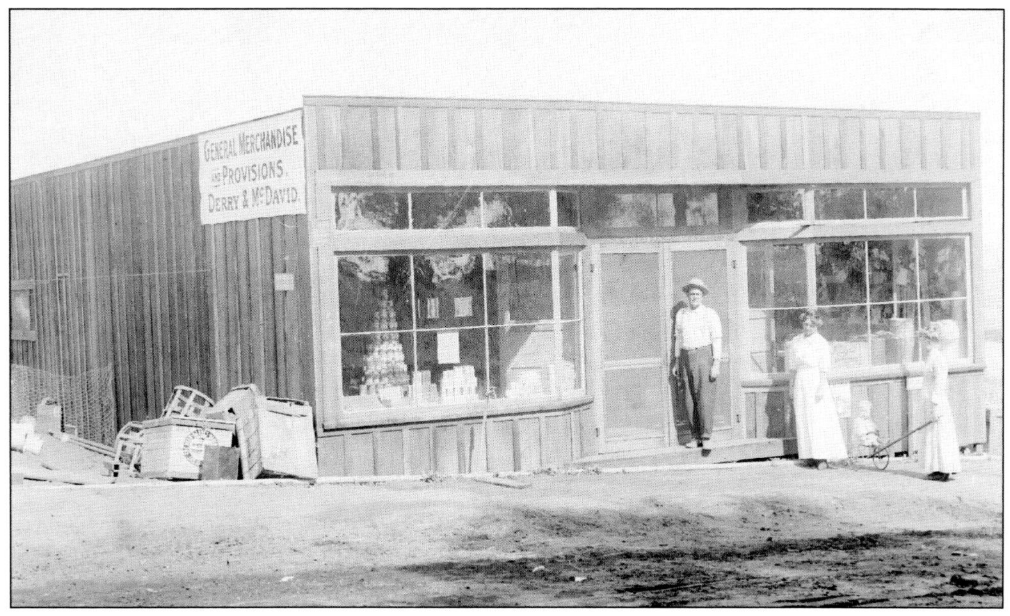

GENERAL MERCHANDISE AND PROVISIONS, DEARY AND MCDAVID, 1912. This postcard image shows Derry and McDavid's General Merchandise and Provisions store. An unidentified man, two women, and a small child (in a stroller) are in front of the building. On the back of the postcard is inscribed: "1912, on El Segundo Avenue between Main and Richmond."

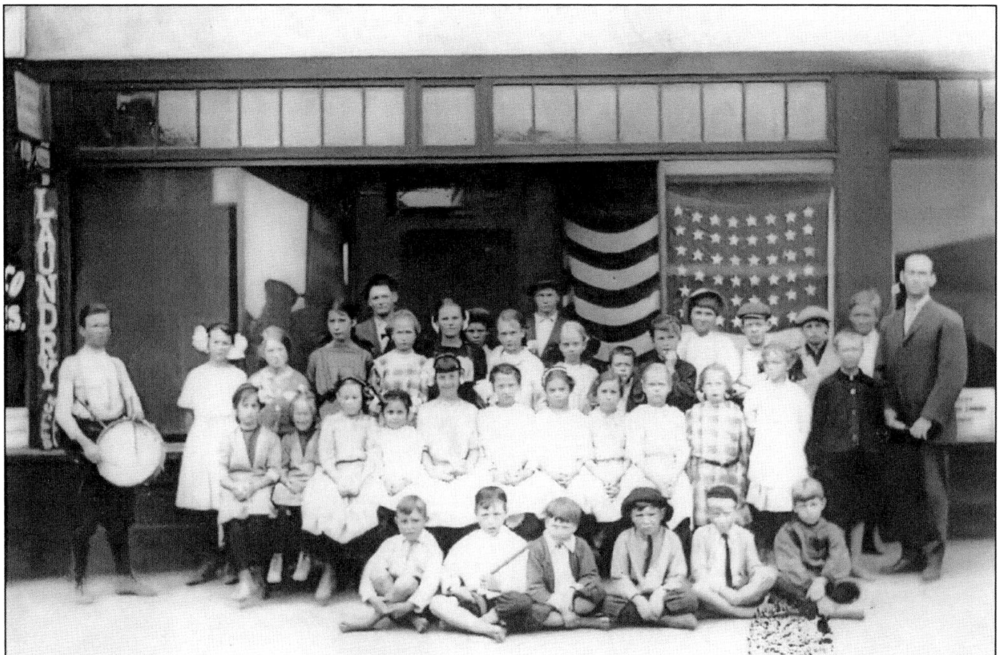

STOREFRONT ELEMENTARY SCHOOL, 1912. The first elementary school classes were held in a store on Richmond Street. The drummer on the far left is Tom Stennett.

EXTERIOR OF MARTIN & ELLIS STORE, 1911. The inscription on the bottom of this photograph boasts of Martin & Ellis as being the "First Store in El Segundo," located on the 100 block of Richmond Street. The signs advertise "Dry Goods" on the left window, "Groceries" on the right window, and "We Sell Every Thing" on the side awning.

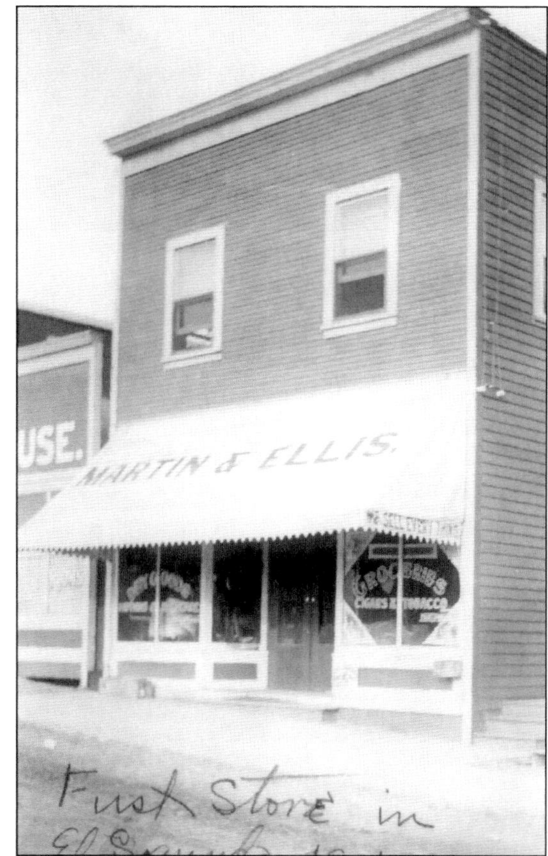

INTERIOR OF MARTIN & ELLIS STORE, 1911. A rare and early photograph of the interior of an El Segundo business includes a handwritten note on the bottom left that reads: "1911 Inside Same Store." The writing on the lower right appears to indicate that "Garner and Nell Ellis" are pictured.

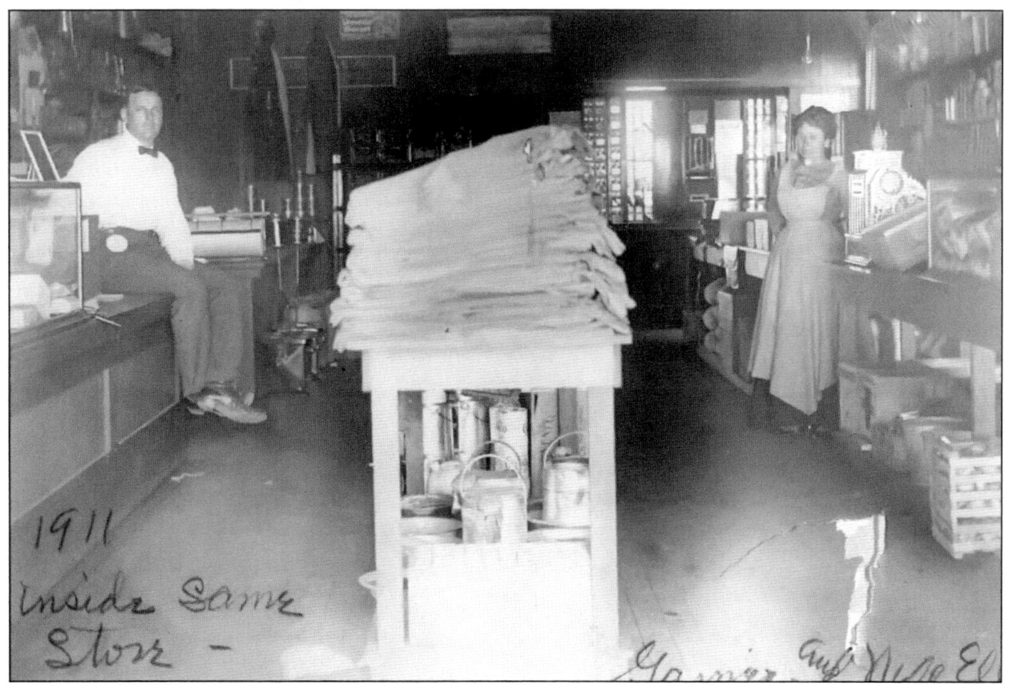

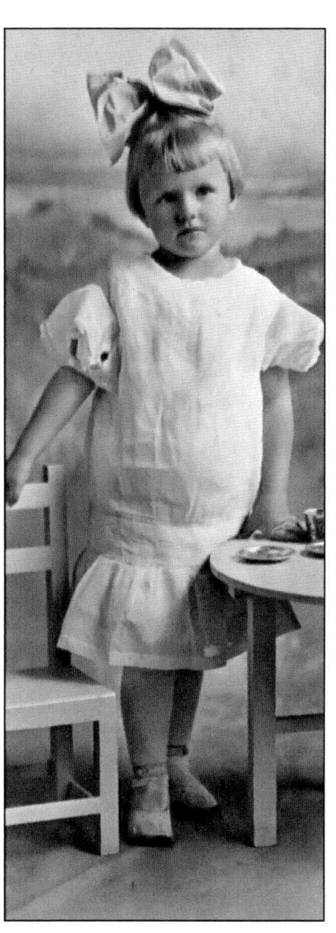

Dorothea Fitzgerald, c. 1916. Little Dorothea Fitzgerald grew up to work at the El Segundo Public Library from 1933 to 1978, becoming the chief librarian in 1954. She was instrumental in expanding the library twice at its current location in Library Park. Her aunt Virginia Fitzgerald was El Segundo's first librarian from 1916 to 1919 in the El Segundo Hotel.

Richmond Street School, 1912. The first grammar school was built at a cost of $12,000. This early site is where the current Richmond Street Elementary School is located at the northwest corner of Richmond Street and Mariposa Avenue.

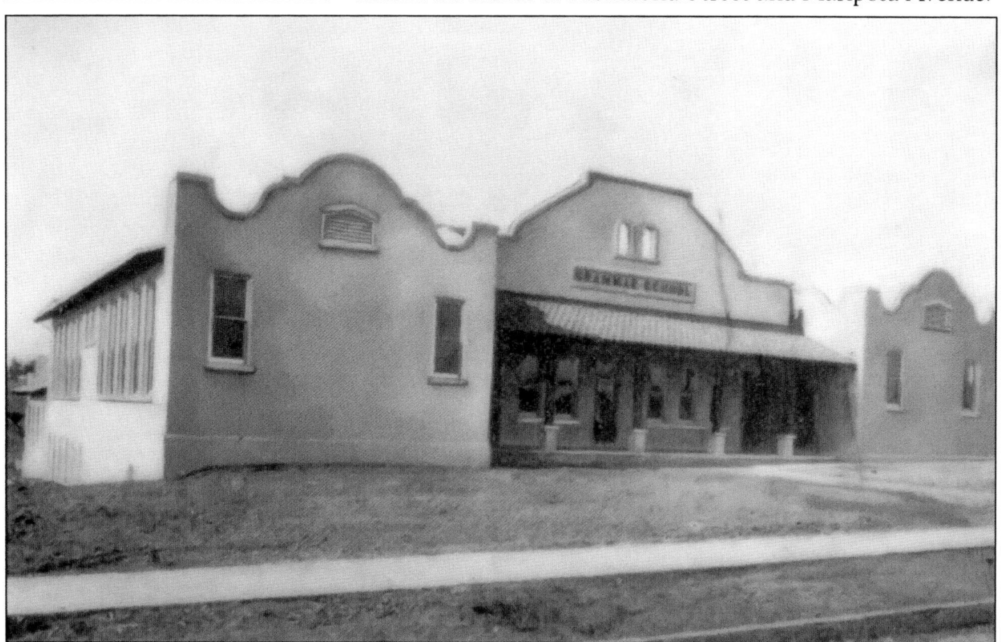

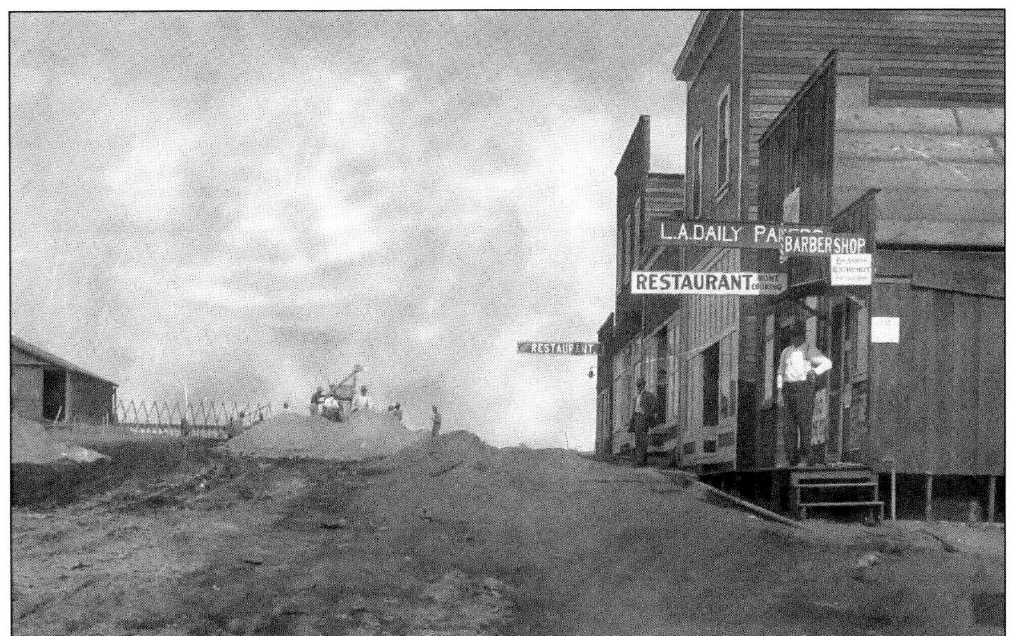

CONTINUED RICHMOND STREET CONSTRUCTION, 1917. Another construction view of Richmond Street looks north with a crew working on paving the street for the expansion of more shops and businesses in town.

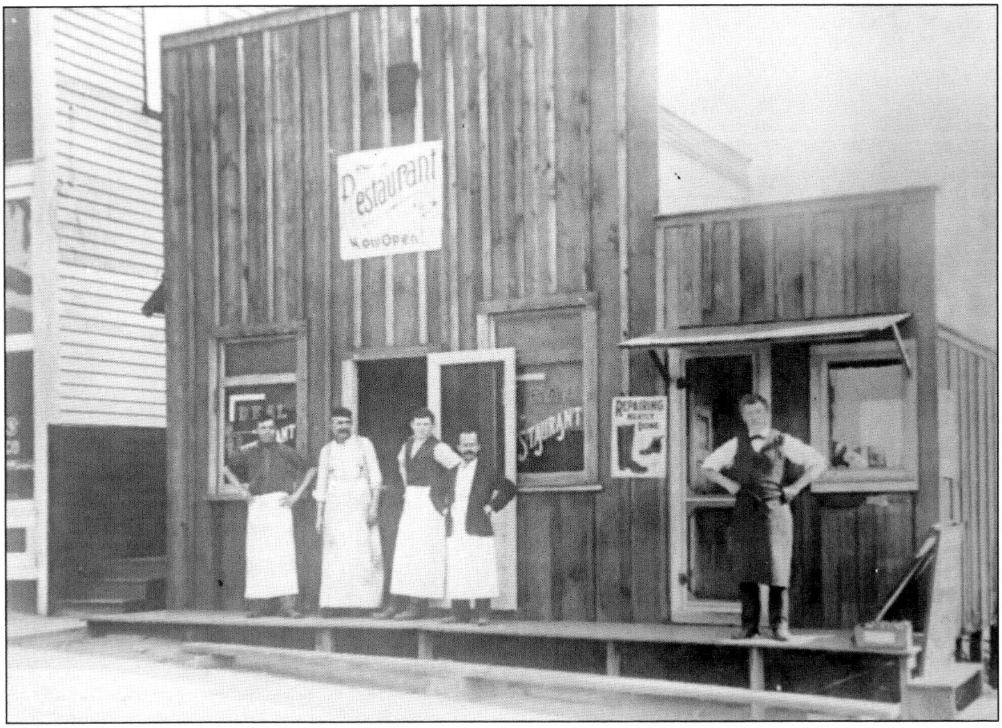

DEAL RESTAURANT WITH ADJACENT SHOE REPAIR STORE, C. 1914. The 100 block of Richmond Street continued to expand with the Deal Restaurant and shoe repair establishment. The sign outside the shoe store reads: "Repairing Neatly Done."

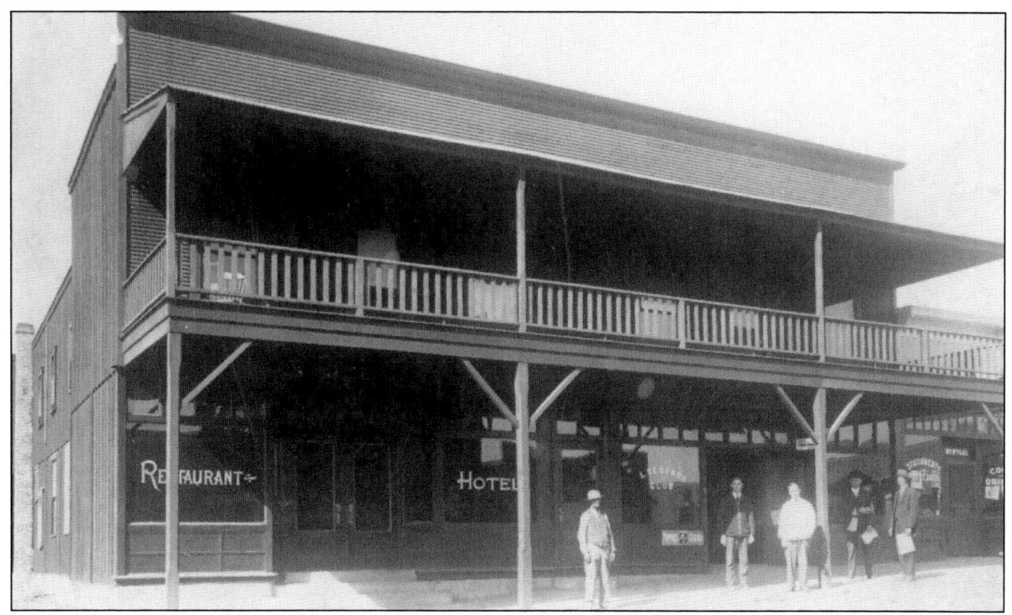

Segundo Club Hotel and General Store, c. 1914. Another hotel and general store opened on Richmond Street after the first El Segundo Hotel. This exact location is unknown.

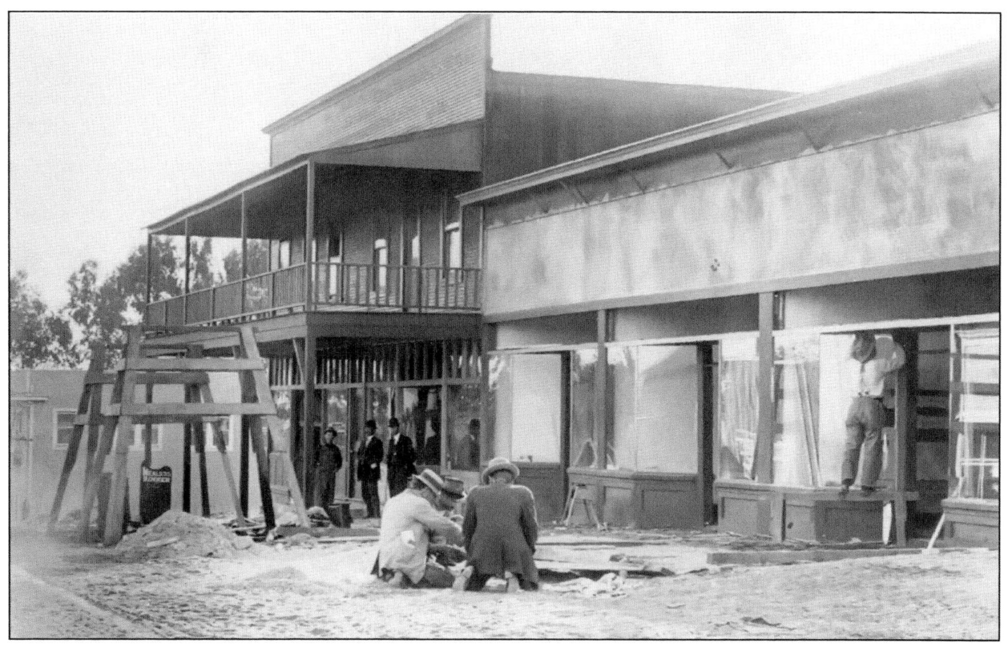

Rebuilding the 100 and 200 Blocks of Richmond after a Fire, 1919. On May 10, 1917, a fire swept through Richmond Street, leaving the downtown section in ashes. Red brick began to replace timber as building material. In June 1917, eighteen men formed a volunteer fire department under the direction of fire chief G.W. Dragoo.

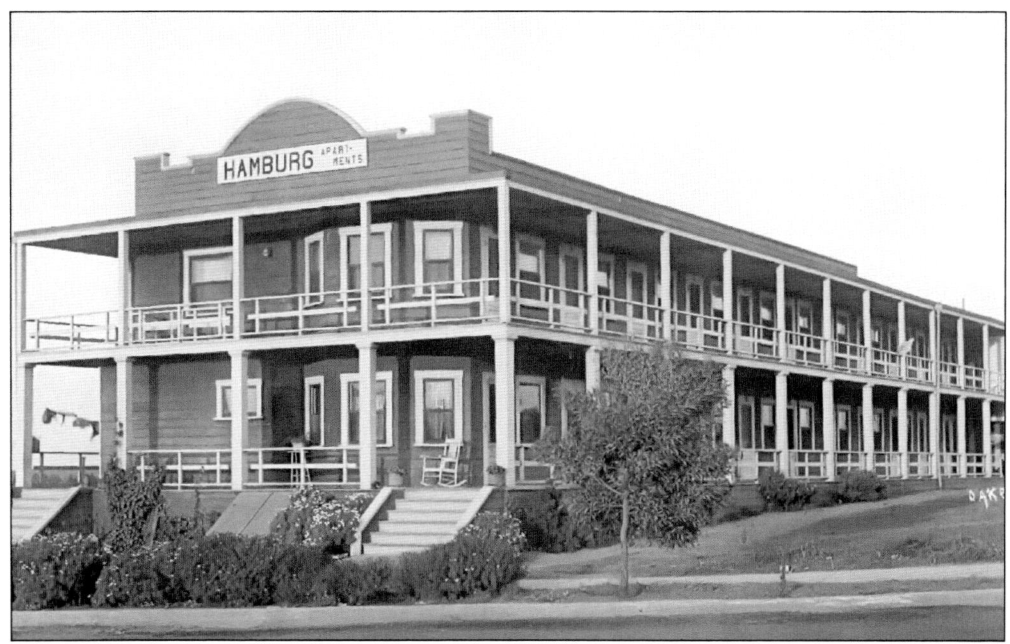

Hamburg Apartments on Concord Street, c. 1911. This apartment building was nicknamed "the Showboat" because it looked like a riverboat when the ditch to the north side of the building flooded during rains. The building still exists today at 210 Concord Street.

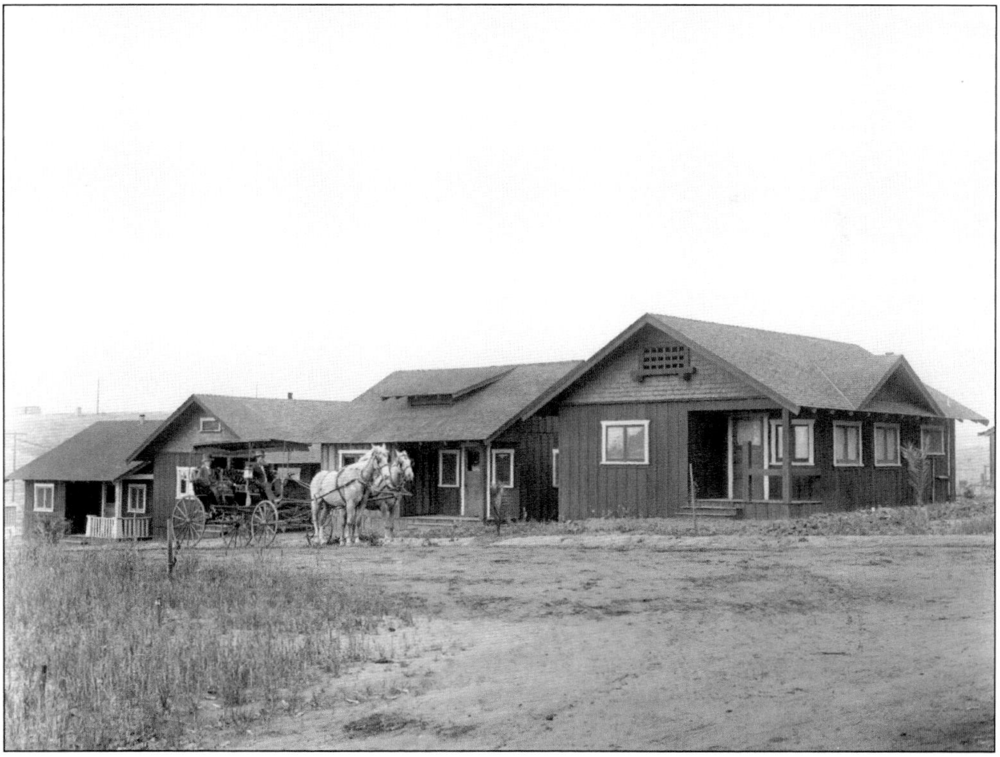

Homes for Standard Oil Workers, 1912. A horse-drawn carriage stands in front of the worker homes at the intersection of Arena Street and Ballona Avenue.

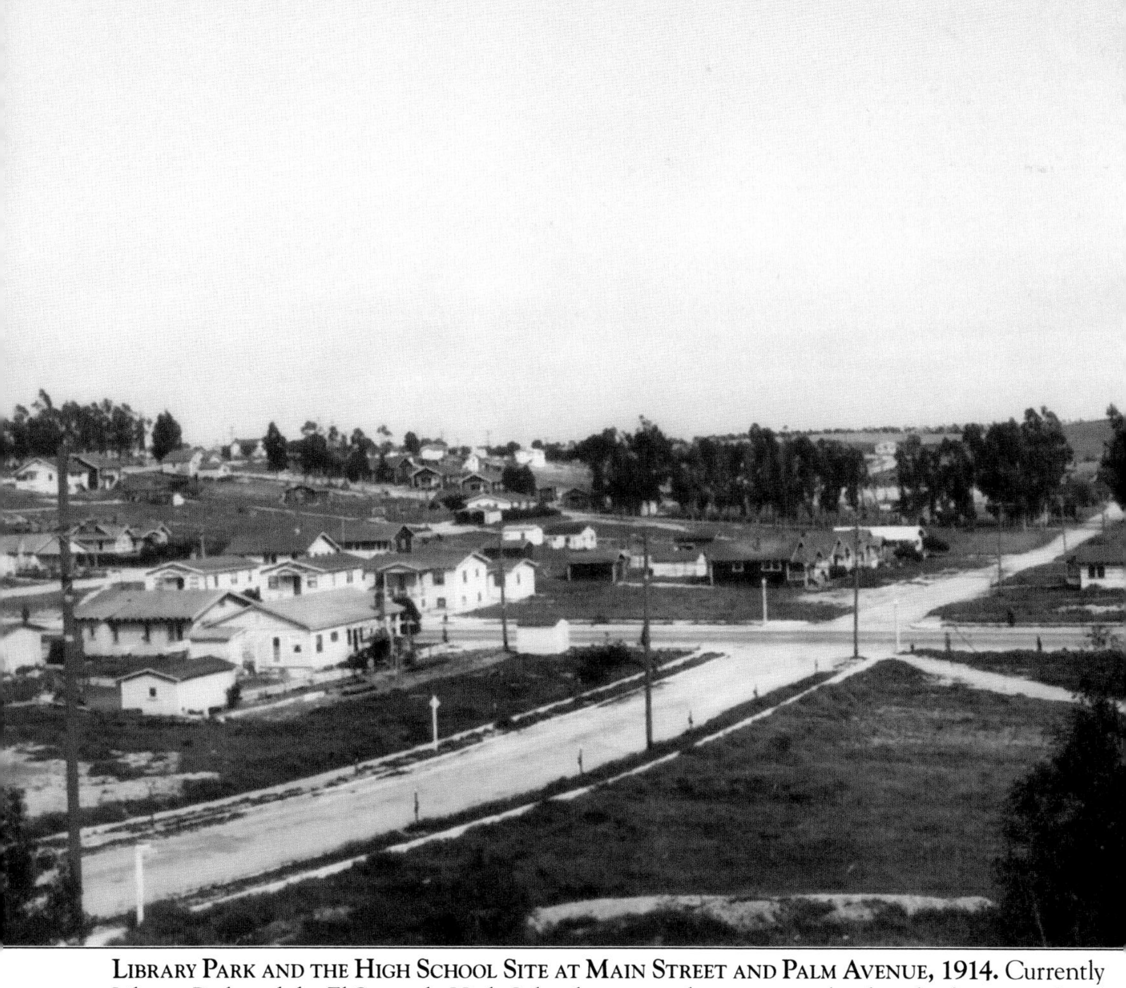

Library Park and the High School Site at Main Street and Palm Avenue, 1914. Currently Library Park and the El Segundo High School campus, the expansive land in the foreground and background predates both the high school and library buildings. The Methodist church, which

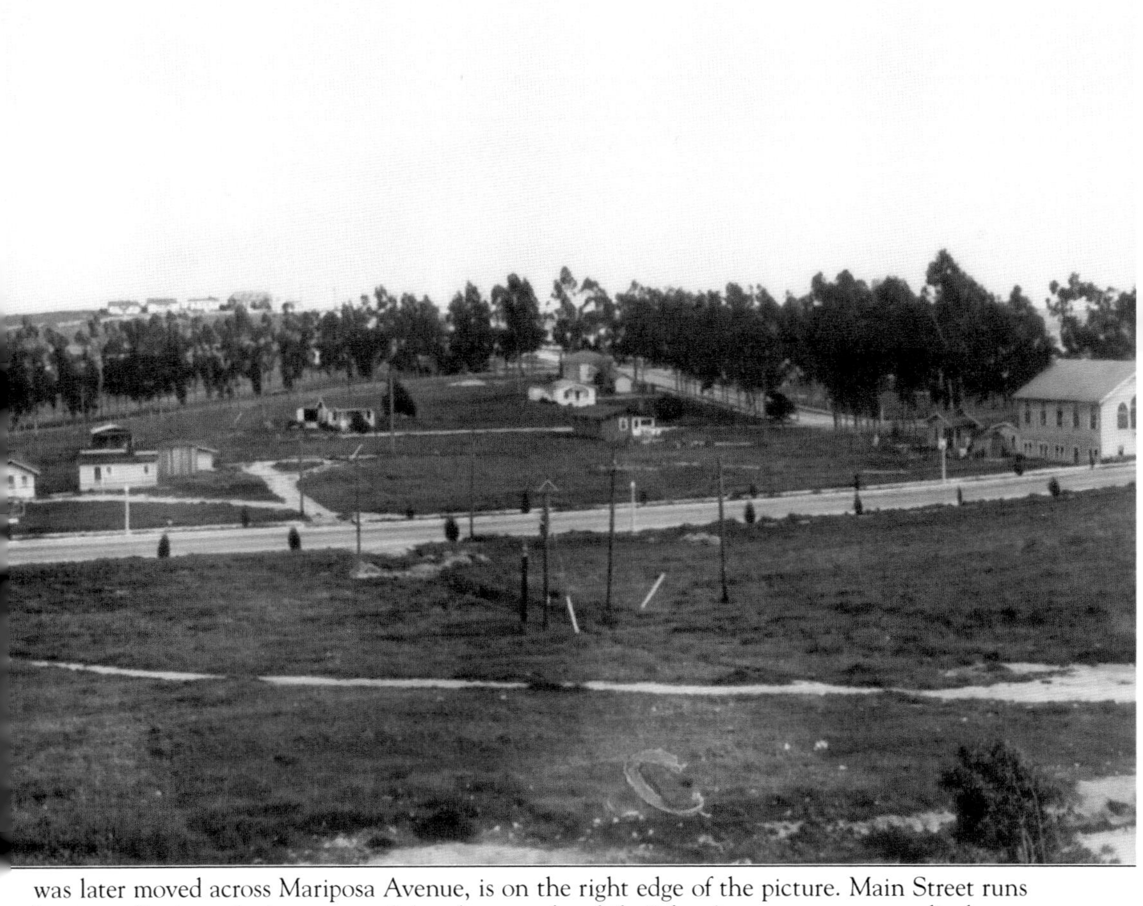

was later moved across Mariposa Avenue, is on the right edge of the picture. Main Street runs horizontally through the center of the photograph, while Palm Avenue runs perpendicular on the left side.

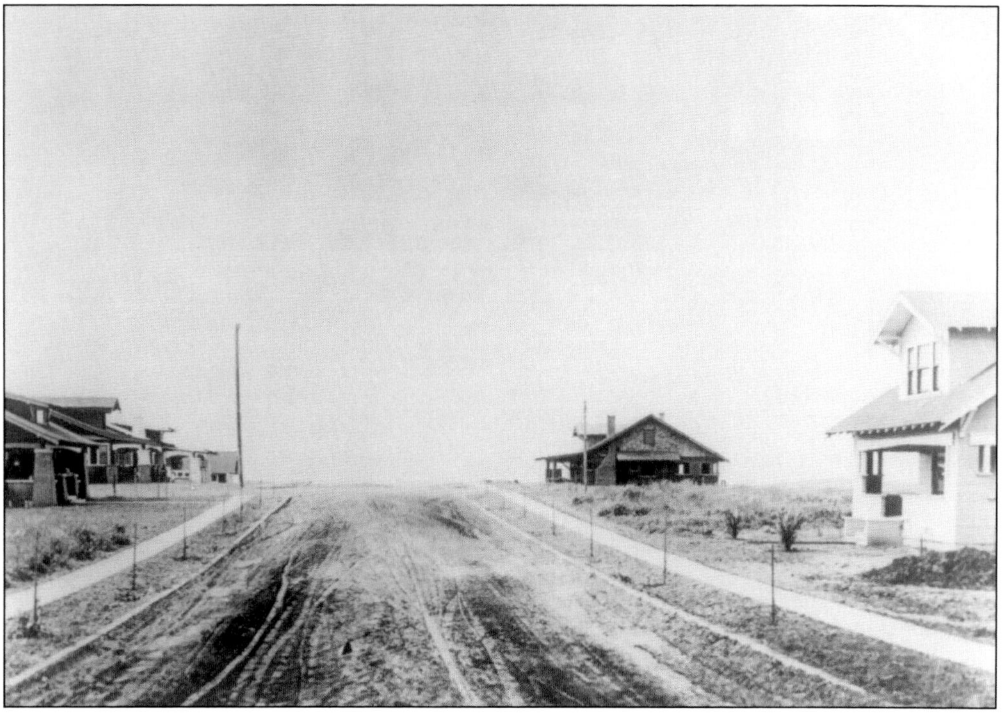

View of Virginia Street Looking North, c. 1912. Text on the back of the photograph states that Virginia Street is "seven months old."

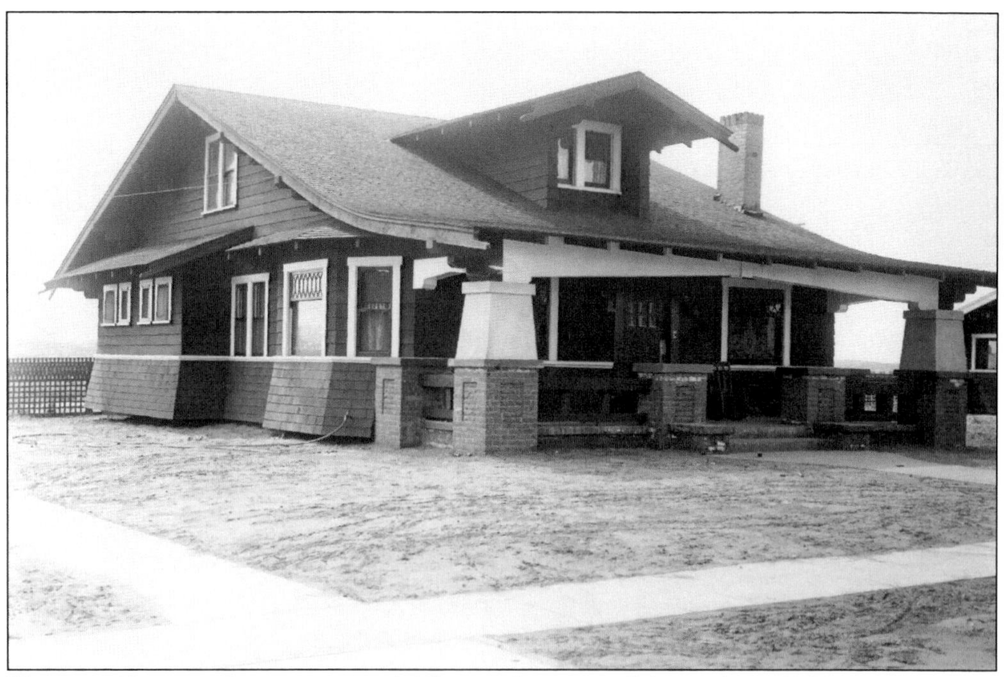

Home on Virginia Street, c. 1915. This residence is still located at 403 Virginia Street at the northwest corner of Holly Avenue. Many of the early homes in this neighborhood still exist today.

"Why You Should Buy a Lot at El Segundo." This advertisement is taken from a 1916 edition of the *El Segundo Herald*.

Why You Should Buy a Lot at El Segundo

"The Standard Oil Pay Roll City"

--THE CITY THAT MUST GROW!

— no two ways out of it — EL SEGUNDO SIMPLY HAS TO GROW!
— location, environment, natural advantages, present activities all demand it!
— El Segundo has already demonstrated that it will, in a few years, be the hub of industrial activity adjacent to Los Angeles.
— business—commerce—manufactures—industries are the real backbone of any community, the creator of real estate values.
— of these El Segundo already has several, either in operation or in course of construction, which will employ several hundred men
— with other big industries to follow!

Here's the "Why" of It-

Here's why these big companies have found El Segundo the only logical spot in the Southland for the location of their manufacturing plants.

STANDARD OIL $6,000,000 REFINERY — with a daily capacity of 30,000 barrels, utilizing the entire output of the Whittier-Placentia-Fullerton oil fields.

LAMBERT MFG. CO. — who will manufacture Steel Tractors in their new factory.

— on the coast! Cheap water transportation!
— near Standard Oil Refinery means cheap fuel!
— three railroads afford ideal transportation facilities!
— low priced factory sites!
— ideal home environment for workmen and families!
— superior educational advantages!
— equable climate that permits work all year 'round!

Don't Flirt With Destiny— Buy a Lot NOW For $500!

These same $500 lots, some of them only six blocks from the refinery, are the future Business Property of El Segundo!

Nothing can prevent it — El Segundo's as sure, as safe as a gold bond!

Read the handwriting on the wall — buy your lot NOW, before prices advance — for every new industry means increase in real estate values.

It's up to YOU whether you will share in the substantial, sure-to-come profits awaiting the wise El Segundo investor.

A little down, a small monthly payment is all you need. El Segundo and its "already-here" activities is its own best argument.

SEGUNDO LAND & IMPROVEMENT CO.
15 Merchants Nat'l Bank Bldg., Los Angeles
Phones Broadway 372. Home F4189
EL SEGUNDO OFFICE: Bank Building, El Segundo

Lots for Sale, c. 1915. Prospective El Segundo residents acquire real estate lots near the El Segundo Hotel at Grand Avenue and Main Street. According to a 1915 edition of *Out West Magazine*, "The soil of El Segundo is a rich, sandy loam very easily worked, and so rich that everything grows most luxuriantly." Pictured in the background is the north face of the Grand Hotel.

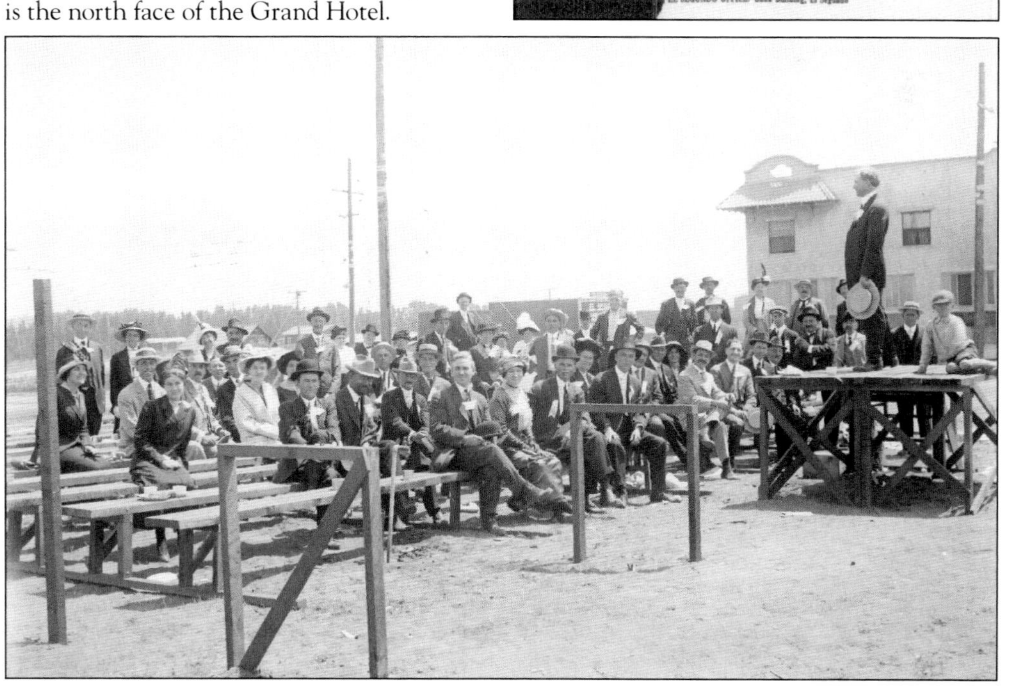

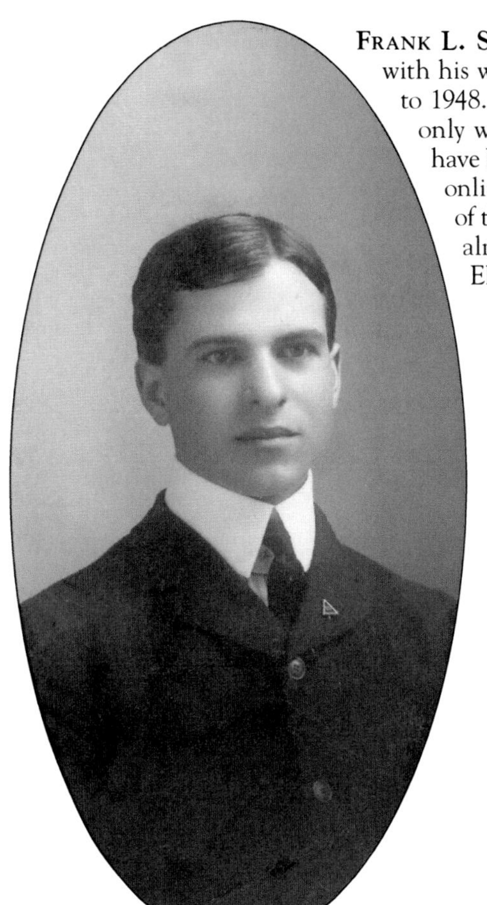

Frank L. Snow, c. 1911. Frank Snow was the co-owner with his wife, Marcia, of the *El Segundo Herald* from 1929 to 1948. This publication still exists today as the town's only weekly newspaper. Recently, issues of the *Herald* have been converted from microfilm and made available online through a generous contribution by the Friends of the El Segundo Public Library. There is accesses to almost 100 years of the *Herald* through a link on the El Segundo Public Library's website.

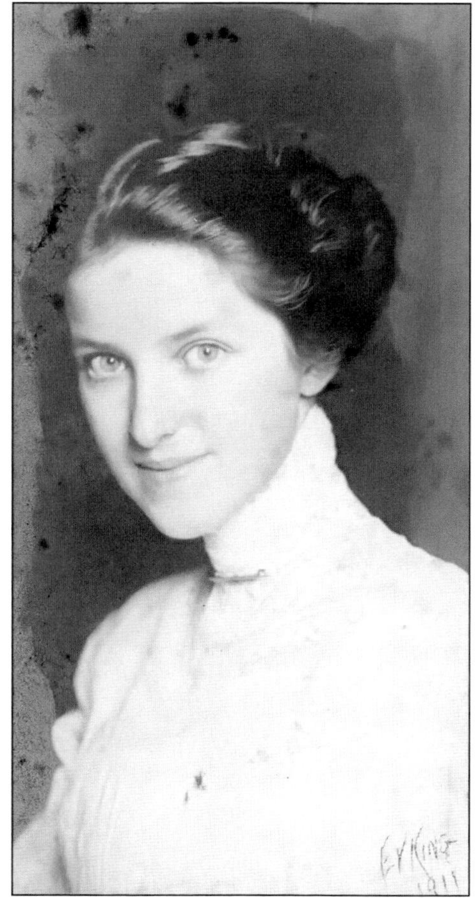

Marcia Snow, c. 1911. This photograph shows a younger Marcia Snow before she became the co-owner of the *El Segundo Herald* with her husband, Frank, from 1929 to 1948.

CITY TRUSTEES TOOK OATH OF OFFICE MONDAY EVENING, JANUARY 19, 1917. This photograph shows a 1917 article in the *El Segundo Herald*.

CITY TRUSTEES TOOK OATH OF OFFICE MONDAY EVE

C. E. Rueger Elected President of Board of Trustees and Many Other Important Offices Filled.—Next Meeting of Board, Wednesday Evening, 7:30

The first meeting of the board of trustees of El Segundo was held Monday evening in the El Segundo Hotel building. A small attendance was present at this organization meeting of the newly elected trustees and city officials.

The business of the first meeting was disposed of in a very efficient manner, and it was evident that careful consideration had been given the affairs of the new city.

City Clerk Victor D. McCarthy called the meeting to order at 7:40. The resolution of the board of supervisors of the County of Los Angeles, dated January 9th, 1917, declaring the City of El Segundo incorporated, and a telegram from Secretary of State Frank C. Jordan, declaring that a certified copy of the above resolution had been filed in his office January 18th, were read, after which the city clerk administered the oath of office to Trustees Carl Ernest Rueger, Sydney R. Martin, Lemuel A. Ward, Alfred M. Smiley and John R. Coward and to Treasurer James E. Howell. Treasurer James E. Howell, a notary public, then administered the oath of office to City Clerk Victor D. McCarthy. The city officials were then full fledged officers and ready to transact the city's affairs.

that his rates had been 50 cents an inch for first insertion and 35 cents an inch for subsequent insertions for the first five years, ever since being established here, and that, compared with the average rate in the county, his rate was reasonable. Trustee Coward suggested that for the first year he might be willing to cut his rate, but the publisher could not see how that could, with justice, be done, also considering the unsettled cost of paper and printing materials of all kinds.

Trustee Smiley moved that such printing matter as the board of trustees may desire to be published shall be published in The El Segundo Herald, at a rate of 50 cents for the first insertion and 35 cents for the second insertion per inch. Unanimously carried.

As there was no written communications regarding the rent of a room for a city hall, Trustee Martin informed the board of his oral arrangements with Mrs. J. A. Davis, lessee of the El Segundo Hotel building and upon the motion of Trustee Smiley the board decided to rent the room from Mrs. Davis to be used as a city hall for the sum of $5.00 per month, city to pay for its own lights.

(Continued on page 4)

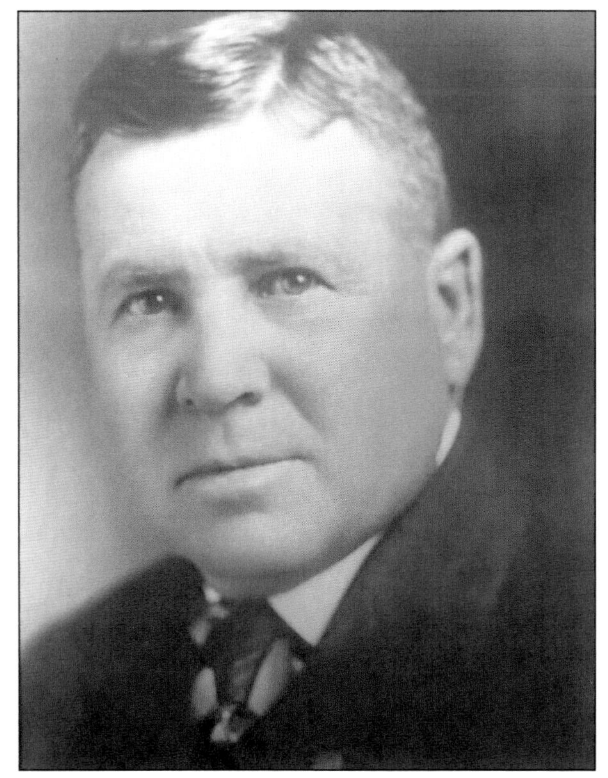

CARL RUEGER, THE FIRST MAYOR, C. 1917. On the city's first day of incorporation, January 19, 1917, Carl Rueger was appointed president by El Segundo's first board of trustees. Due to illness, he resigned during his second term. He was elected two more times but died in the middle of his fourth term on May 20, 1924.

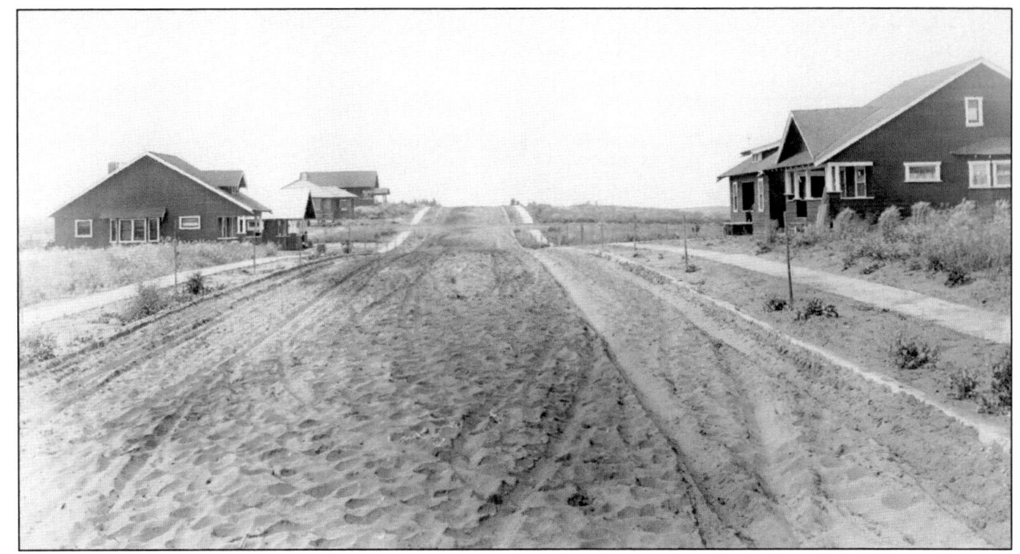

Whiting Street, c. 1912. Whiting Street was another well-traveled street in El Segundo.

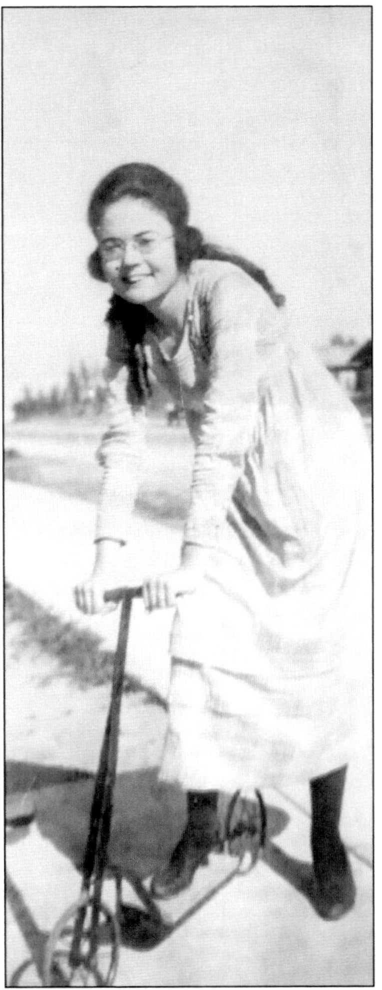

Mildred "Maggie" Spargo, 1917. Maggie belonged to another prominent family in town. She was 17 years old when this photograph was taken during the year the city incorporated. In 1987, she was honored as an El Segundo pioneer.

Marieum Gilbert Tuck, 1917. Marieum and her husband, Arthur, were city pioneers and longtime residents who arrived with their families. Marieum was born in 1898; her father, John W. Gilbert, owned one of the first grocery stores in town and made daily deliveries. She became a teacher until she married Arthur. Later, she worked at Wiseburn School for 38 years and was a principal for five years. She died in 1988, four years before her husband.

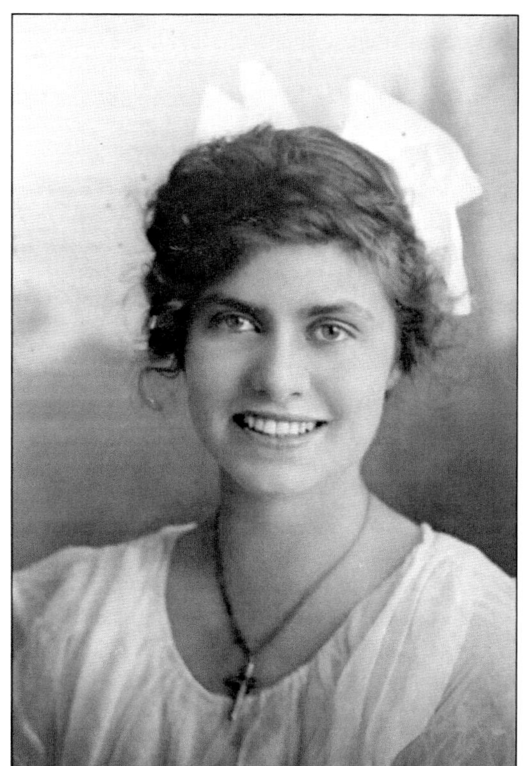

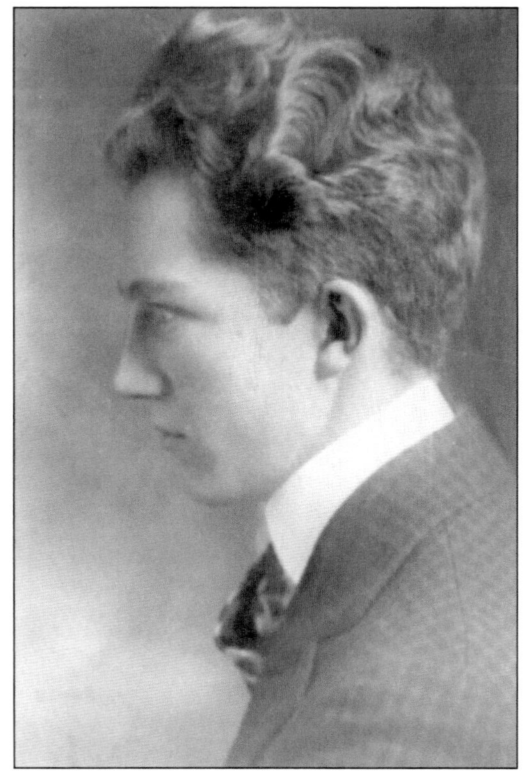

Arthur R. Tuck, 1917. Arthur was born in 1897, and his family came to town in 1912. He worked for Standard Oil and claimed to work 50 different jobs. He and Marieum went to school together, were married, and lived their whole lives together in El Segundo. He died in 1992.

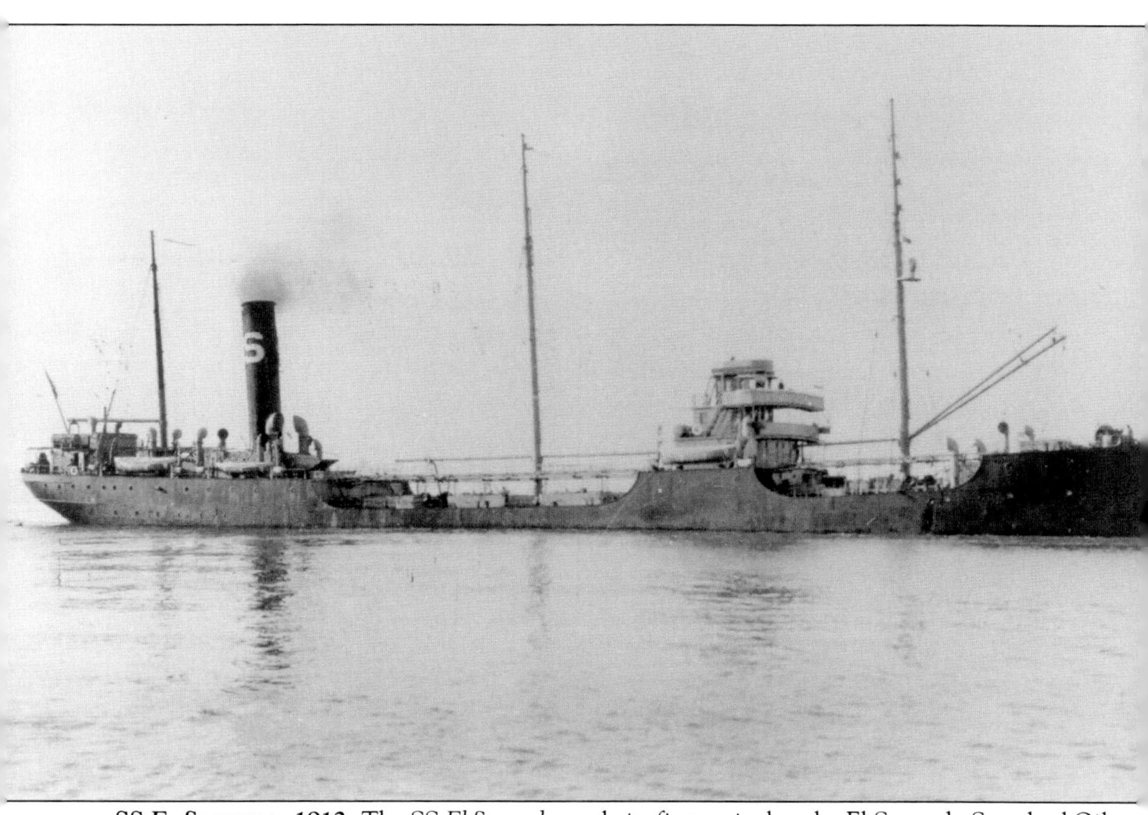

SS *El Segundo*, 1912. The SS *El Segundo* made its first arrival at the El Segundo Standard Oil Refinery's wharf on December 13, 1912. The following year, it joined the company's fleet.

Two

Early Expansion and Growth 1920–1939

Most of the streets adjacent to the Standard Oil Refinery, such as Richmond Street, Ballona Avenue (now El Segundo Boulevard), Franklin Avenue, and Main Street, experienced a rapid development of stores, restaurants, markets, hotels, a car dealership, a barbershop, an ice company, and many other small businesses to support the influx of nearly 2,000 employees coming into town to work at the refinery. A city hall to govern this growing population was built on Franklin Avenue and Richmond Street by the early 1920s and housed council chambers, a city clerk office, police department, volunteer fire department, and small library. The volunteer crew became a paid fire department in 1930 after being organized by Chief Cecil K. McConnell.

Those traditional institutions that provided the social connections of a town also quickly followed, with churches, a post office, the Woman's Club and American Legion, sports teams, Camp Fire Girls, and Boy Scout troops. This era also saw the expansion of school facilities, including a new El Segundo High School completed in 1927. A new grammar school to replace the one-room schoolhouse (now the Woman's Club building on Mariposa Avenue) was also built at Richmond Street and Mariposa Avenue.

Besides Standard Oil, other large industrial plants had their beginnings during this time. In 1925, General Chemical Company was the top consumer of Standard Oil products. The Northrop Division of Douglas Aircraft Company would be instrumental—along with its major competitors, Hughes, McDonnell Aircraft, and North American Aviation—in putting El Segundo on the map as the "Aerospace Capital of the World" by the 1950s.

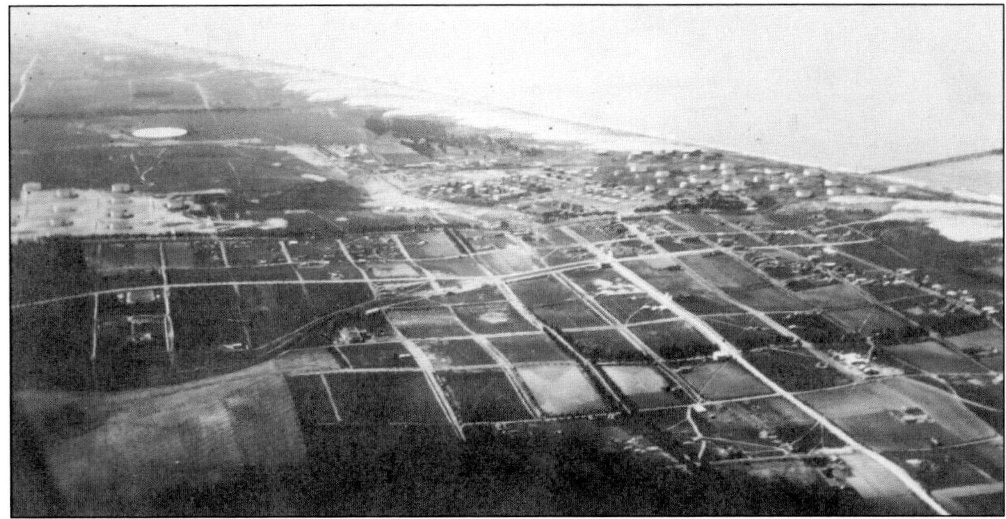

Aerial View Looking Southwest of the City, 1919. This early aerial view of the city streets shows homes and businesses starting to sprinkle the land north of the refinery. Already, Richmond Street, Main Street, Grand Avenue, Franklin Avenue, and Ballona Avenue (now El Segundo Boulevard) were clearly visible, and other lots in town were well drawn out. The population was close to 3,000, and there were 15 miles of paved streets and an assessed valuation of the city of $15 million.

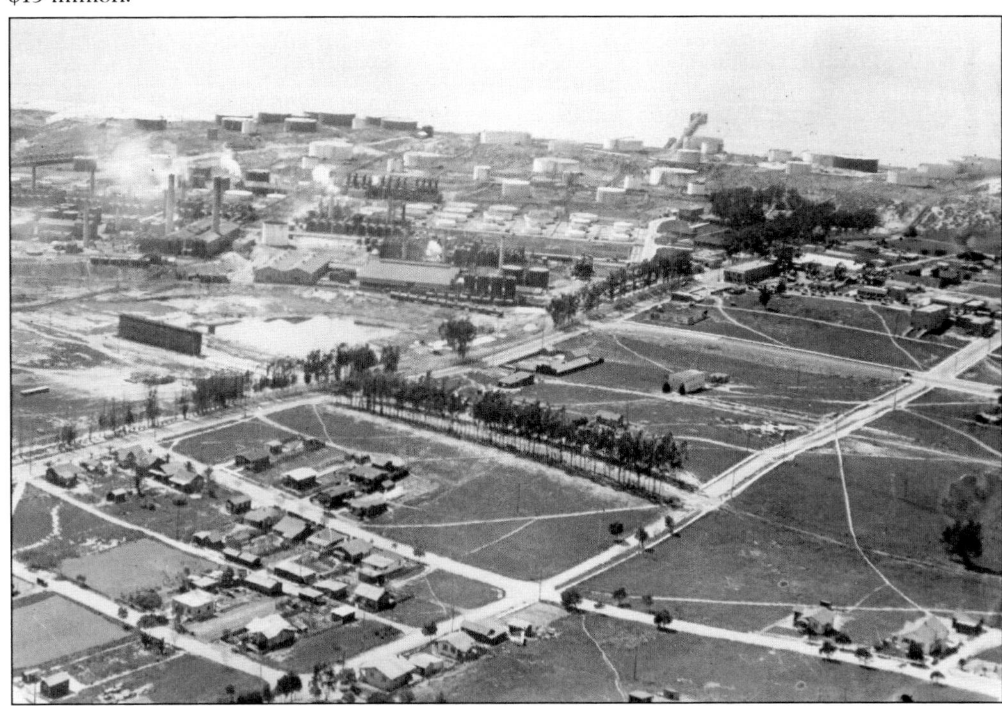

The Refinery and the Center of Town, 1923. This zoomed-in aerial photograph of the northwest portion of El Segundo shows the tree-lined Eucalyptus Drive in the center. The main road running east-west is Franklin Avenue, with Arena Street, Sheldon Street, and Penn Street ending at Ballona Avenue, which bordered the south of town. This area is known as "Smokey Hollow" because of the light industrial shops that later formed in this location.

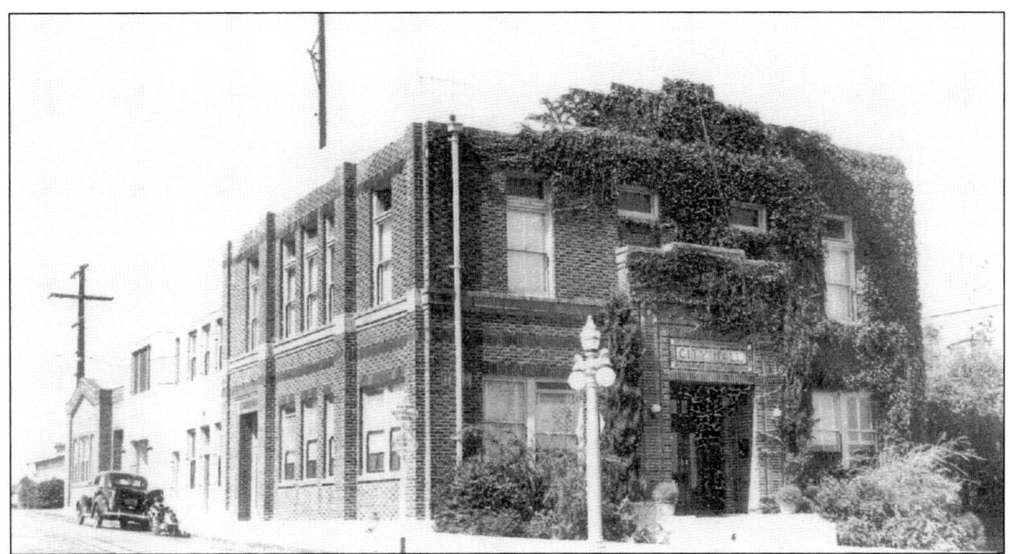

City Hall in 1930. A side view of the expanded city hall complex on Franklin Avenue and Richmond Street includes the police and fire departments. The city hall building was constructed at a cost of $15,900. The current site is a parking lot for small businesses along Richmond Street.

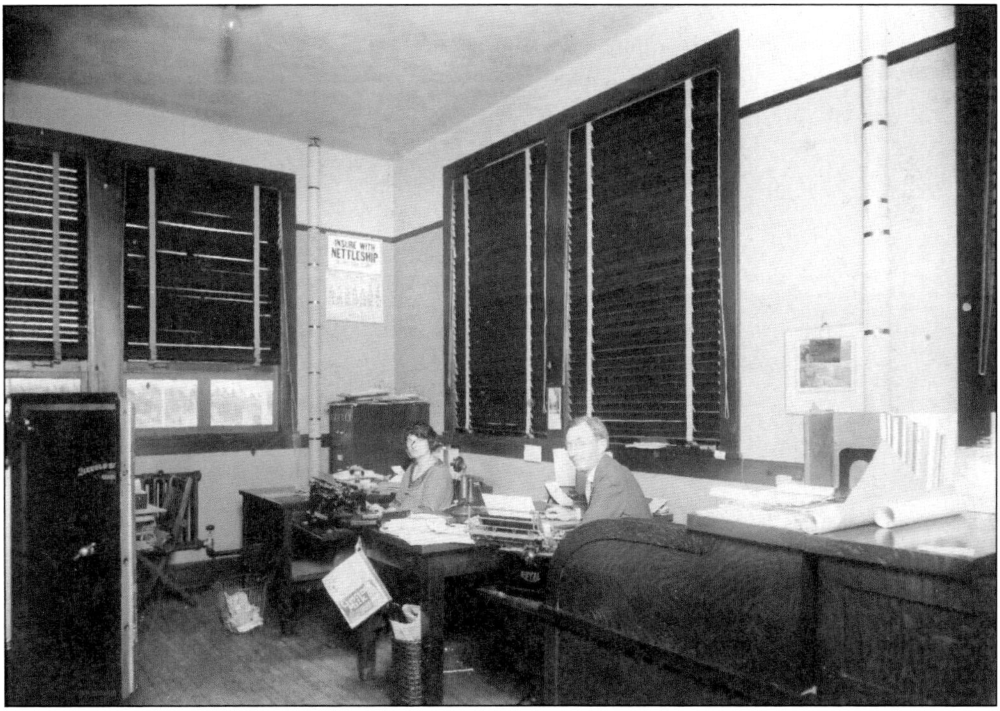

City Hall Clerk's Office, 1923. Victor D. McCarthy was the city clerk from 1917 to 1951. Neva Elsey, sitting next to him on the left, followed him as city clerk from 1951 to 1957.

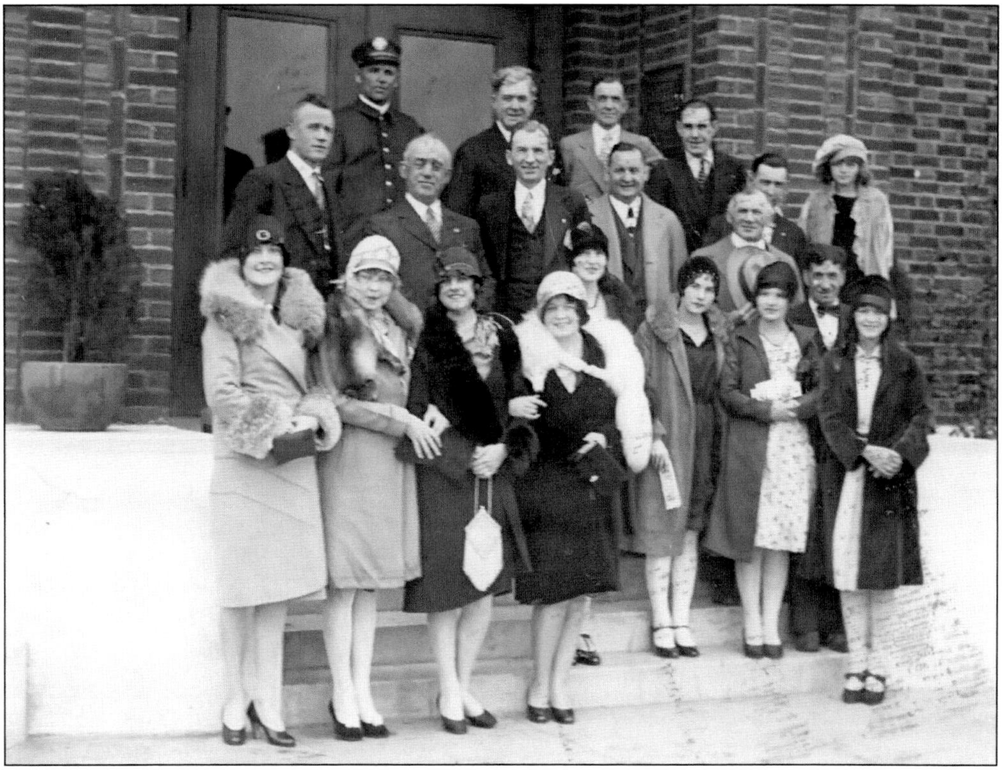

WORKERS IN FRONT OF THE FIRST CITY HALL BUILDING, 1928. The offices in the new city hall were ready by early 1918, and the first year, 50 business licenses were issued. The operation budget that year was $33,400.

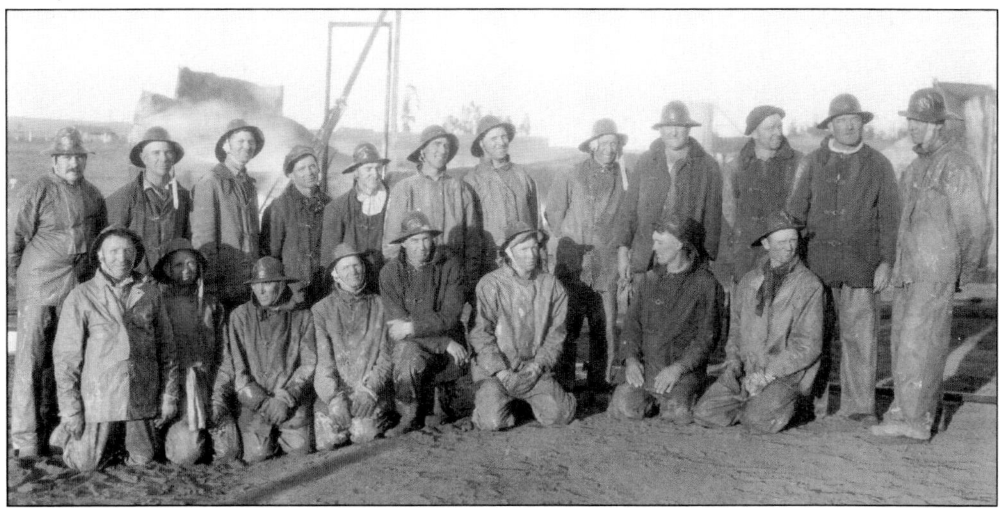

VOLUNTEER FIRE DEPARTMENT, 1926. Volunteers from the Standard Oil Refinery and the city fought fires until a paid city fire department was formed in 1947. In this photograph are, from left to right, (first row) Fred Hope, Art Crosby, Tony Seote, Elmer Peterson, Cecil McConnell, Arnold Schleuniger, Bert Dimwiddie, and Cliff Bixler; (second row) Bill Lenon, Hal Barbara, Glen Todd, Jack Lowe, Ward Miller, George Neschke, Leo Dessert, Casey Hancher, Bob Campbell, Jerome McDonald, Art Blair, and Walter Pierce.

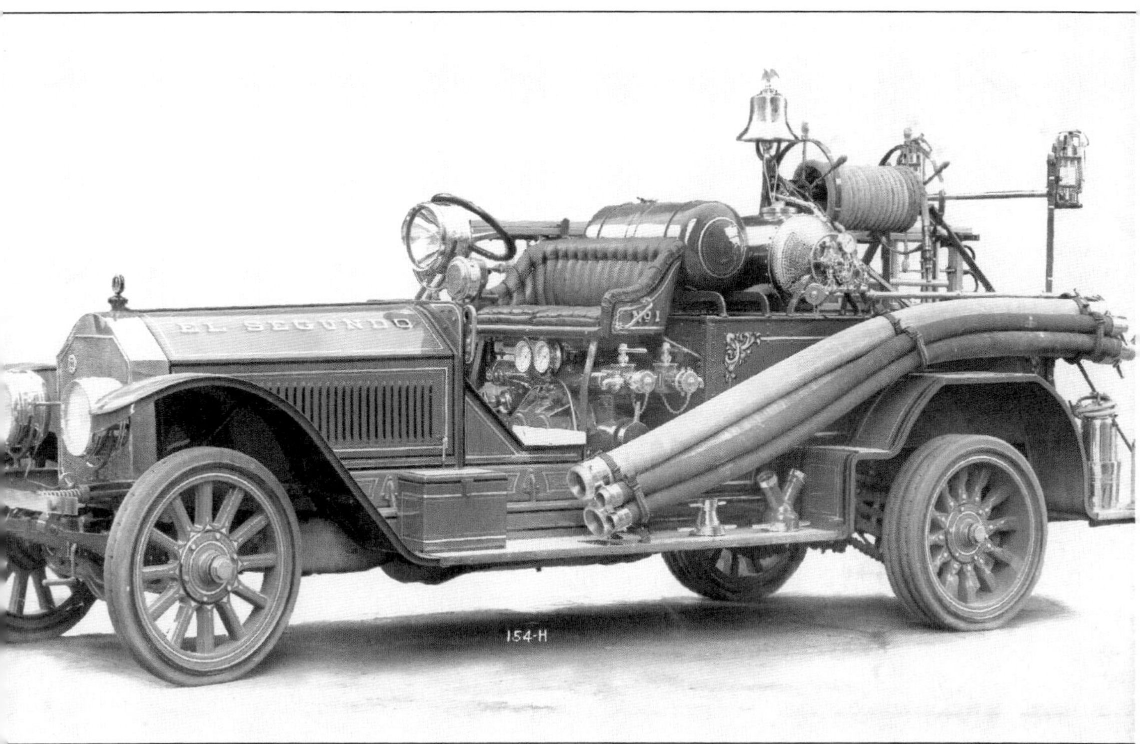

American LaFrance Fire Truck. The back of the original photograph lists this as a "Type 75 Triple Combination Pump Chemical and Hose Car; 105 Horse Power, 6 Cylinder Motor, 750 G.P.M. Rotary Gear Pump, 1200 feet, 2 ½ inch Hose Body, and a 40 gallon chemical tank. 'Specials' include 2 Lengths of 2 ½" suction hose and 1 suction Siamese." It was in service from 1924 to the 1960s.

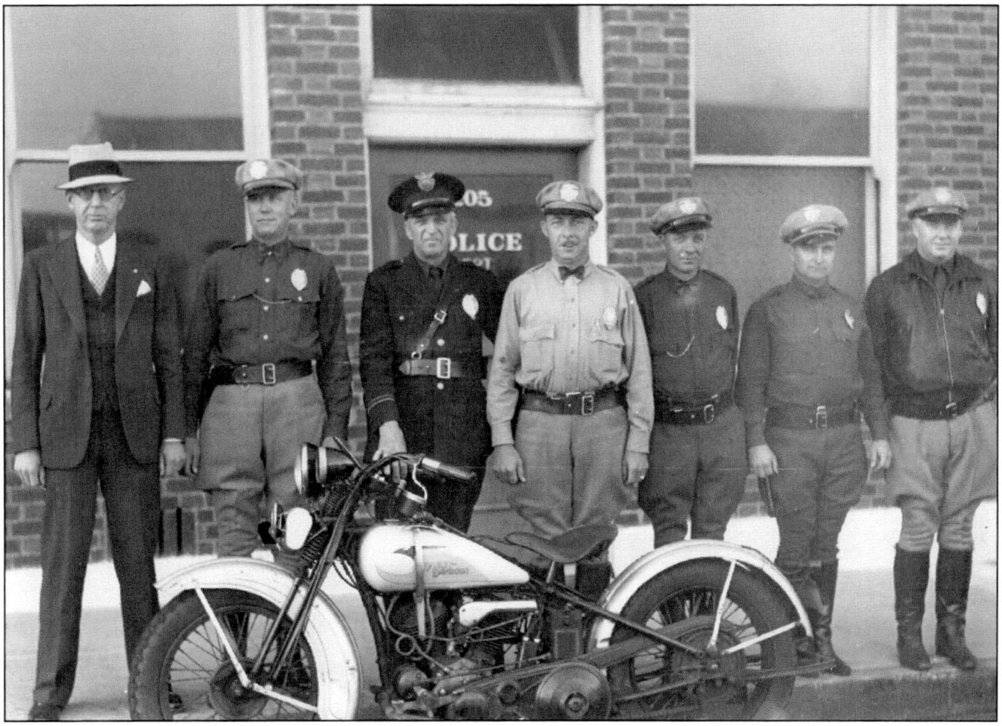

The Police Department, 1935. The police department was located at 205 Franklin Avenue and was behind the city hall building. Although the city hall structure has not survived, the brick building that was the police department still stands today as a local business. From left to right are Chief R.T. Hutchins, J.A. "Bert" Cummings, K.E. Campbell, Thomas DeBerry (who became police chief the following year), William Allee, M.H. McIntire, and C.C. Mavens. Later, Cummings's grandsons would become a police chief (David) and a director of recreation and parks (Bob).

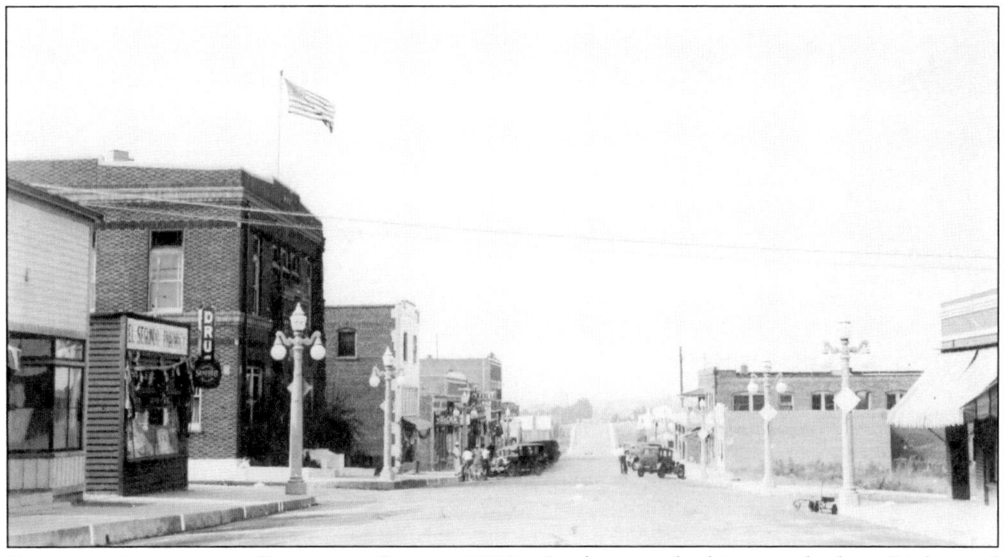

Franklin Avenue and Richmond Street, 1920s. In this view looking north along Richmond Street, a flag sits on top of the early city hall building. El Segundo Pharmacy, the first drugstore, is pictured south of city hall, and several of the buildings along Richmond Street still exist today.

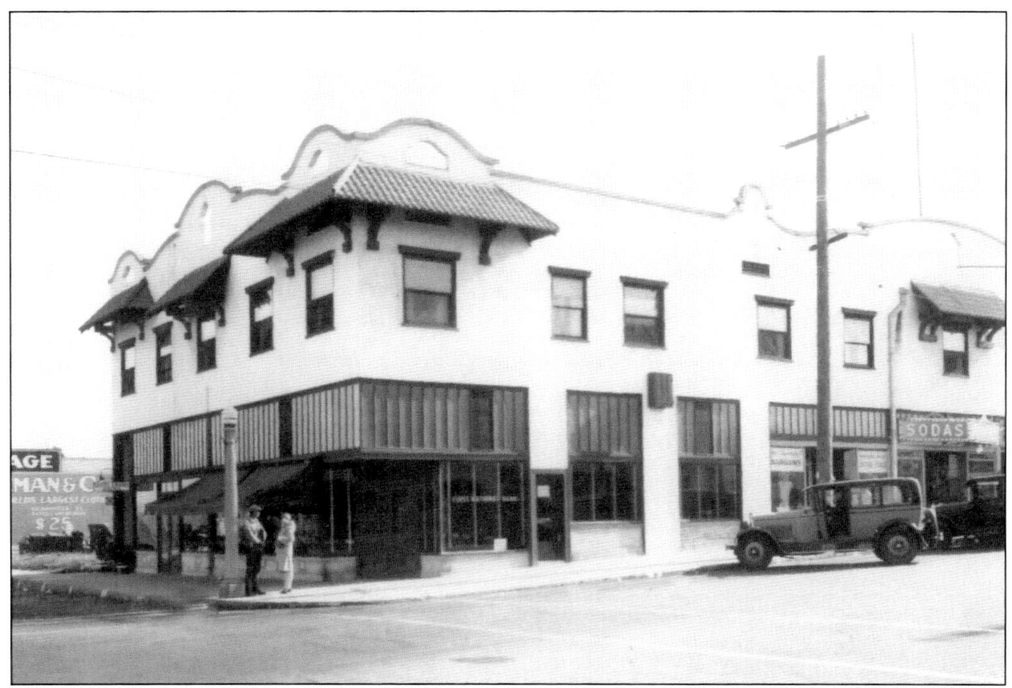

Grand Hotel, c. 1920. Although the building no longer exists, it was located on the southwest corner of Grand Avenue (where the cars are parked) and Main Street.

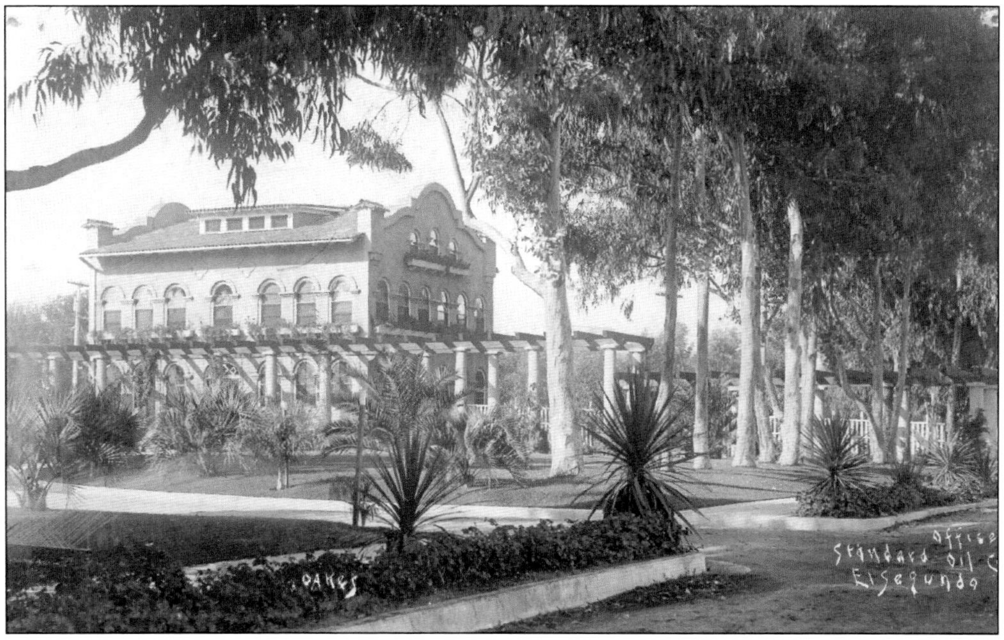

Standard Oil Administration Building, c. 1915. Outside this structure completed in 1912, the palms and newly constructed columned arbors create a scenic view through multiple arched windows for workers inside. A majestic entryway welcomes those visiting the main office. This is another of the early postcards promoting the city.

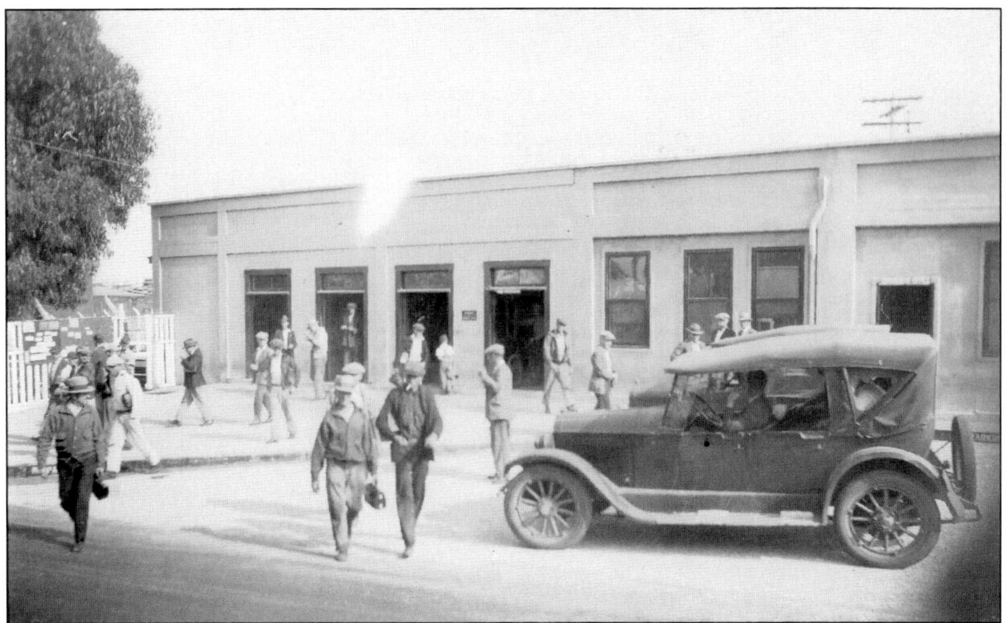

Main Gate at Standard Oil, c. 1920. Workers are depicted here finishing their shift with lunch pails in hand and a couple of automobiles waiting to pick up passengers. According to the book *Chevron El Segundo Refinery: Energizing California for 100 Years*, by the early 1920s, Standard Oil completed an expansion program that made the refinery one of the largest in the world. Extending over an area of more than 1,200 acres, the refinery employed nearly 2,000 men and women and manufactured approximately 100 petroleum products for shipment as far away as Asia, South America, and Europe.

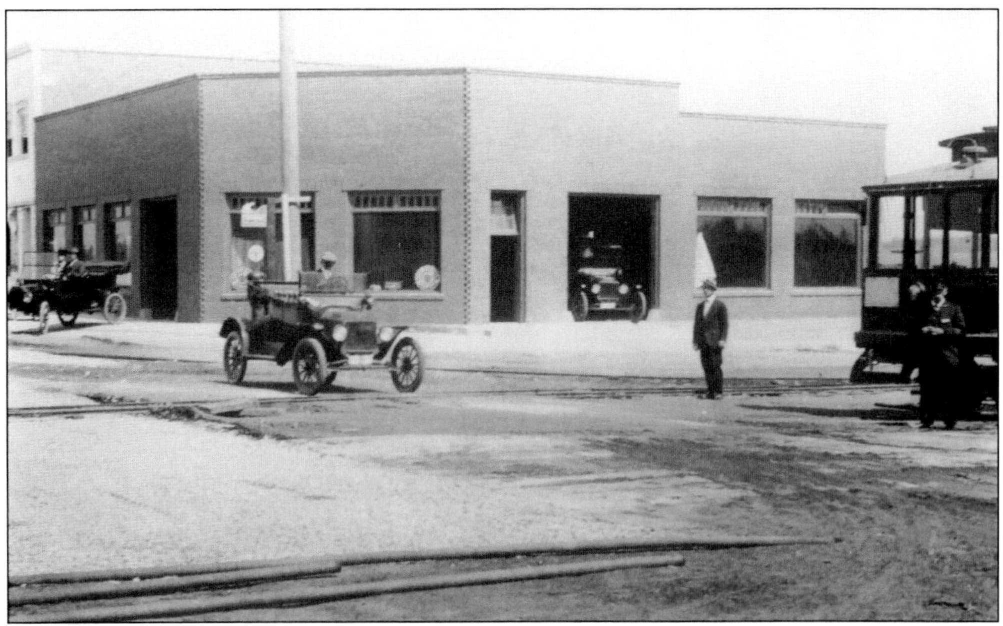

Ford Automobile Dealership, c. 1925. This early Ford dealership at the northeast corner of Main Street and Grand Avenue would later become the Ira E. Escobar Ford dealership.

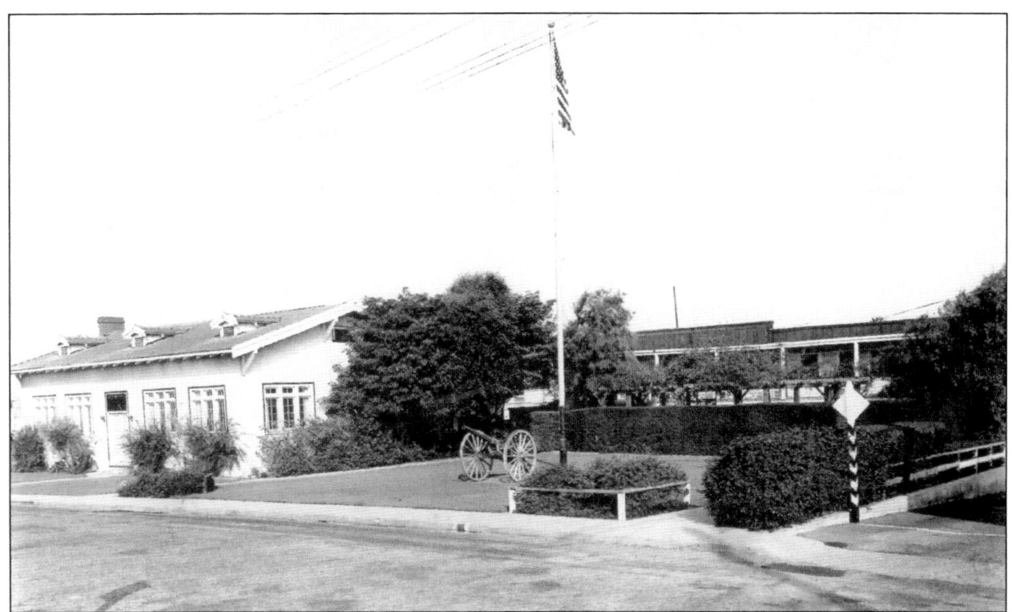

American Legion Clubhouse, c. 1923. Located at 223 West Franklin Avenue (at Concord Street), the American Legion focused on war veterans and the betterment of community life. Central to the Legion-sponsored events was baseball for adolescents. The Hamburg Apartments building, or "the Showboat," is visible behind the clubhouse. It is now the El Segundo Christian Church.

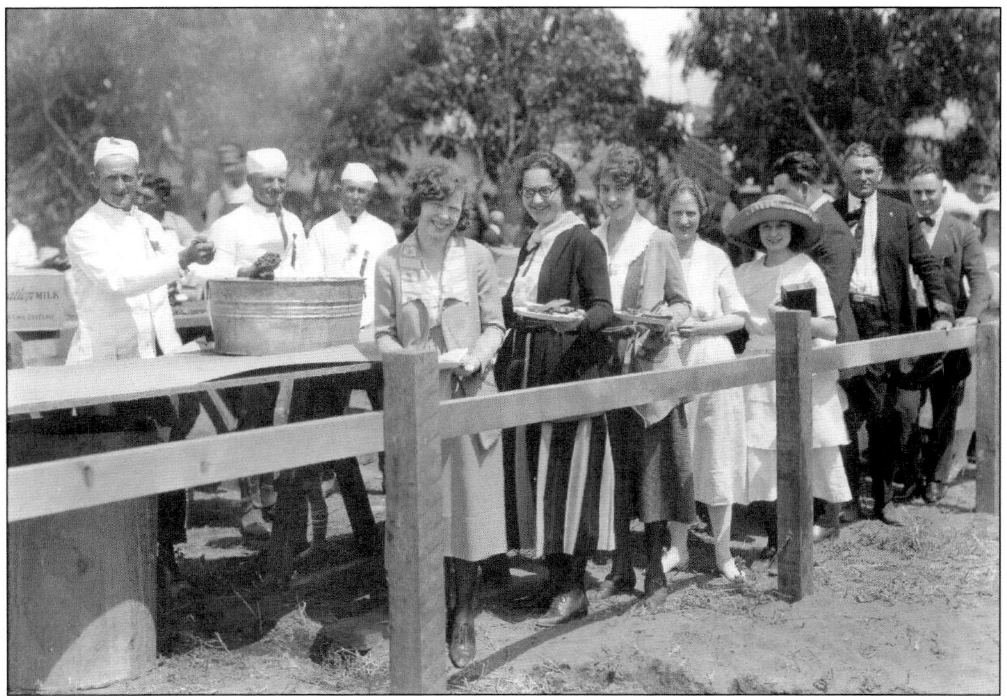

Standard Oil Refinery Ladies, 1920s. This photograph is labeled "Some of our fair office force taking on the chow." From left to right in line are Viola Gregory Gadso, Emily Rueger, unidentified, Eleanor Griffin Johnston, and Ernestine Abshier Penny. George Merritt is one of the men behind the tub.

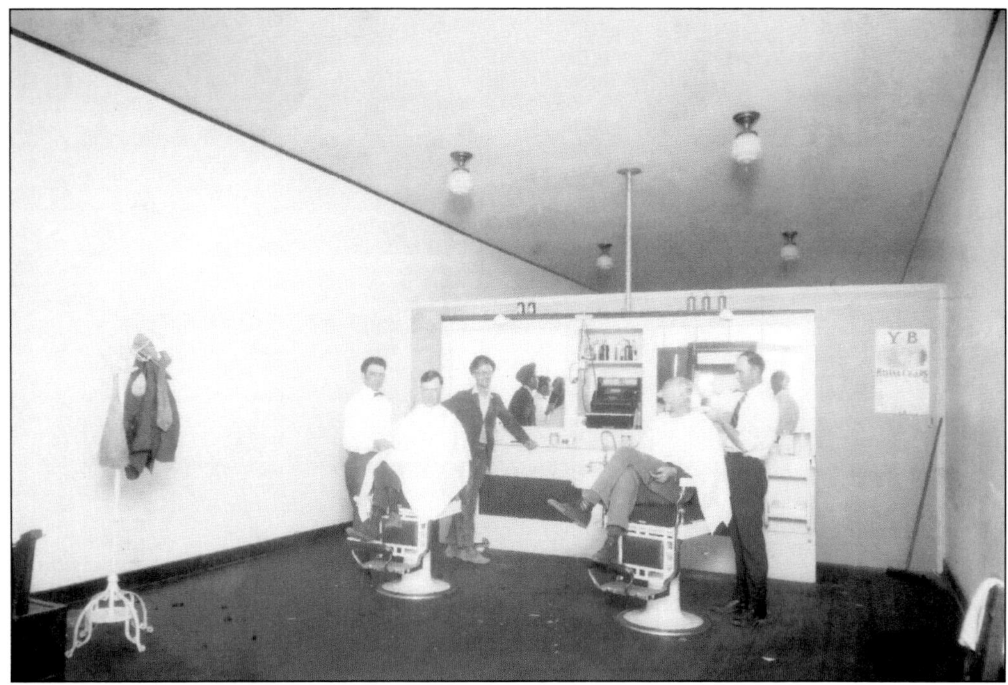

Floyd's Barbershop, c. 1925. This is another rare photograph of the interior of a small business in the 1920s. Floyd Carr Sr. is pictured on the far right. The shop was located on Richmond Street.

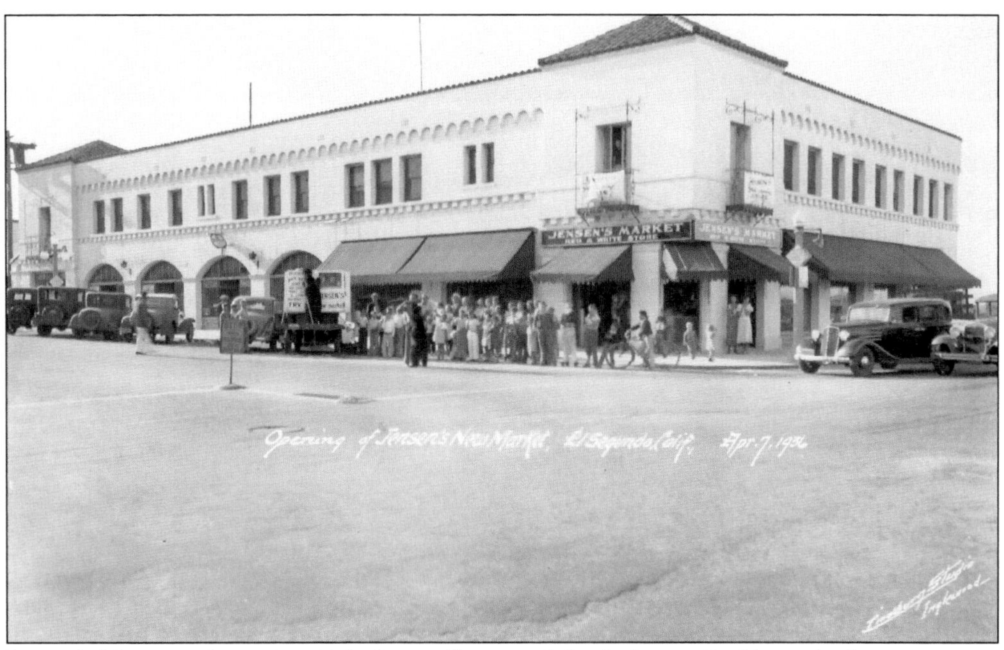

Jensen's Market, April 7, 1936. Originally named the Lafayette Building, the large structure still exists today as a cornerstone of downtown at the northwest side of Grand Avenue and Main Street. The opening of Jensen's Market was on April 7, 1936. The name of the photographic studio written on the photograph is illegible. This was later named the Hollingsworth Building.

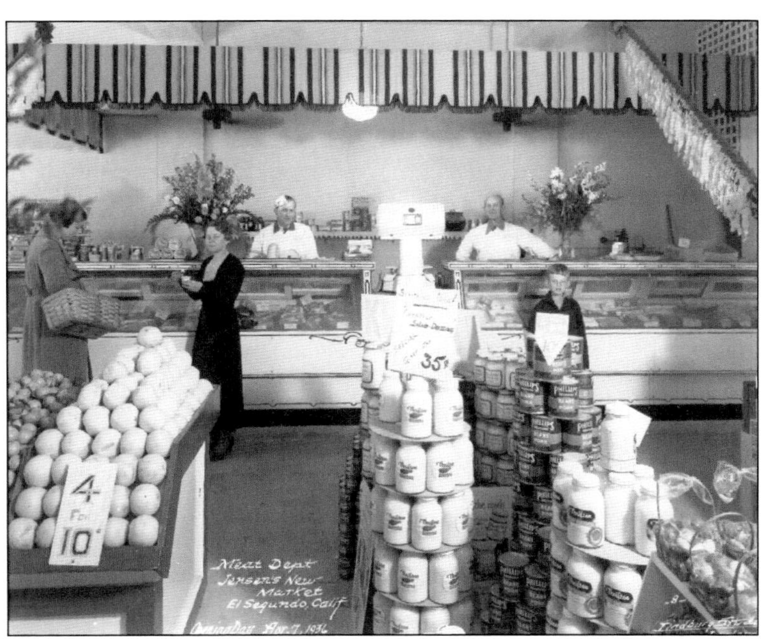

JENSEN'S MEAT DEPARTMENT, APRIL 7, 1936. Another opening-day photograph shows the interior of Jensen's Market with produce and canned goods in the foreground and the meat counter in the back. One of the two men behind the counter has been identified on the back of the photograph as Neal Stevenson, butcher, but it does not reference which man is Stevenson.

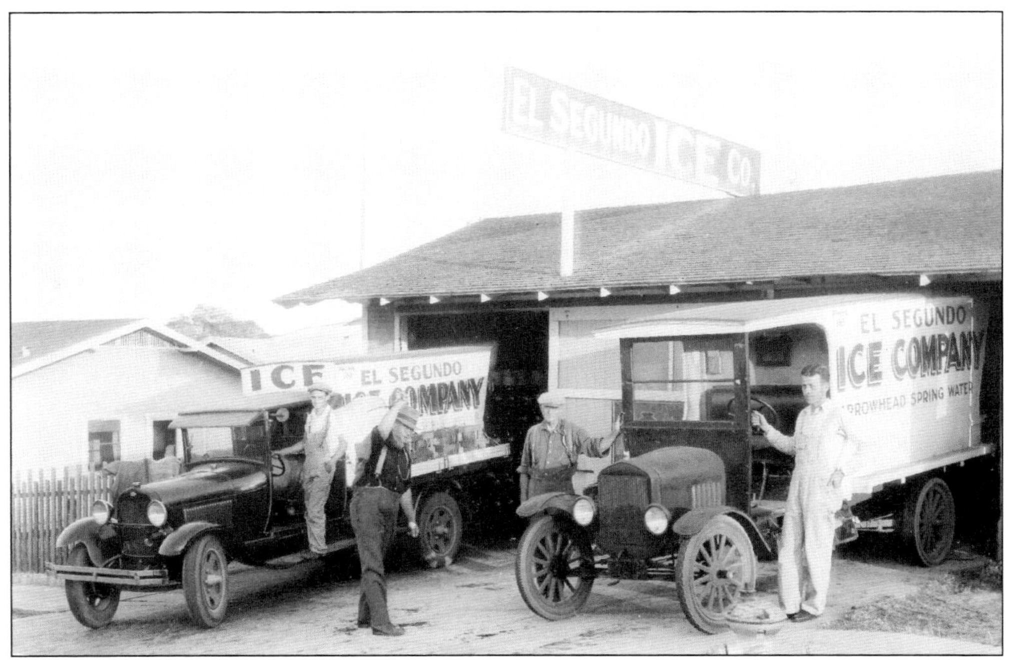

EL SEGUNDO ICE COMPANY, 1920s. Spreading out from the center of town at Ballona Avenue (El Segundo Boulevard) and Richmond Street, many small businesses sprang up. The Pinkerton family owned the El Segundo Ice Company on Pine Avenue west of Virginia Street. Notice the Arrowhead Spring Water sign on the side of the truck and the phone number (133) with only three digits.

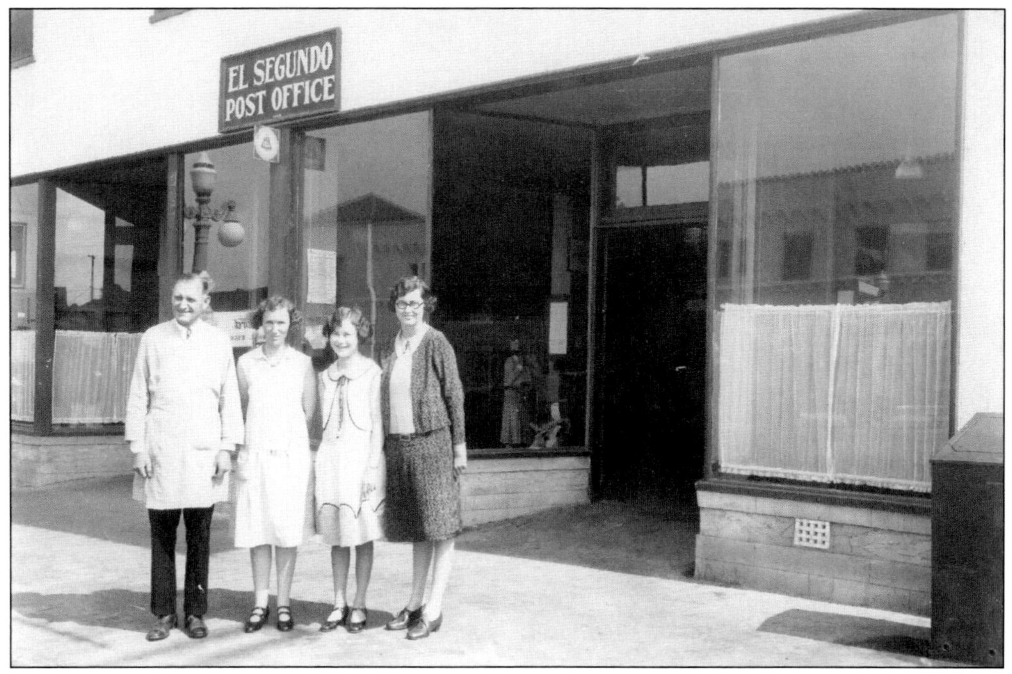

EL SEGUNDO POST OFFICE, 1930S. This view shows the exterior of the El Segundo Post Office, south of Grand Avenue between Main and Richmond Streets. Pictured are, from left to right, postal clerks Fred James, Mildred Marshall, and Florence Hauge and postmistress Lila James.

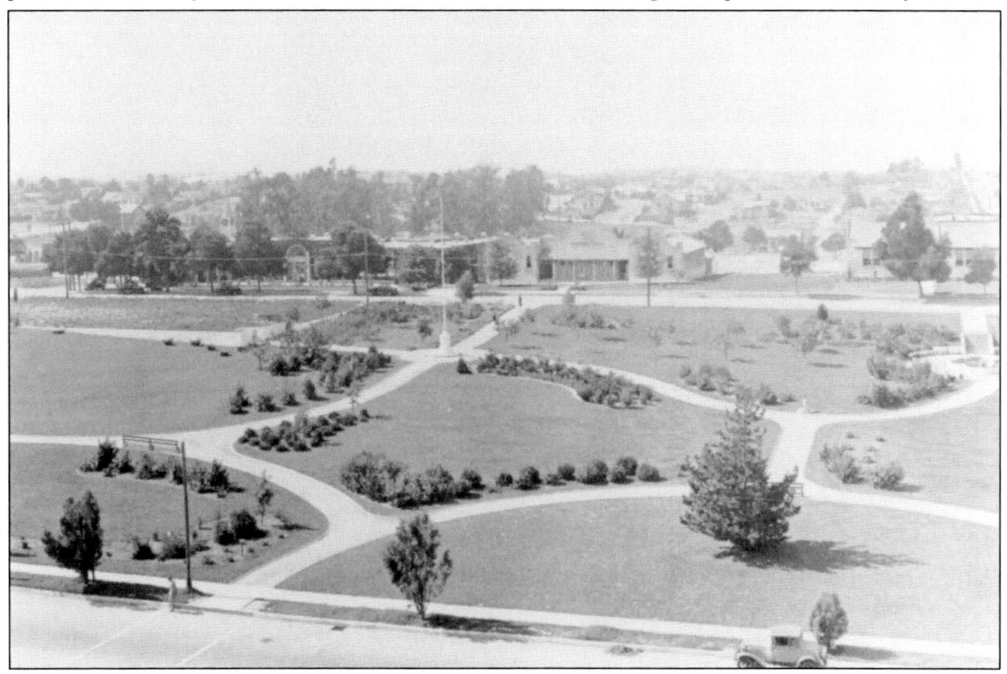

LIBRARY PARK, C. 1930. Looking west from the newly constructed high school bell tower, this view of Library Park was taken a decade before the construction in the 1940s of the current public library, which is now at the center left of the scene. The first Richmond Street Elementary School is surrounded by trees in the left background.

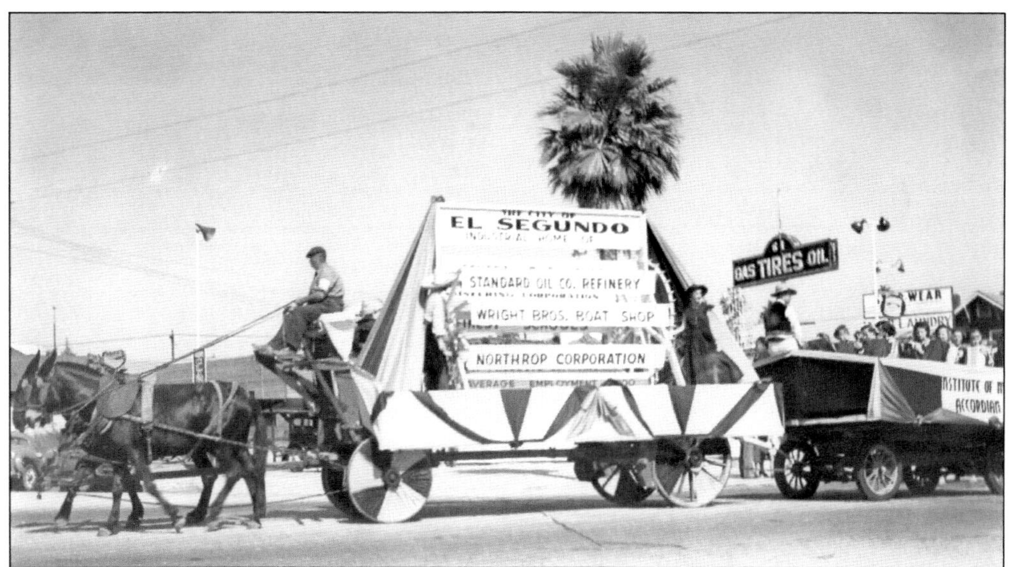

Parade on Grand Avenue, 1930s. A mule-drawn cart of local advertisers is part of a community parade. The sign at the top reads, "The City of El Segundo / Industrial Home of," with the following company names revolving into view: Standard Oil Co. Refinery, Wright Bros. Boat Shop, and Northrop Corporation.

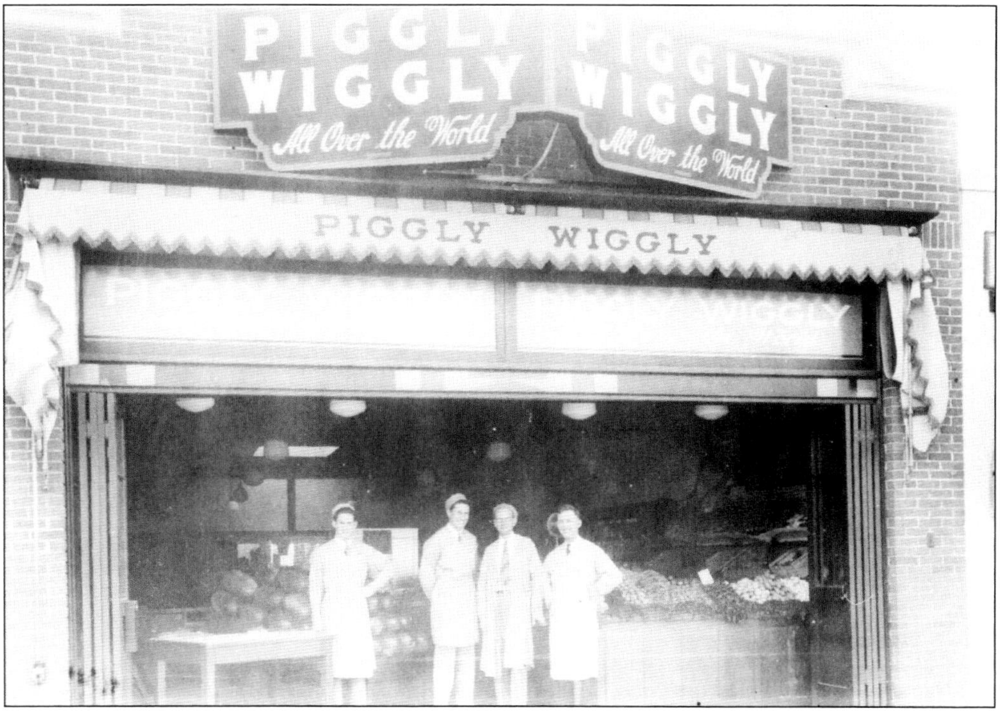

Piggly Wiggly Store, 1930s. The sign above the entrance claims, "Piggly Wiggly All Over the World." This store was located in the 200 block of Richmond Street. The current website for the company states that Piggly Wiggly was "America's first true self-service grocery store." It was founded by Clarence Sanders in Memphis, Tennessee, in 1916. Today, there are more than 600 stores in 17 states, mostly in the Southeast.

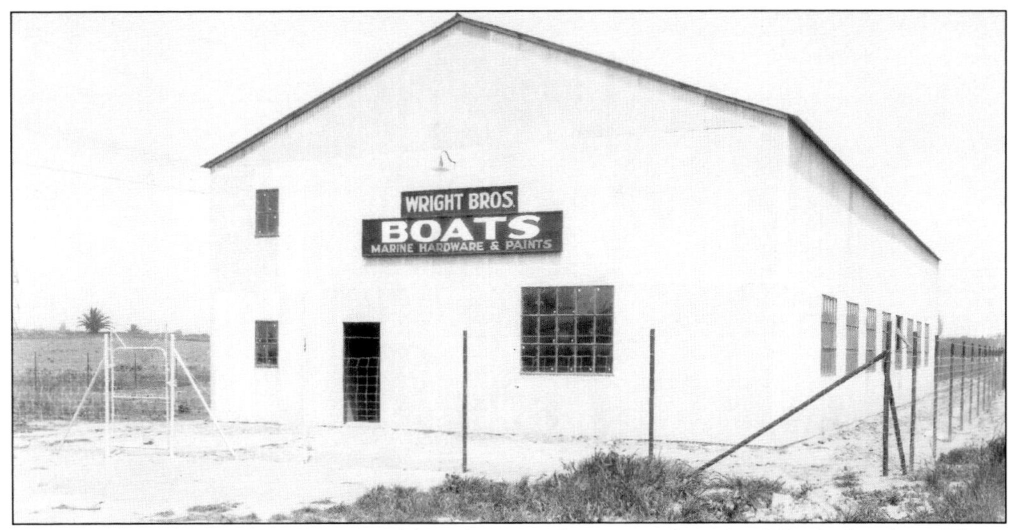

WRIGHT BROTHERS BOATS, 1930s. Although not as famous as the other Wright brothers, Elmer and Lefty owned Wright Brothers Boats at 1817 East Grand Avenue.

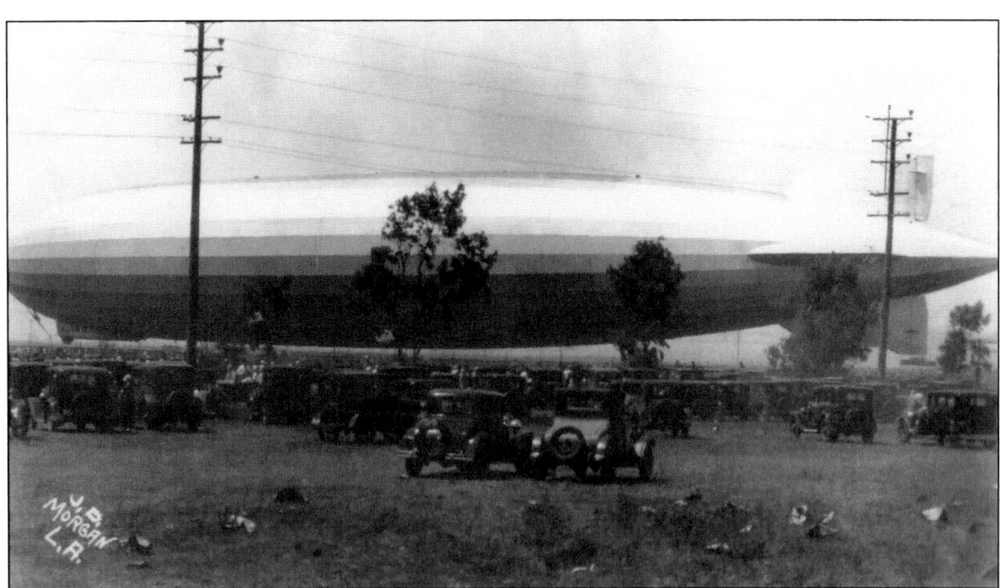

GRAF ZEPPELIN AT MINES FIELD, 1930s. Now the Los Angeles International Airport, this was known as Mines Field in the late 1920s and hosted national air races. According to Hunter's book *El Segundo Seventy-Five Years*, Watt L. Moreland built his aircraft factory on a 15-acre tract just south of Mines Field. He found the "wind conditions are excellent, as evidenced by the choice of this field for the mooring of the *Zeppelin* on its visit to Los Angeles." Unfortunately, his company went out of business in 1931.

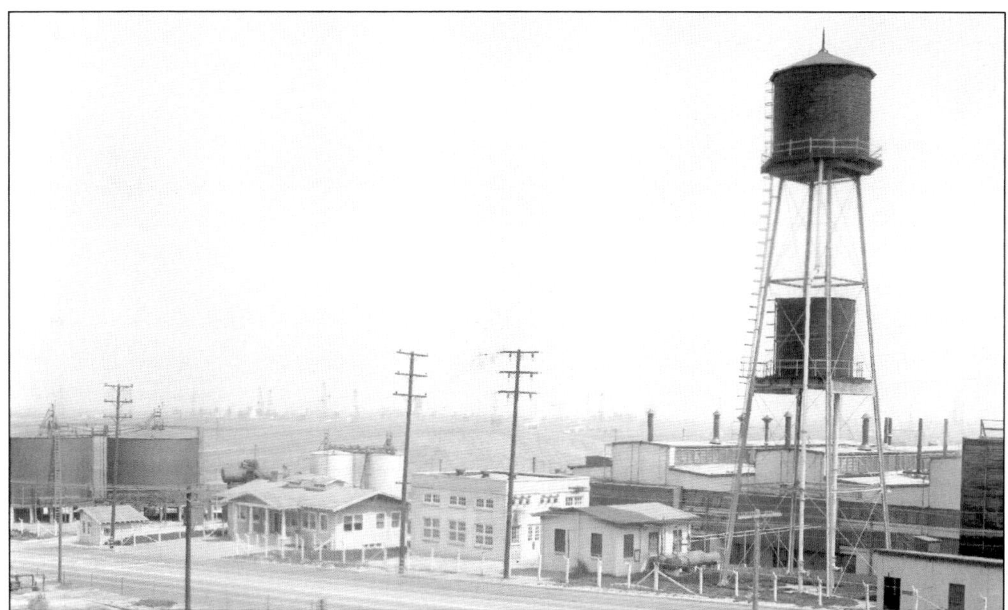

General Chemical Company, c. 1925. General Chemical Company built its plant on the east side of Sepulveda Boulevard near Rosecrans Avenue. It was the largest consumer of the Standard Oil Refinery's products. By 1925, product demand was increasing and General Chemical was planning to expand its facility. It remained a major manufacturer until the first decade of the 21st century, when it was dismantled. The site is now a shopping and restaurant area called the Point.

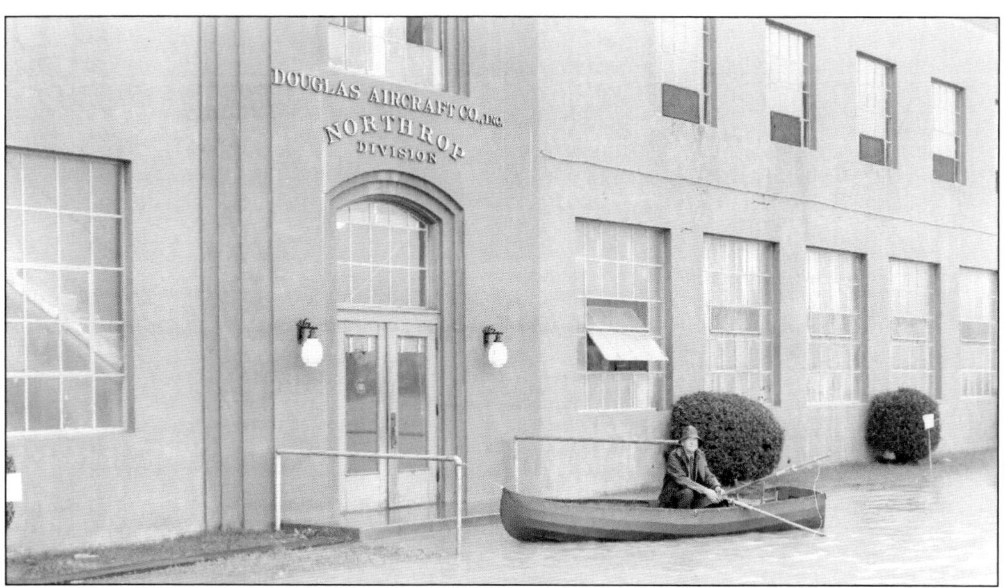

"Lake" Northrop, March 2, 1938. A rowboat with an unidentified man holding a fishing pole is tethered to the entrance of the Douglas Aircraft Company, Northrop Division, during a flood. Jack Northrop was never formally trained, but he had an intuitive eye for design and economy. By the time Douglas Aircraft opened its plant in El Segundo in the 1920s, Northrop was already Donald Douglas's partner. Northrop's first design was the fuel system for the Douglas World Cruisers, large, heavy biplanes that were the first to circumnavigate the world.

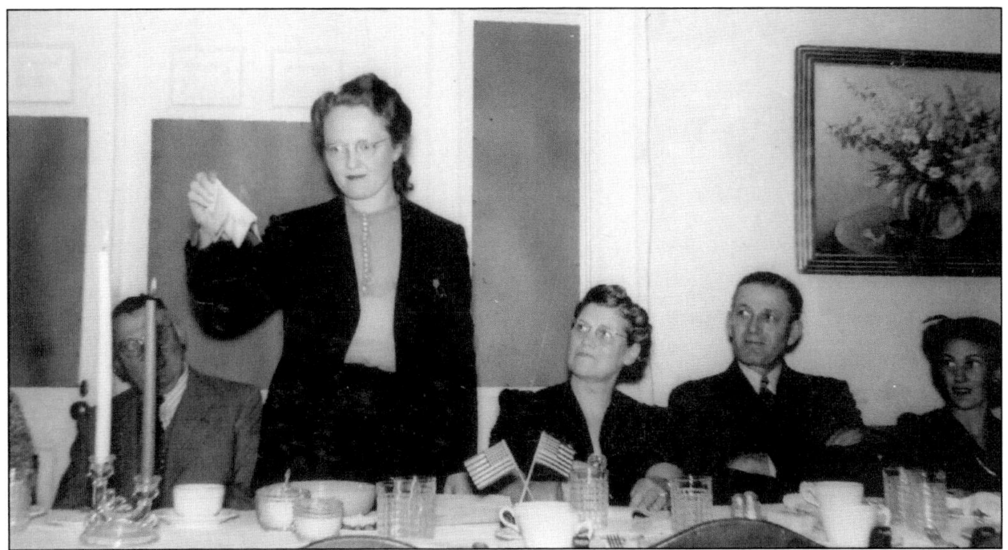

TREASURER OF THE WOMAN'S CLUB, 1935. Lorna Tilton, Woman's Club treasurer, burns the mortgage. The property is still located near the southwest corner of Mariposa Avenue and Standard Street, behind the Methodist church. To her left are the club's president, Edythe Burgett, and her husband, Clyde Burgett, the El Segundo postmaster.

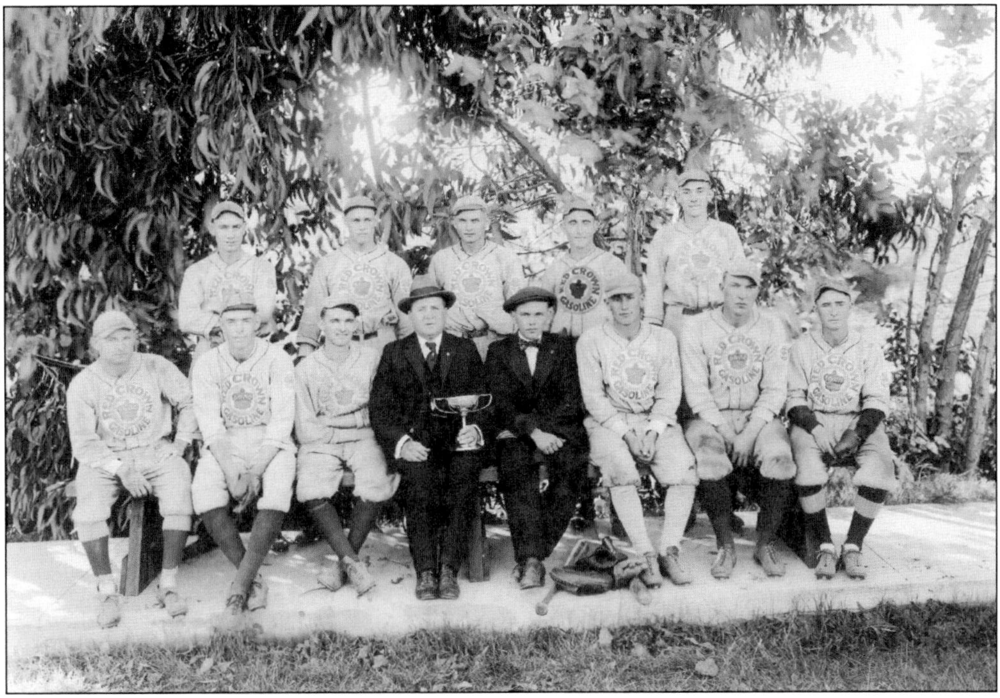

THE FIRST MAYOR AND THE RED CROWN GASOLINE BASEBALL PLAYERS, 1920s. Hunter's book states that "baseball was big in the early days and competition keen between Standard's Richmond and El Segundo refineries. . . . The father of baseball in El Segundo was Mayor Carl Rueger—or 'Daddy' [center with trophy]." His team in this photograph has been identified as, in no known order, Billie Lee, Jake Kipe, Red Schleunger, Geo Kessler, Frank Wireman, Oscar Palmer, Lefty Bell, Geo Duncan, Danny Daniels, and Jimmy Delany.

PAULINE "POLLY" GILBERT, 1929. Pauline was one of four daughters of the Gilbert family whose father owned an early grocery store on Richmond Street across from the current Old Town Theater. Before the self-service Piggly Wiggly set up shop, Pauline's father drove a horse and carriage around the city asking ladies what they wanted on a daily basis because they did not have refrigeration. According to her sister, Marieum, "After making the rounds, he would return to the store, pack up each order, and delivery the day's groceries. His regular customers would pay him on Standard Oil's pay day."

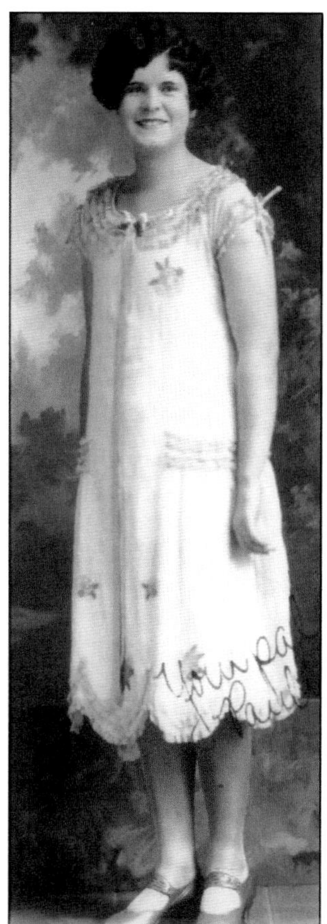

MAE LEWIS AND FAMILY, c. 1925. Mae Lewis, third from the left, proudly stands with her family in front of their California Craftsman–style home at 537 Whiting Street. She was the first realtor in El Segundo and, for many years, her business office was at 201 West Grand Avenue.

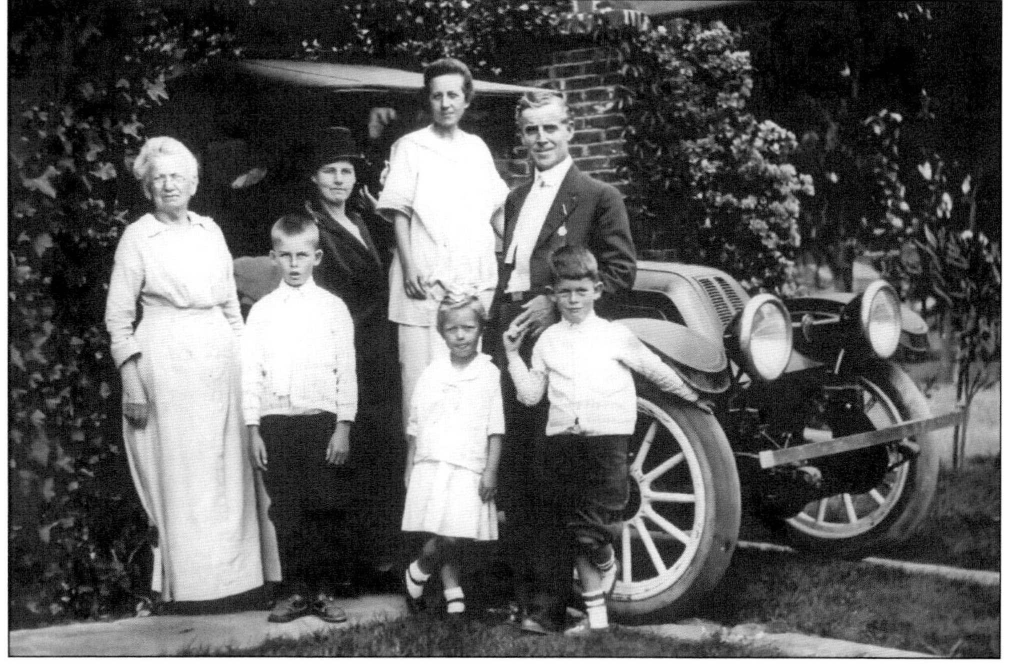

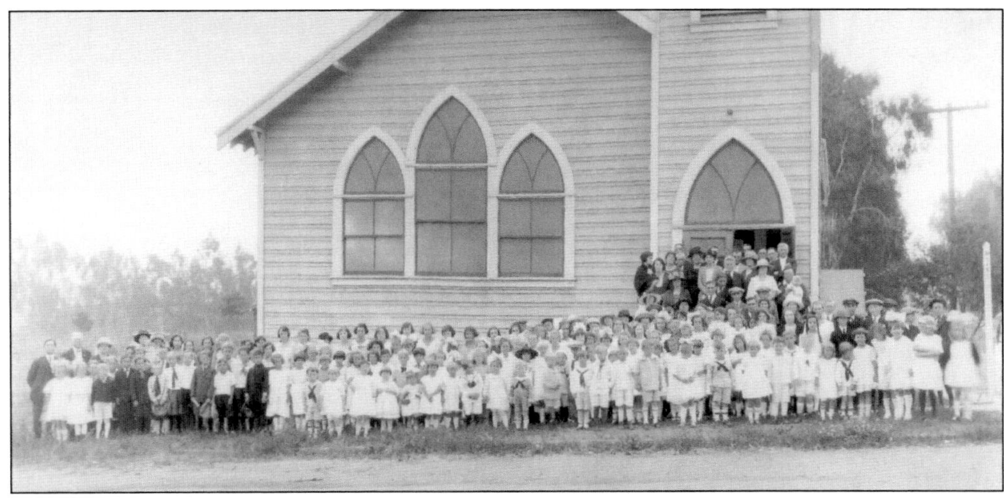

COMMUNITY METHODIST CHURCH, C. 1920. Originally built on the southwest corner of Mariposa Avenue and Main Street, now part of the high school campus, the Community Methodist Church was dedicated on August 30, 1914, and was El Segundo's earliest known church building. Although El Segundo had a strong churchgoing community that met in public rooms, halls, and private residences, many churches were not built until the 1940s and 1950s. This structure was moved to Richmond Street during the building of the high school in the late 1920s, and the new United Methodist Church opened at its present site on January 28, 1928.

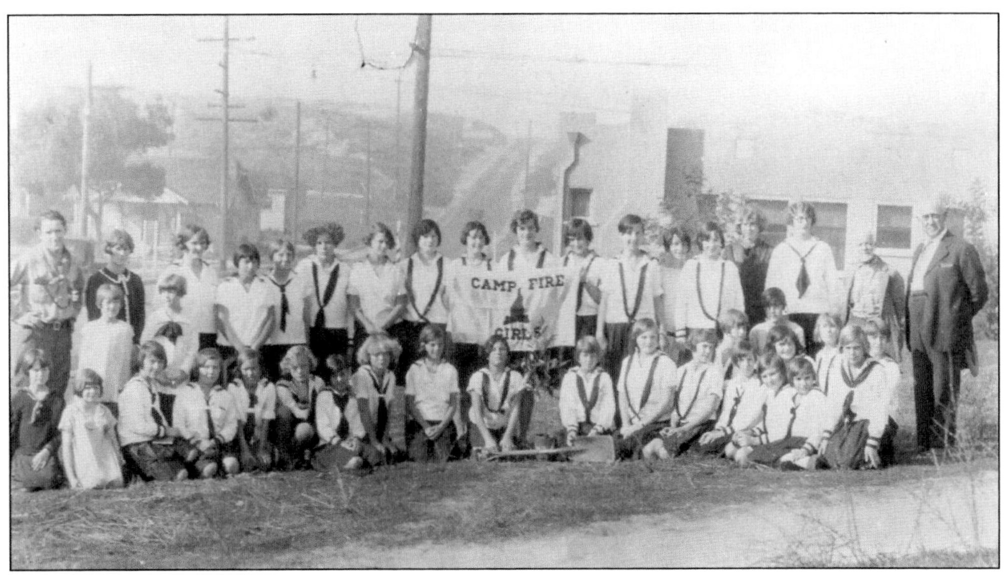

FIRST CAMP FIRE GIRLS, 1926. The Camp Fire Girls was the first youth group to organize in town. During the summer of 1926, Ruth Cracroft, head nurse at the refinery hospital, organized a group of a dozen girls. Within three years, more than 140 had joined. Dance and music lessons of a mixed variety were part of Cracroft's teachings.

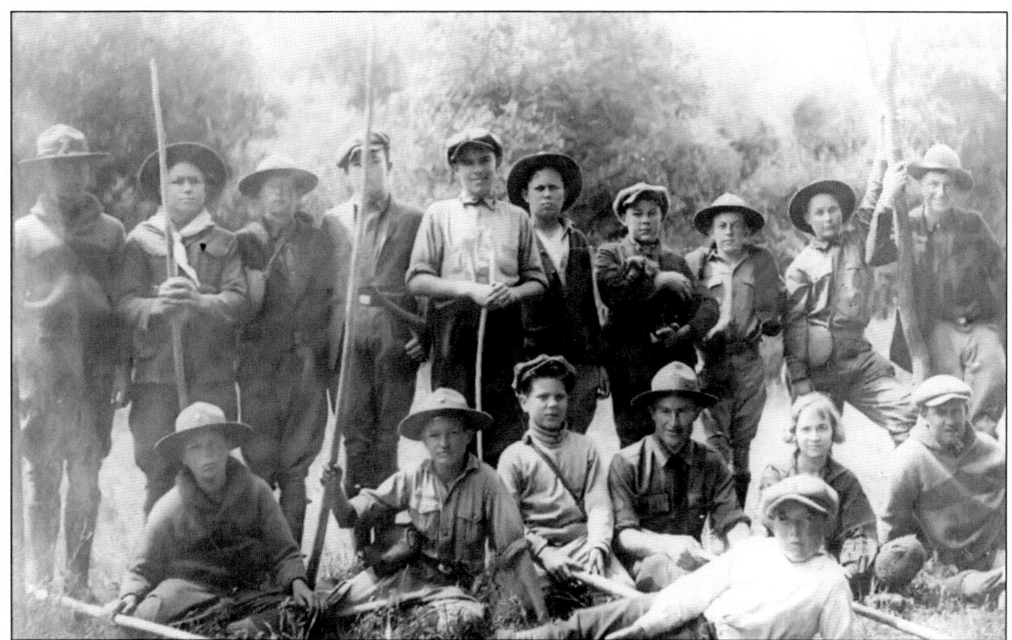

Boy Scout Troop 267, 1928. Not to be outdone by the Camp Fire Girls, the Boy Scouts completed a 14-mile hike around the Topanga Canyon area in 1928. The Scoutmaster, Mr. Hastings, is seated fourth from left. Those identified are, from left to right, John Kelly (reclining); (seated) Frank Booth, Richard Cramp, an unidentified Scout, Hastings, Mrs. Hastings, and Clint Howell Sr.; (standing) James Hall, Julian Christensen, ? Larson, Roy Magee, Horace Cartland, Elton Ericsson, Carl Mullin, Paul Griggs, Clint Howell Jr., and Elmer Ford.

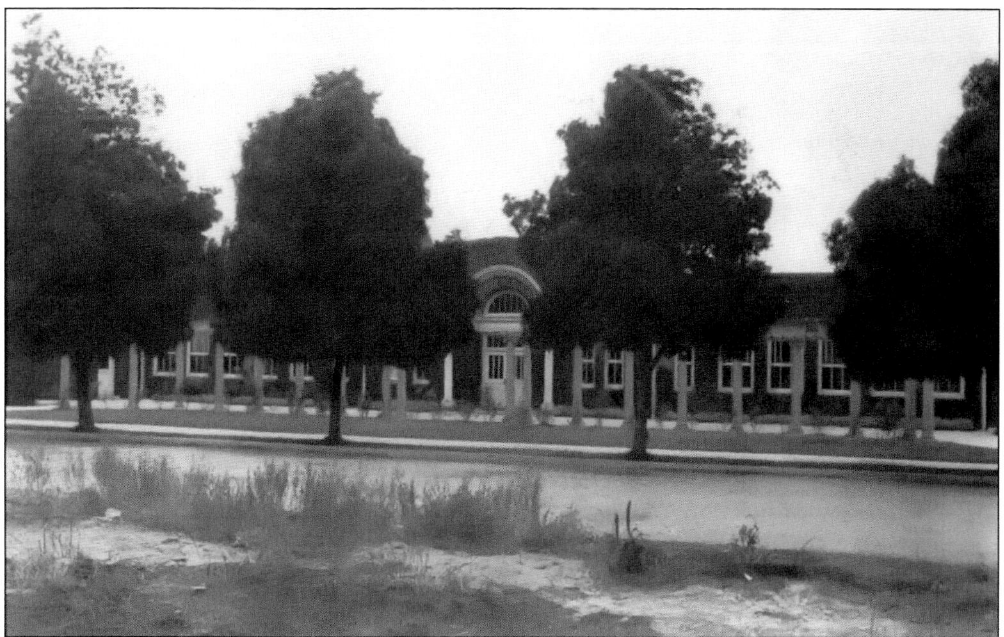

Richmond Street School, c. 1930. This is El Segundo's second grammar school at Mariposa Avenue and Richmond Street facing east. This facility replaced the elementary school that is the current Woman's Club building on Mariposa Avenue and Standard Street.

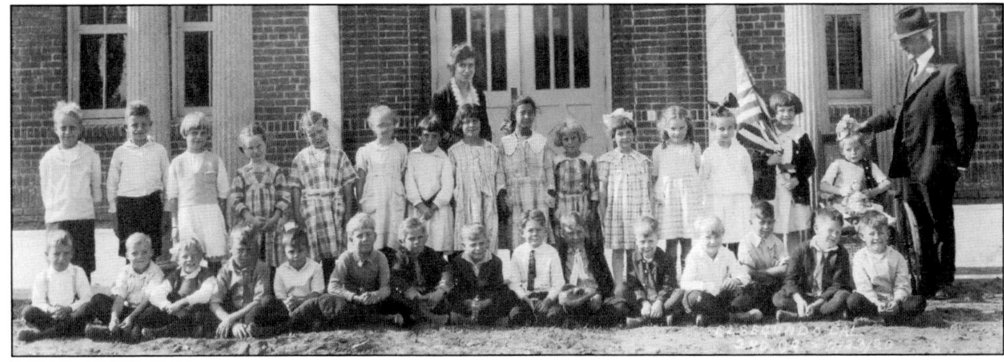

SECOND-GRADE CLASS, NOVEMBER 23, 1920. The teacher was Marieum Gilbert Tuck, mentioned in chapter 1. Charles Mills, at the far left, was the second principal of the school. Here, he is admiring a girl's large hair bow. Plaid in many of the girl's dresses also seemed to be the fashion for the day.

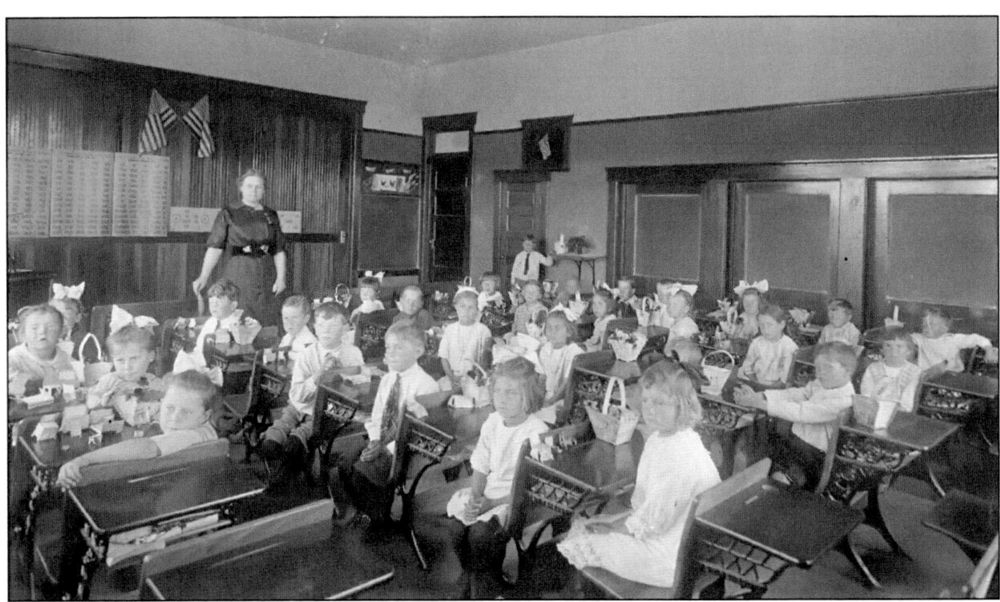

THIRD-GRADE CLASS, C. 1917 (OR 1928?). Although the teacher is unidentified, this is another rare but popular photograph of the inside of a classroom of this era. The bows and dresses make a strong case for the earlier period, although there has been some debate among history buffs that the photograph was taken around 1928. The children are displaying some handmade baskets and miniature paper furniture. One young lady on the far left in the fourth row has made a good start on a dollhouse.

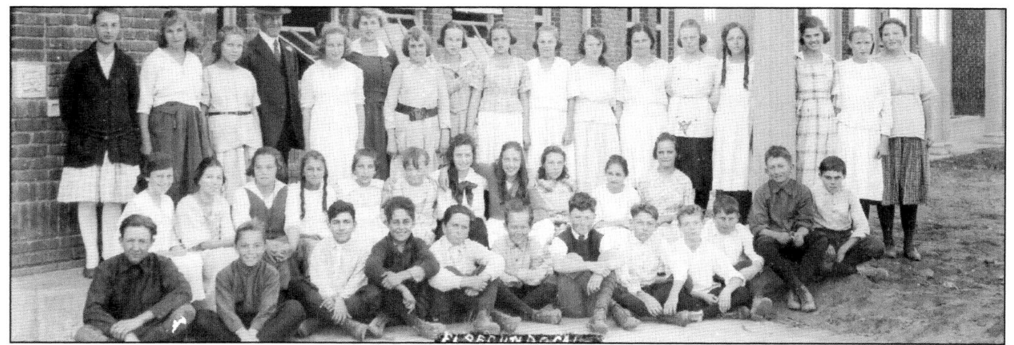

SEVENTH-GRADE CLASS, C. 1920. Charles Mills, the principal, seems to be a standard fixture in many of the classroom pictures. Here, a large seventh-grade class poses in front of the Richmond Street School.

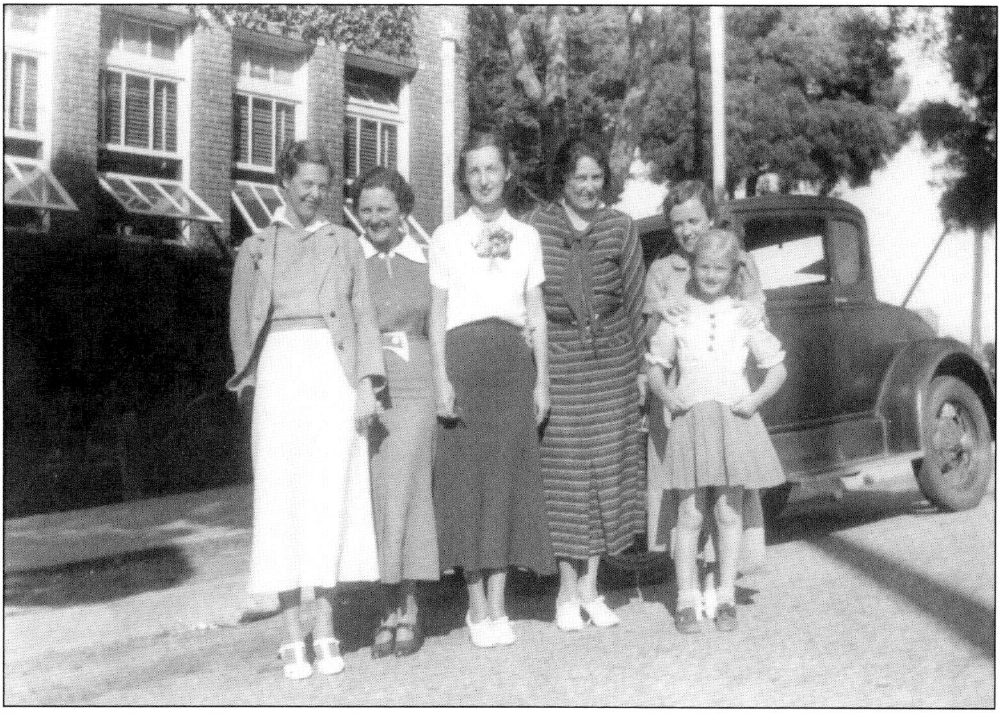

RICHMOND STREET ELEMENTARY SCHOOL, FEBRUARY 1936. The teachers are identified as, from left to right, Miss Huber, Miss Yelman, Miss Shell, Miss Elbert, and Miss Robertson. Later a parade queen and city employee, Yvonne Burgett Wills seems to be a teacher's favorite.

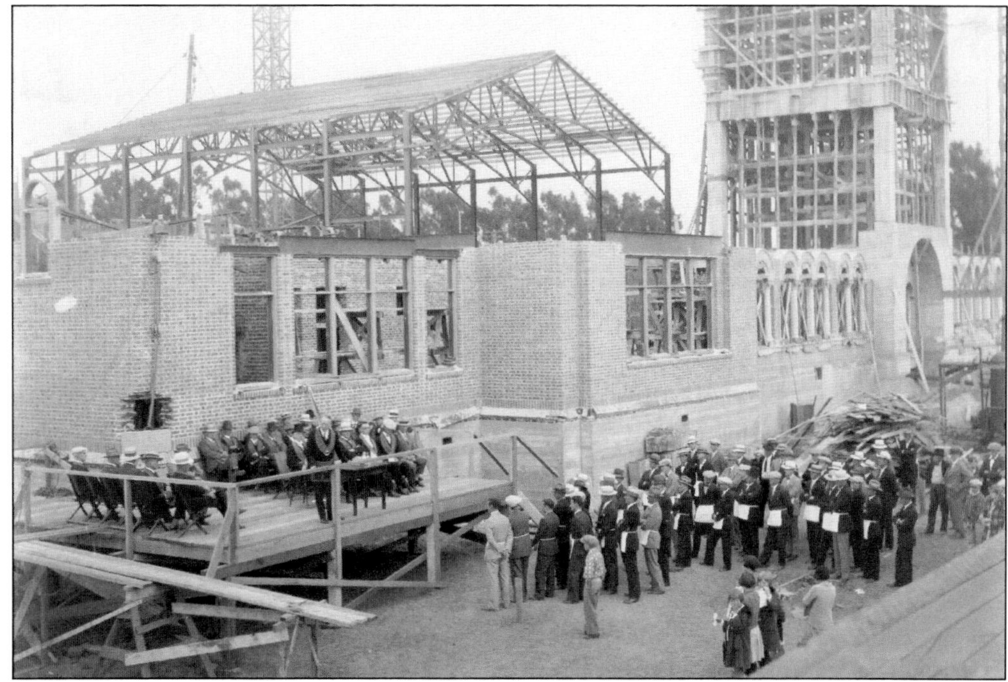

HIGH SCHOOL CORNERSTONE CEREMONY, JUNE 18, 1925. During the construction of the El Segundo High School on Main Street, El Segundo students still attended Inglewood High. A $500,000 bond measure was passed to finance the new facility. In the fall of 1927, one hundred twenty-four students entered their new school—although reluctantly, according to an early student, Clyde Walker, in Hunter's book. Charles L. Broadwater was the first high school principal and district superintendent, at a starting salary of $4,320. The architects were Alfred W. Rea and Charles E. Garstang; the contractor was Herbert M. Baruch.

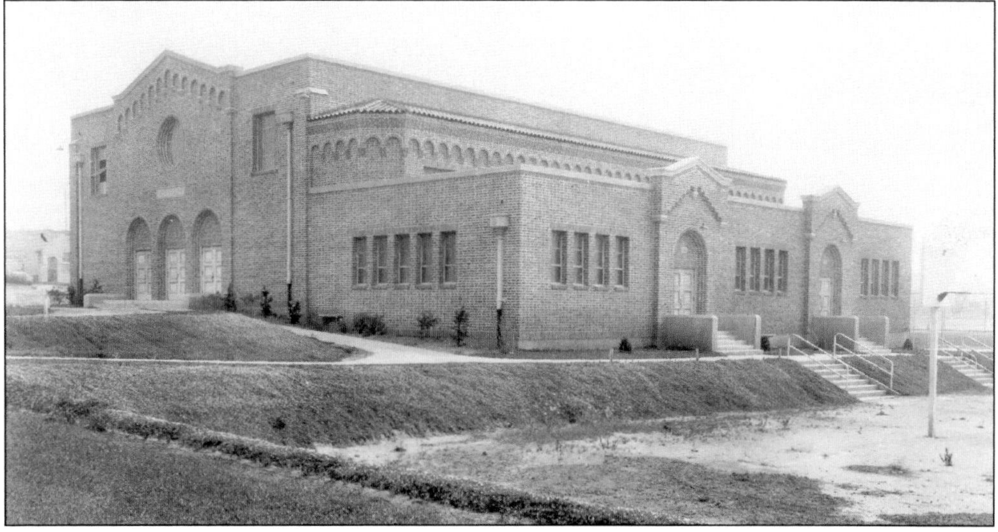

EL SEGUNDO HIGH SCHOOL GYMNASIUM, C. 1932. This is a photograph of the original gym before the March 1933 earthquake. The quake caused minor cracks and structural damage to some of the buildings on the campus, as reported after an investigation by the superintendent, Charles L. Broadwater.

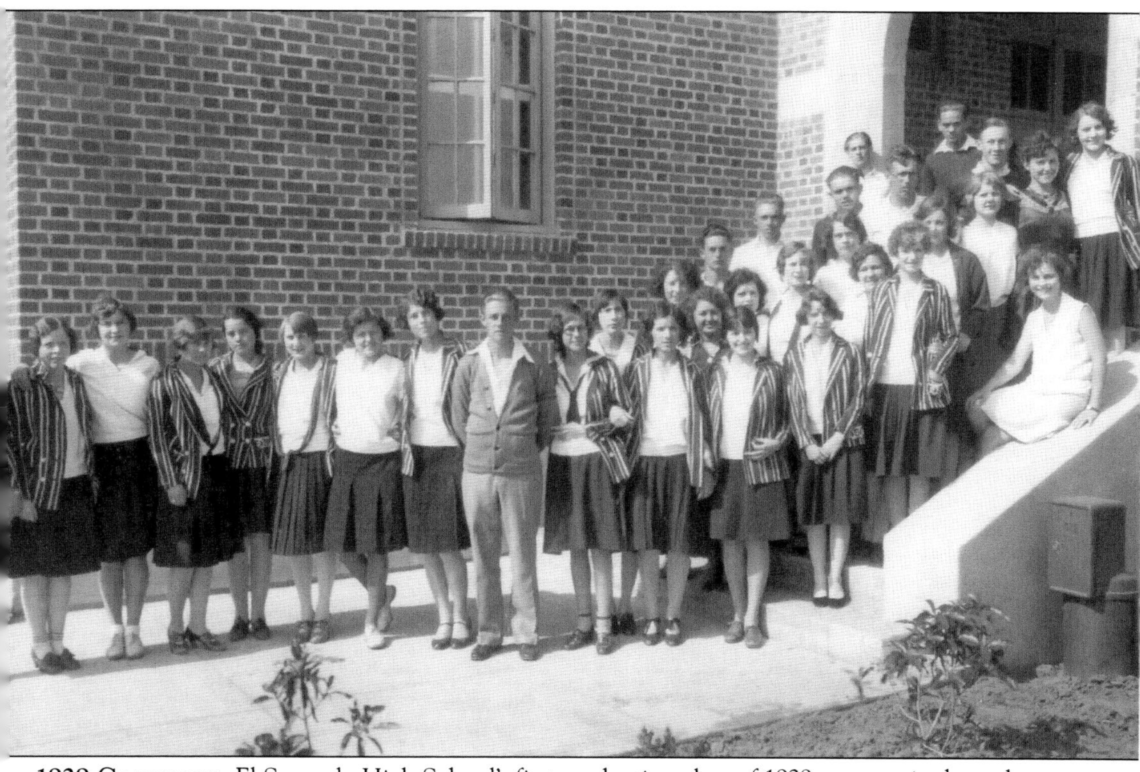

1929 Graduates. El Segundo High School's first graduating class of 1929 was required to take English, American history, civics, laboratory science, and physical education. According to Hunter's book, electives included Spanish, Latin, woodwork, metal work, auto mechanics, business training, typing, stenography, home economics, music, and art. And a big concern was senior "ditch day." A report by Charles L. Broadwater states, "teachers must teach and not take any part in 'ditch day,' and pupils must find other means of entertainment . . . instead of doing something which is a loss to the district."

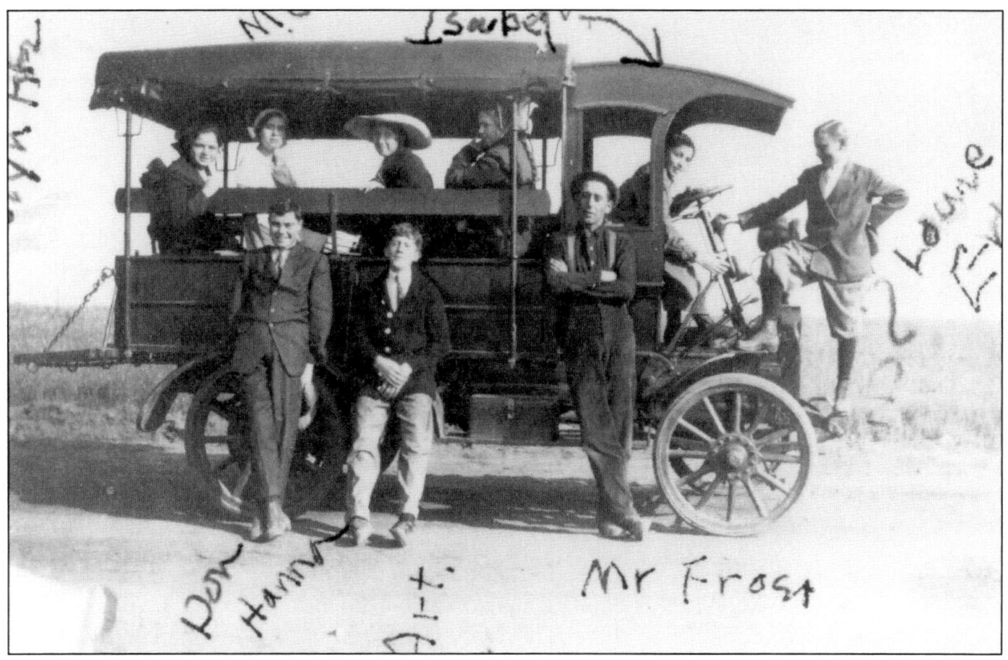

First School Bus, 1920s. The original owner of the photograph was young high school student Marieum Gilbert (Tuck), who apparently self-identified the riders of the bus from left to right as Evelyn Fitz (Fitzgerald), herself, Daisy Stege, Rachel Hanna, Isabel Fitzgerald, Louie Erb, Mr. Frost (?), Art Tuck, and Don Hanna.

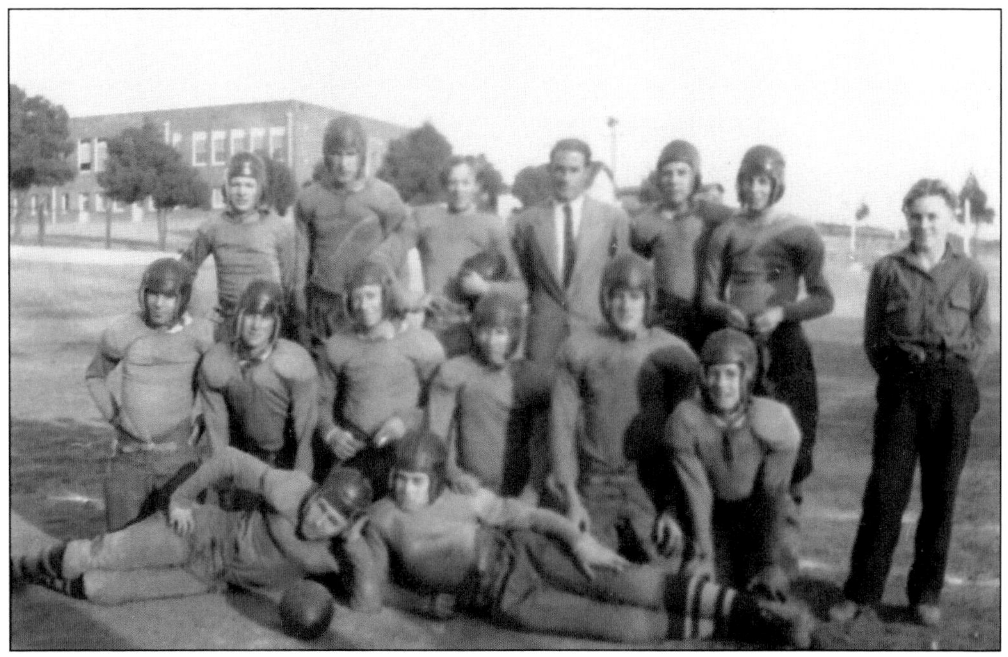

First Football Team, c. 1926. From left to right are (reclining) Carl Grimes and Harold O'Connell Fedderson; (kneeling) George Sueto, Jack Woods, Bert Cobb, Lloyd Fleming, Bob Cosby, and Harry Hoefle; (standing) unidentified, Bud Newman, Elgin Short, coach Harvey Hazeltine, Charles Russell, and unidentified. Out of uniform at the end is Harry Booth.

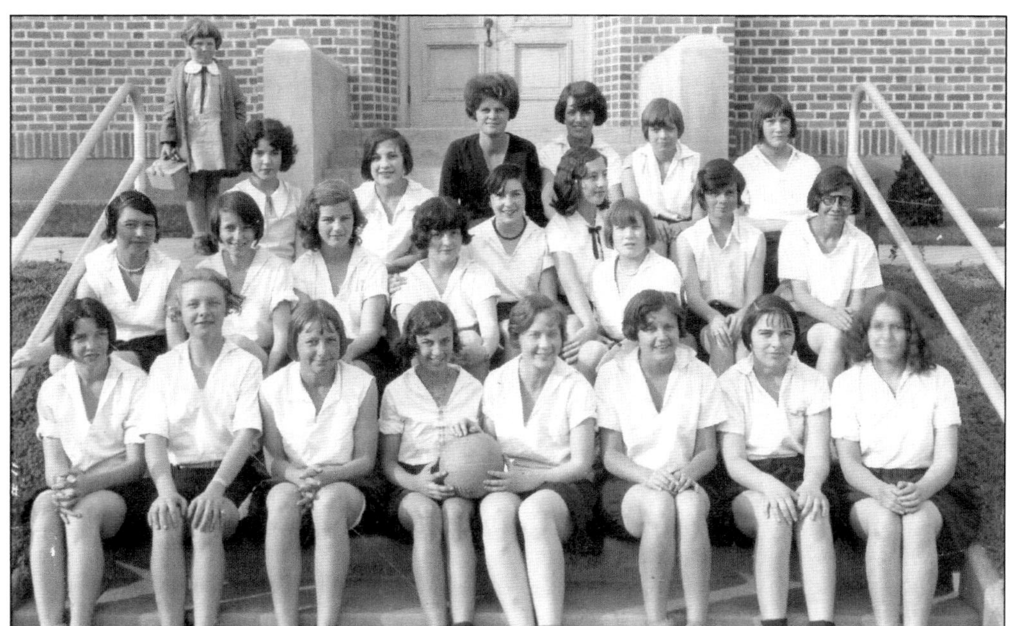

Girls' Volleyball Athletes, 1928–1929. The teacher, Florence Chambers, is at center in the back row. From left to right are (first row) unidentified, ? Reich, Virginia Martin, unidentified, Nina May Kevanfer, unidentified, Virginia Jape, and Viola Groger; (second row) Vera Chancel, Winifred Graham, Betty Hanna, Frances Krummel Kidd, Eleanor Griffith McCay, Jane Hornell, unidentified, Lenore Turner, and unidentified; (third row) all unidentified except for Chambers.

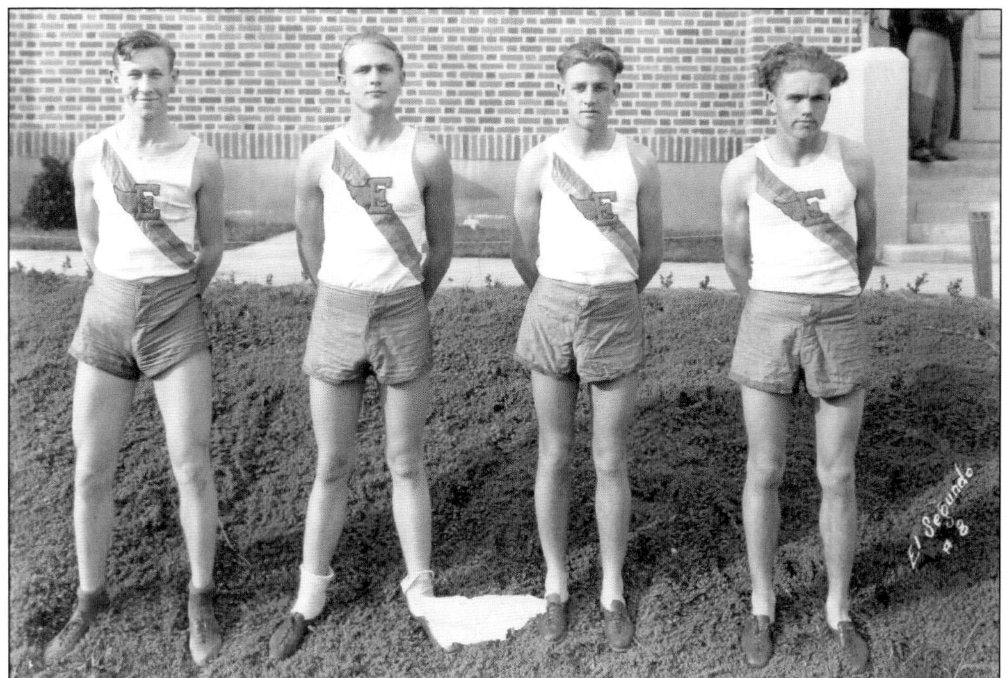

High School Track Team, 1929. From left to right are Lowell Nutting, Bill Lane, Clyde Walker, and Bert Smith.

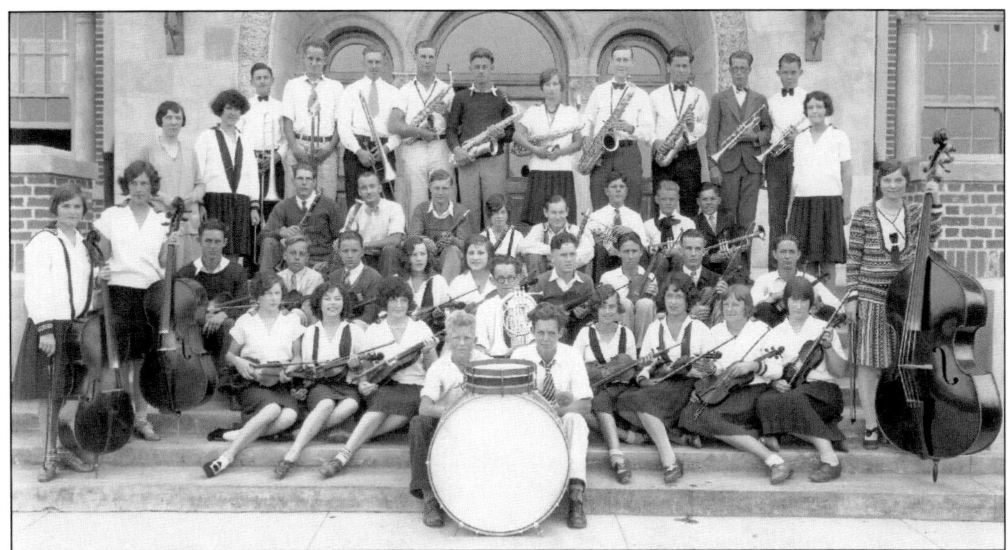

HIGH SCHOOL ORCHESTRA, 1930. Pictured on the high school's front steps are, from left to right, (first row) unidentified violinist, Dorothy Meads, Francis Krimmel, unidentified drummer, Burdette Foster, unidentified horn player, two unidentified violinists, Helen Cartland, and Ruth Ainsworth; (second row) Bernard Lawler, Wayne Fleming, George Eason and the rest unidentified; (third row) Donovan Fisher, Sam Heintz, unidentified clarinetist, Lenore Turner, George Binder, Wilbur Bailey, George Merritt, and Jack Moore; (fourth row) Ruth Fitzgerald, Artimesa Wilson, unidentified, Charlotte Clybourne, unidentified, Glen Foster, unidentified, Jack Woods, Clyde Walker, unidentified, Lowell Nutting, Harold Clybourne, John Shaffer, Bill McCoy, Shirley Martin, and unidentified cellist.

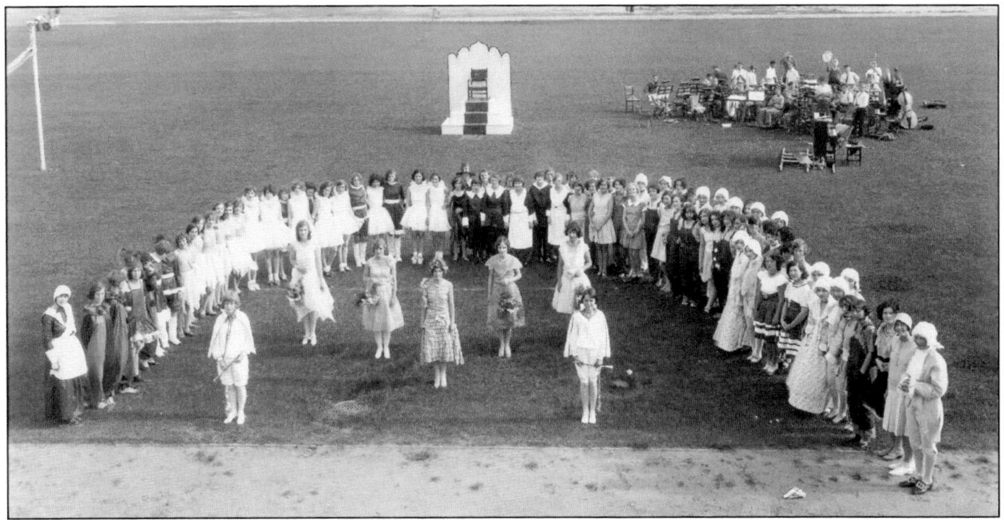

MAY DAY CELEBRATION, 1929. May Day celebrations were common in the United States at women's colleges and academic institutions in the late 19th and early 20th centuries. Baskets were filled with flowers or treats and left on doorsteps. This view was taken facing north from the stands in the high school athletic field. The larger street in the background behind the band is Eucalyptus Drive. The maypole is located on the left corner, midway up the field. Besides the baton holders and girls holding flowers in the middle, there appears to be a variety of costumes from early colonial and pioneer days to celebrate the first days of spring.

Three

World War II and Beyond 1940–1949

With the start of World War II, Victory bond drives, women entering the local workforce, and the escalation of fighter planes being built at Douglas Aircraft and North American Aviation on the east side of town, the city continued to expand its civic pride on the west side or downtown area. The 1940s brought several community development projects to completion, including a plunge, a public library, and a fire station.

The Urho Saari Plunge was well known for Coach Saari and his victorious swim teams, including finalists for the 1952 Olympics in Helsinki. Although a new public library was planned and partially constructed in the early 1940s, completion of the facility had to wait until after the war. The first fire station was built in 1947, in the city hall complex on Franklin Avenue and Richmond Streets, next to the police station.

For fun activities, a host of local parades, Woman's Club events, singing groups, dances, and even golf matches all tried to offer a balance between the horrors of a world at war and the social needs of a growing town. It is well documented in a pristine scrapbook that in the summer of 1942 the children of El Segundo took full advantage of a wide range of activities offered by a robust parks and recreation department.

More businesses came to town, including auto service stores, a gas station, and a very popular drive-in. The El Segundo refinery was expanded further, and the Los Angeles International Airport was developed across the north side of Imperial Boulevard, which later generated numerous aerospace support industries in El Segundo.

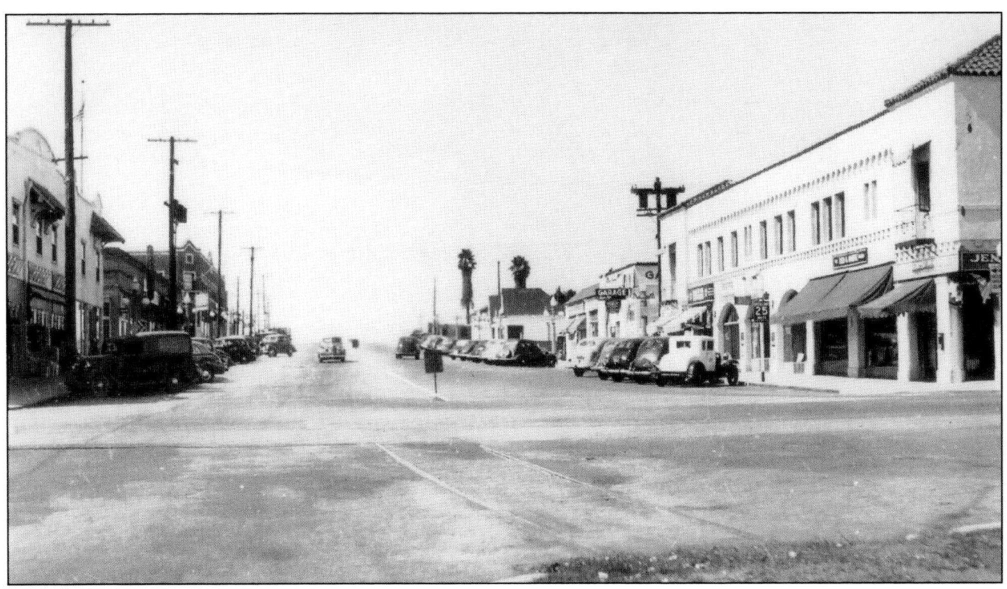

Intersection of Grand Avenue and Main Street in a View Facing West, 1940s. The impressive Lafayette Building on the right, later known as the Hollingsworth Building, and other distinctive businesses along Grand Avenue still make up the center of downtown today, 75 years later.

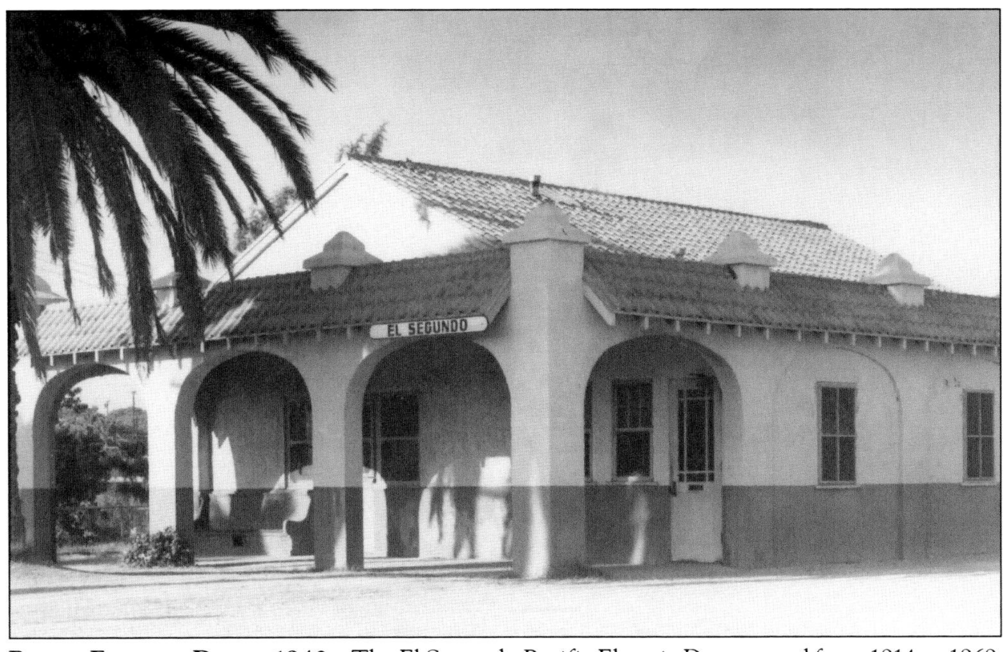

Pacific Electric Depot, 1940s. The El Segundo Pacific Electric Depot stood from 1914 to 1969. It was located at what is now the site of the Joslyn Center parking lot along Grand Avenue.

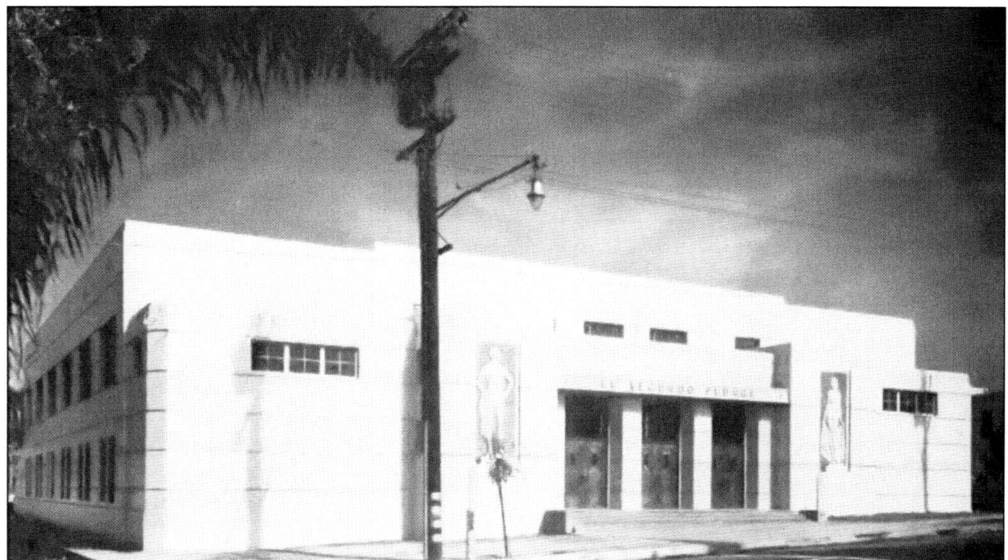

Exterior of the El Segundo Plunge, 1941. The El Segundo Plunge, also known as the Urho Saari Stadium, at 219 West Mariposa Avenue, was completed in the fall of 1941. Although major repairs are needed for the existing facility today, it still provides swimming instruction for El Segundo schoolchildren and recreational swimming for the community.

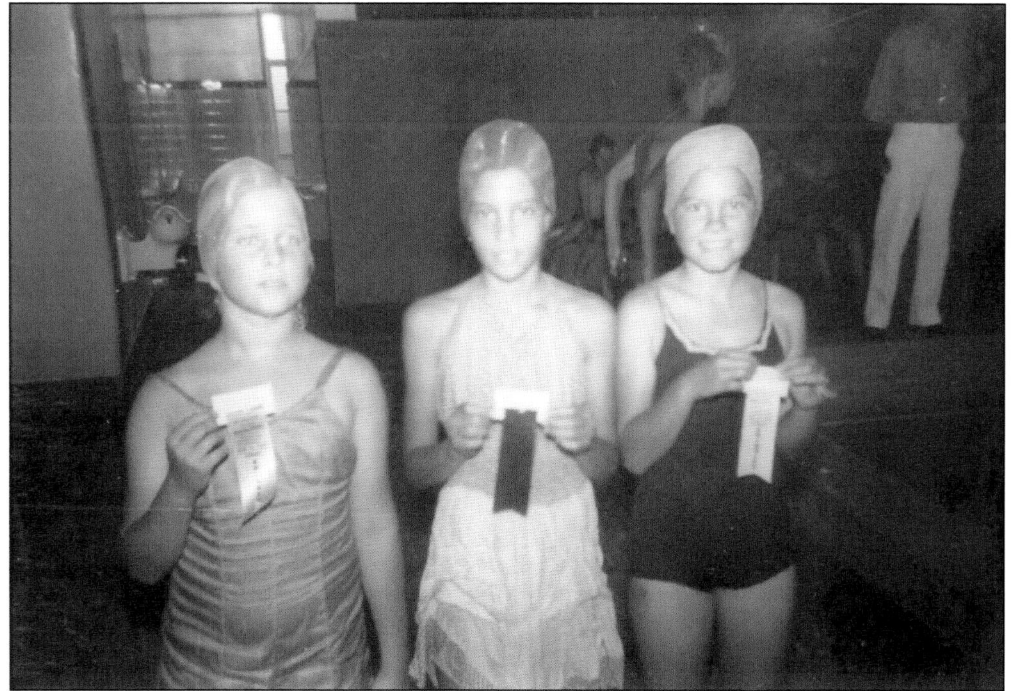

First Annual Swim Meet, August 1942. Seventy local boys and girls competed in the first annual El Segundo swim meet, sponsored by the recreation commission. The ribbon winners in the girls under 10 years 20-yard backstroke are, from left to right, Bobby Eiche, Marion Myers, and Ruth Wilson.

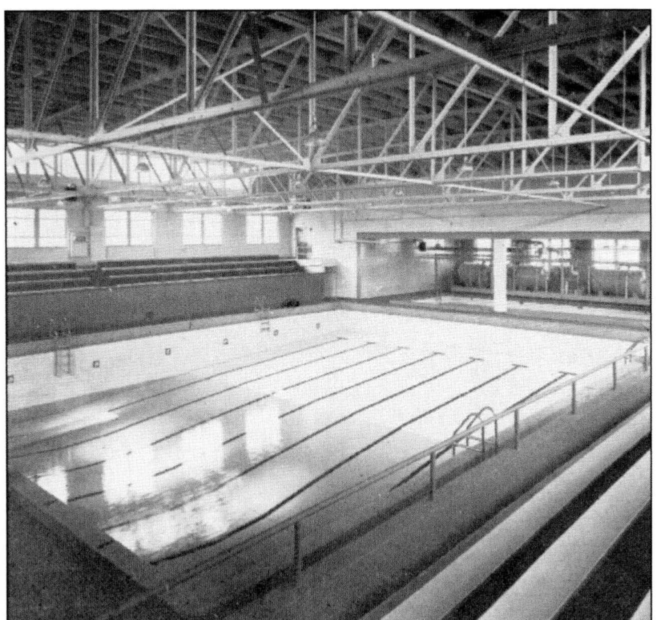

INTERIOR OF THE EL SEGUNDO PLUNGE, 1941. The 75-by-60-foot tiled pool holds 250,000 gallons of water. In 1948, the water polo team won the first California Interscholastic Federation (CIF) championship for the high school. Jack Spargo, Bob Hughes, and George Allen all won CIF titles in swimming. Coach Urho Saari continued to lead a string of victories for the high school swim team in the 1940s before he served in World War II. In the early 1950s, his El Segundo Swim Club won a US Olympic Water Polo final in Helsinki, finishing fourth among 21 other countries.

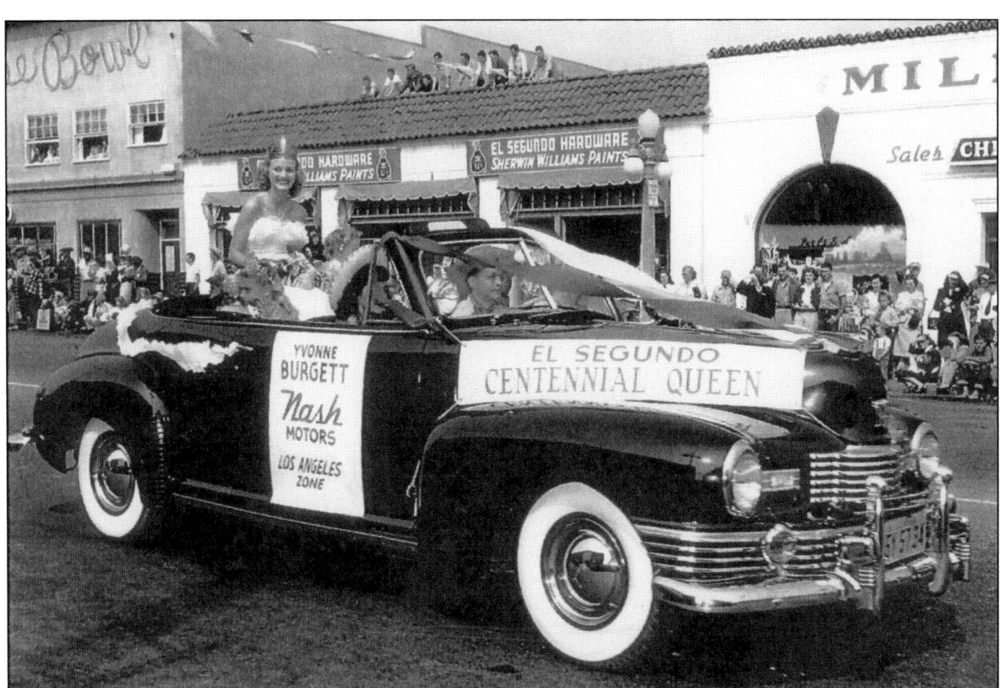

EL SEGUNDO CENTENNIAL QUEEN YVONNE BURGETT WILLS, 1948. Nash Motors of El Segundo sponsored an entry in the city's first Fiesta Parade, celebrating the 100th anniversary of the discovery of gold in California in 1848 at Sutter's Mill. Yvonne Burgett Wills served as queen of the event. The Rose Bowl bowling alley, in the background, unfortunately later burned and was demolished.

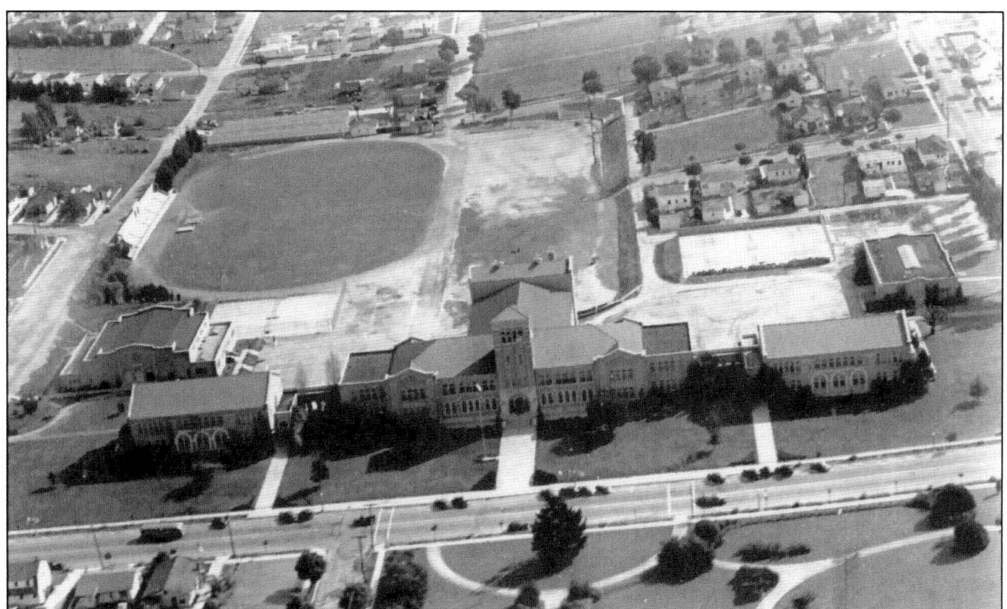

Aerial View of El Segundo High School, 1940. In this view facing west above Library Park, although the library has not been constructed yet, main buildings of the high school in front of Main Street are flanked by the gym on the back left and the manual arts building on the back right off of Mariposa Avenue and Standard Street. The smaller grandstand faced south at this time, and there were still many open lots behind the school.

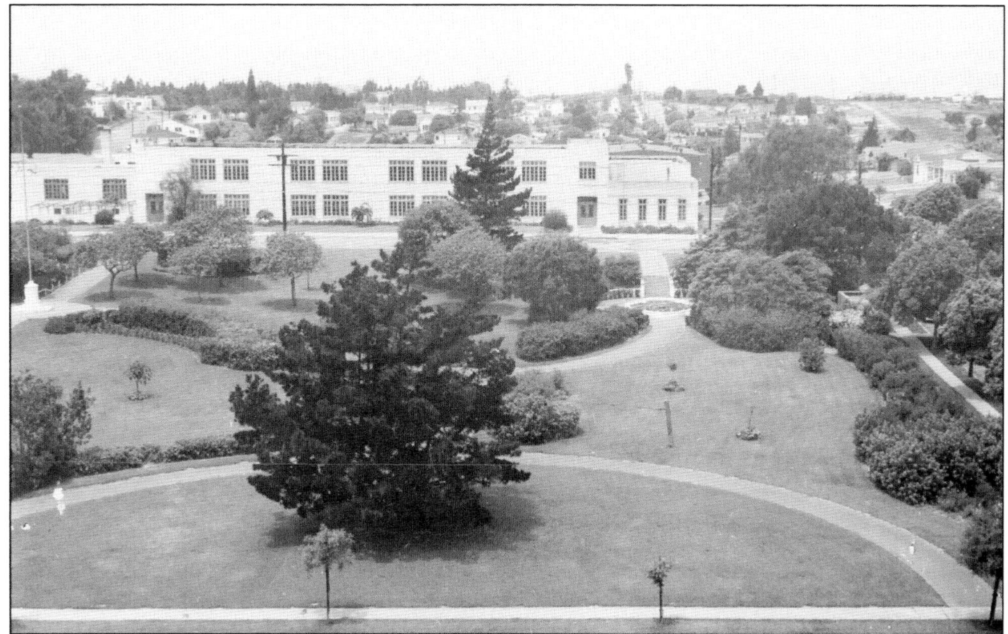

Aerial View of Library Park and Richmond School, 1940s. A note on the back of the photograph claims that this view was taken from the bell tower of the high school. Richmond Street School is very much as it looks today, but it is uncertain whether the library was built yet, since the view of the park does not extend far enough to the southwest corner, where it was started in the early 1940s, halted during the war, and then completed in 1948.

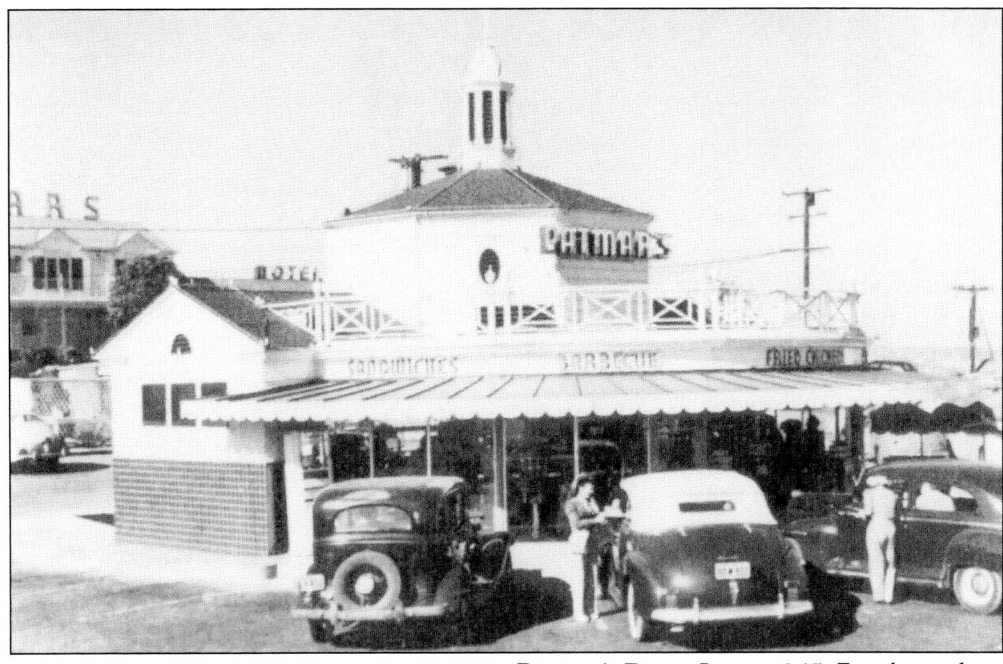

Patmar's Drive-In, c. 1945. First located at the southwest corner of Sepulveda Boulevard and Imperial Highway, from 1939 to 1959, Patmar's was the social hub for South Bay teenagers, a resting spot for weary travelers, and a cheap place for family dining.

PATMAR'S DOUBLE-DECKERS
(Please Order by Number)

1. SLICED CHICKEN AND BACON .75
Lettuce, Tomato, Mayonnaise and Shoestring Potatoes

2. AVOCADO AND BACON .70
Lettuce, Tomato, Mayonnaise and Shoestring Potatoes

DINNER SPECIALS

TENDER N. Y. STEAK PLATE, Chef's Salad, Shoestring Potatoes, Toasted Bun 1.35
Large Half Fried Chicken, Shoestring Potatoes, Honey, Toasted Bun, Salad 1.25
Ground Round Steak (a generous portion) Freshly Ground from the Finest Steer Beef, Salad, Shoestring Potatoes, and Toasted Bun 85
Barbecued Beef or Pork Plate, Spaghetti, Bar-B-Q Sauce, Shoestring Potatoes, Salad and Toasted Bun 85
Omelets — Denver, Ham or Cheese 85
Meat Loaf Plate, Chef's Salad, Shoestring Potatoes and Toasted Bun 80

HOT BEEF OR PORK SANDWICH 75c
Shoestring Potatoes Salad

SPECIAL STEAK SANDWICH,
Tender, Lean and Juicy 55c
Served with French Fries

FRESH STRAWBERRY SHORTCAKE 35c
with Whipped Cream

SPECIALTY DISHES

Delicious Hot Turkey Sandwich, Giblet Gravy, Dressing, Shoestring Potatoes and Cranberry Sauce 80
Spaghetti Italienne, Toasted Bun 50
Spaghetti, Chili, Toasted Bun 50
Spaghetti with Meat Loaf, Toasted Bun 55
Spaghetti with Meat Balls, Toasted Bun 55
Spaghetti Size with Chili 60
Grilled Chicken Liver on Rye 35
Tenderized Steak Sandwich on Toast, Shoestring Potatoes 55
Cold Sliced Chicken Sandwich, Lettuce and Mayonnaise 55
Oven Baked Beans 35
With Frankfurters 50
Chili and Beans 40

All Prices Are Our OPS Ceiling Prices or Lower. A List Showing Our Ceiling Prices for Each Item is Available for Your Inspection.

Menu of Patmar's Drive-In, 1940s. An early menu from Patmar's features spaghetti served in a variety of ways for 60¢ and under, double-decker sandwiches up to 75¢, half a fried chicken for $1.25, and a New York steak dinner, which today can easily cost over $30, for a whopping $1.35.

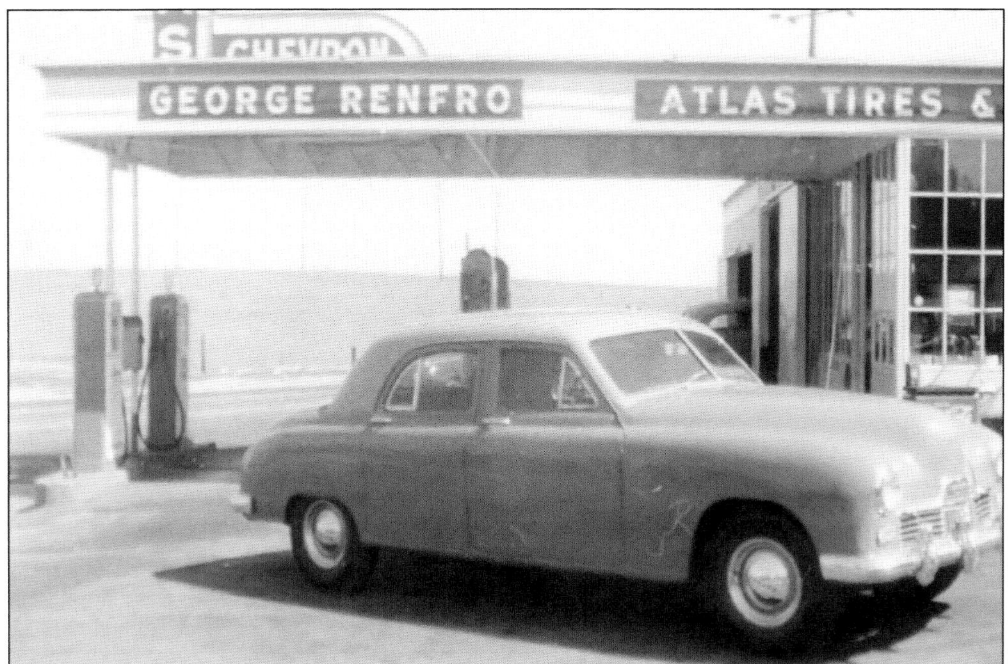

GAS STATION, 1945. George Renfro Jr. opened his Chevron gas station in 1945 at the southeast corner of Main Street and Imperial Highway. He continued as the proprietor until 1951, when he became a realtor. Today, there is a donut shop, a Hawaiian restaurant, a shoe repair, and a Subway shop in this location.

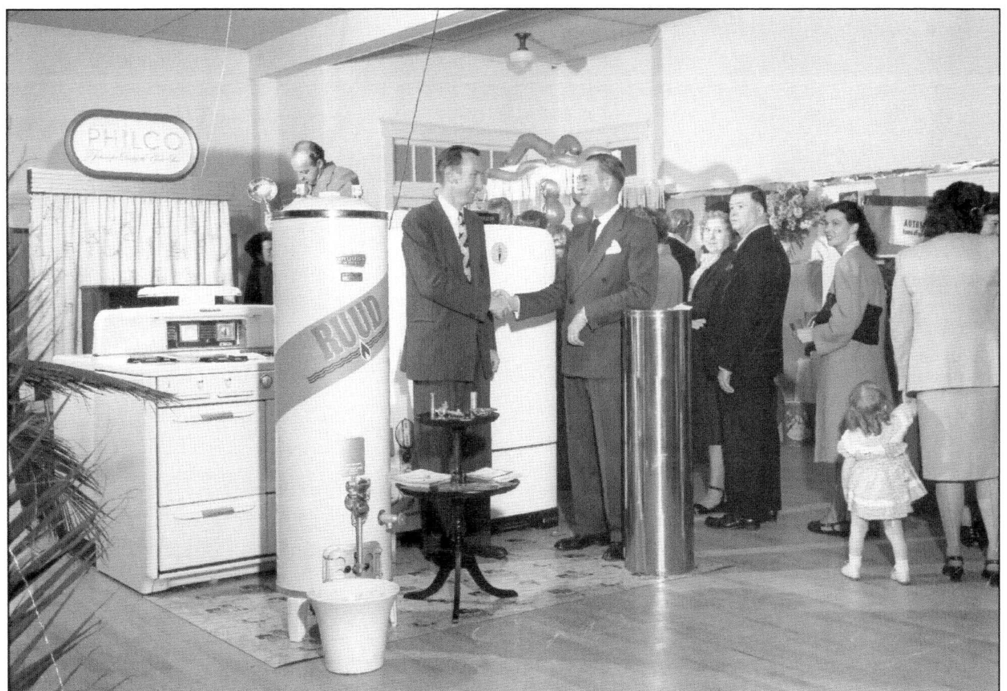

WOMAN'S CLUB EVENT, APRIL 29, 1948. A small "Home Show," sponsored by the Woman's Club, showed off the latest in home appliances.

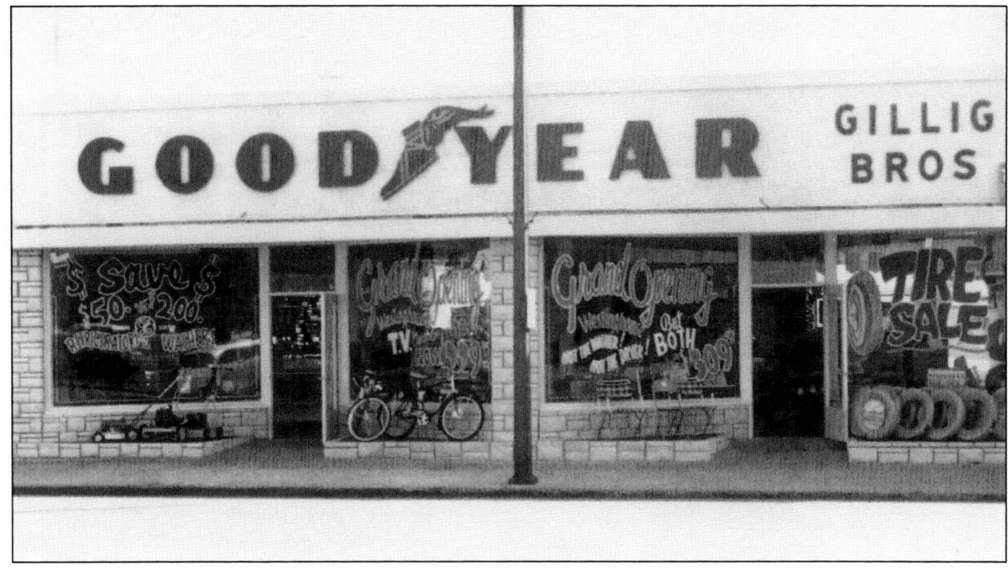

Gillig Brothers Goodyear Auto Store, 1947. After running an auto repair business at the southwest corner of Grand Avenue and Concord Street at Fredrick's Gas Station, James and Howard Gillig opened their own Goodyear tire and auto service stores on the east side of the 200 block of Main Street. The stores closed in the late 1950s and no longer exist. Today, this is the site of the Chevron gas station at Main Street and Grand Avenue.

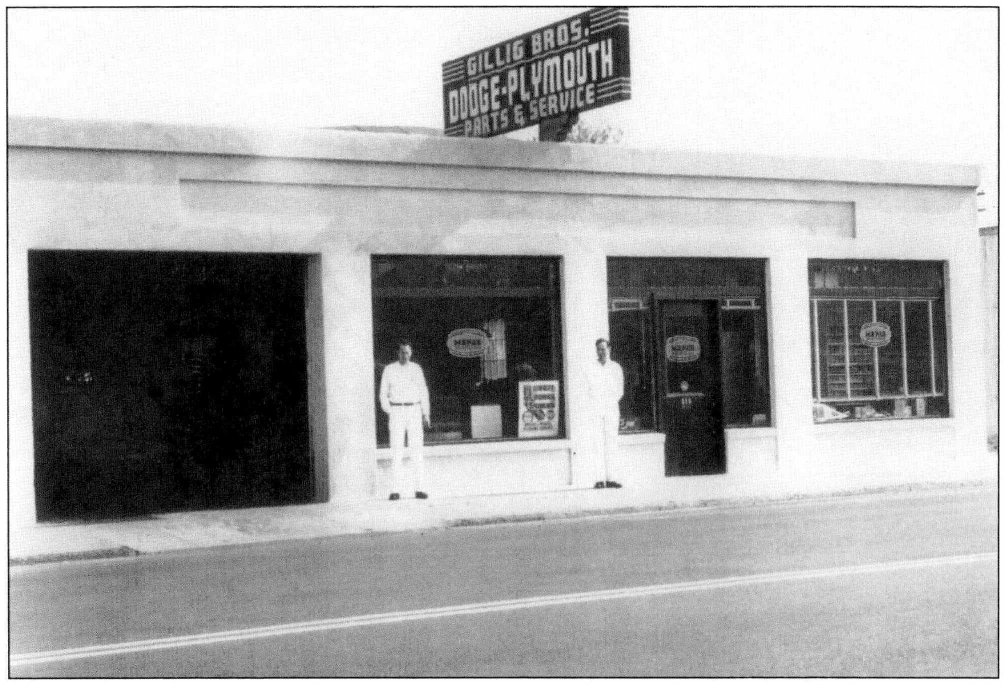

Gillig Brothers Parts and Service, 1947. The two brothers pictured (not identified by name) also opened an auto parts and service store near their tire store in 1947.

STANDARD OIL WORKERS UNLOADING DRUMS, FEBRUARY 1944. By 1949, the refinery processed 115,000 barrels of crude oil daily and manufactured 40,000 barrels per day of motor gasoline, plus more than 3,000 barrels per day of aviation fuel. By 1951, the workforce consisted of 1,700 employees.

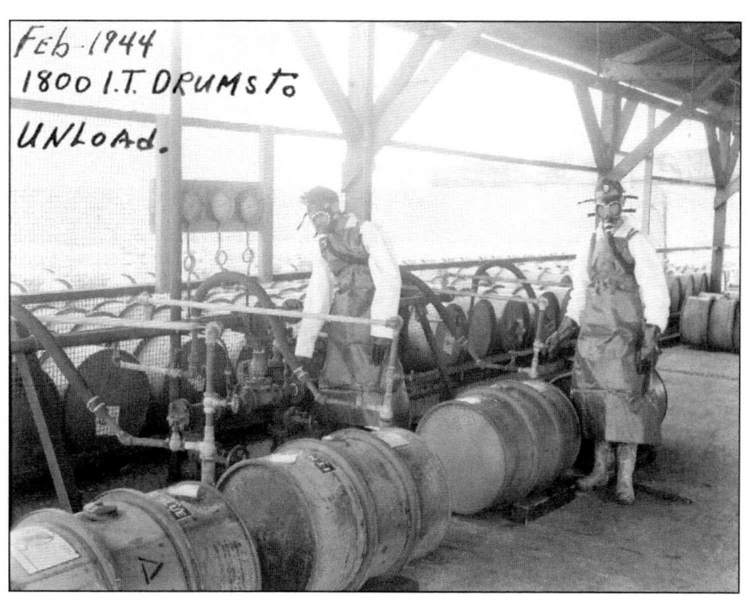

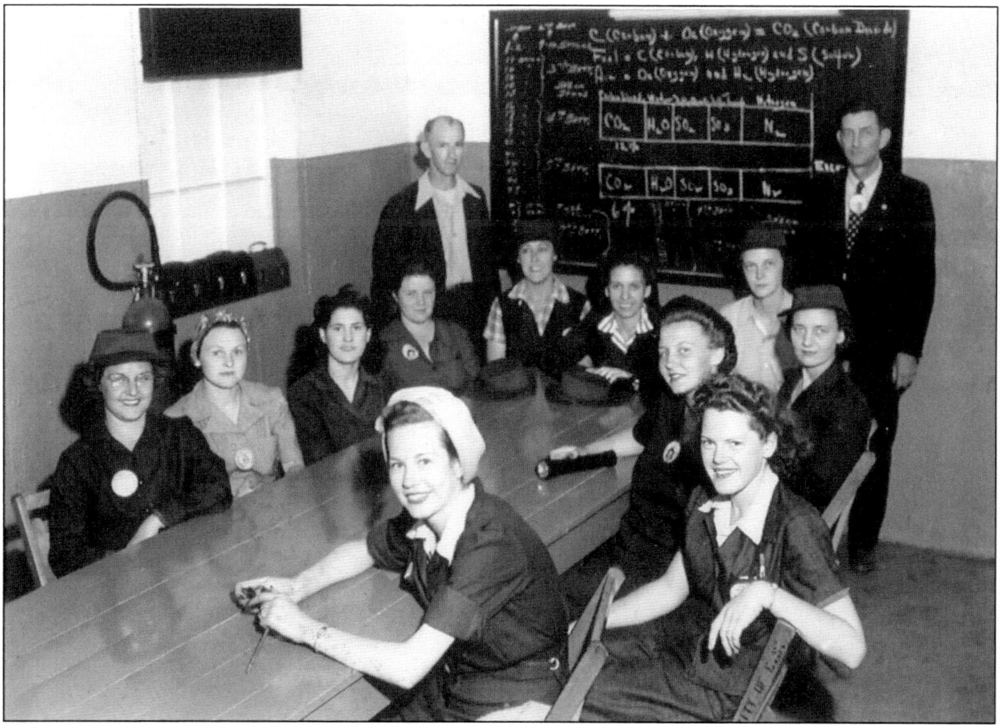

FIRST FEMALE MACHINE OPERATORS, AUGUST 26, 1943. During the war, women were hired to perform driving jobs and become low-pressure still operators. This is the first graduating class of female still operators at the Standard Oil Refinery. Clockwise from left are Jane Kiels, Dorothy Sanders, Shelly Ashworth, Jackie Gunn, Harold Mercer (standing), Bonnie Shilling, Mary Colesman, Rea Thompson, an unidentified man wearing a tie, Winoma Butler, Hazel Stewart, Jannadale Brodie, and Ruth Larson.

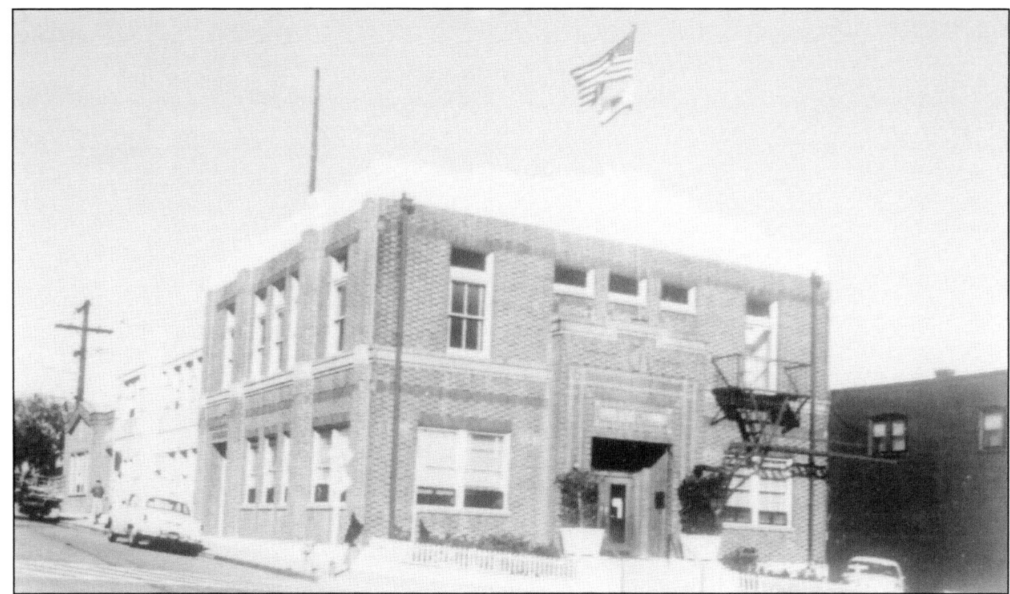

City Hall in the Mid-1940s. A cleaned-up exterior shot of city hall illustrates more of the front facade than the 1930s version of the same view, in which it is covered in ivy. It was still located at the northwest corner of Richmond Street and Franklin Avenue with the police and fire stations behind it to the left.

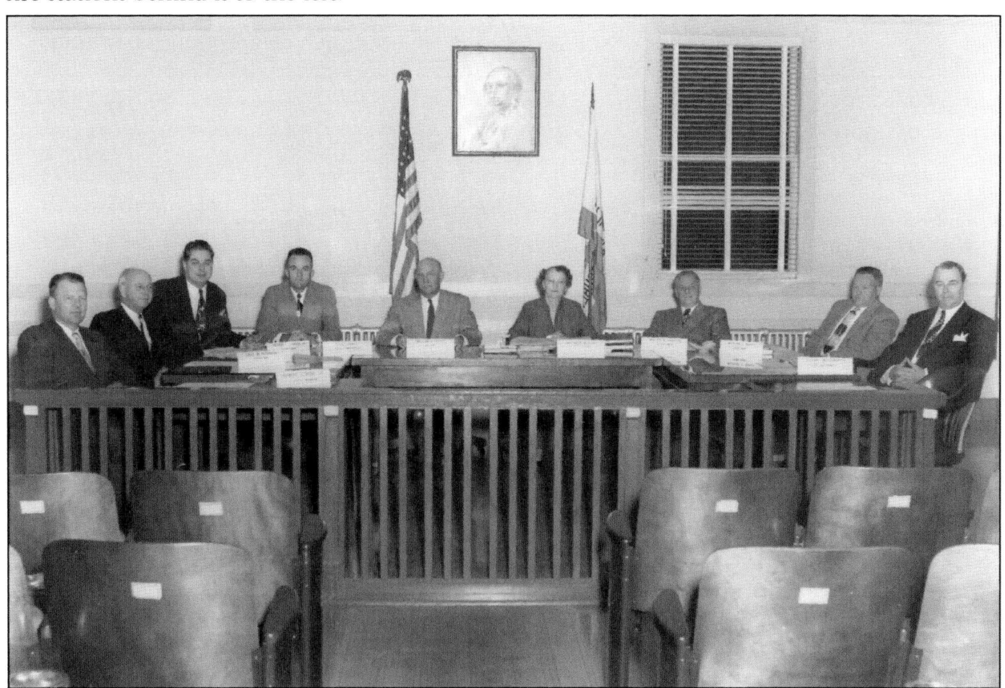

City Council Meeting, 1940s. A city council meeting conducted at the Richmond Street location includes, from left to right, Bob Webb, city engineer; Don Peterson, council member; George Gordon, council member; Earl Udall, city administration; Mayor Roy Selby; Deputy City Clerk Neva Elsey (later city clerk); Walter W. Swanson, council member; Wilburn Baker, council member (later mayor); and Clyde Woodworth, city attorney.

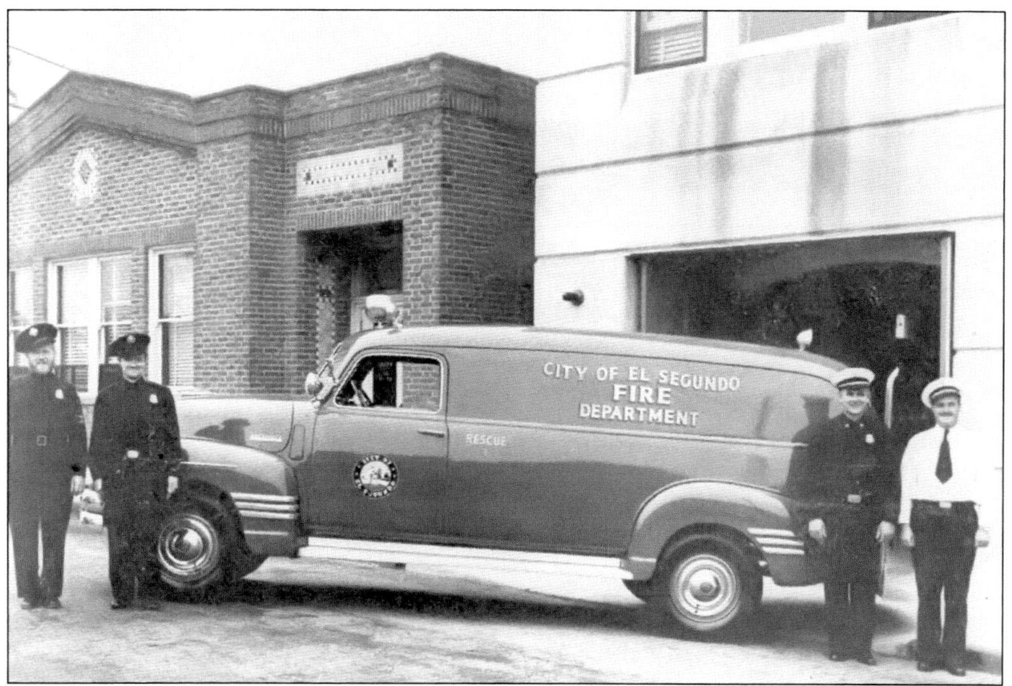

FIRE DEPARTMENT, 1947. In November 1947, the city built its first fire department building (no longer standing), which faced the 200 block of Franklin Street and was next to the brick building (still standing) that housed the El Segundo Police Department. Although the other individuals are not identified, the man in the white shirt, Don J. Farrar, is the city's first fire chief.

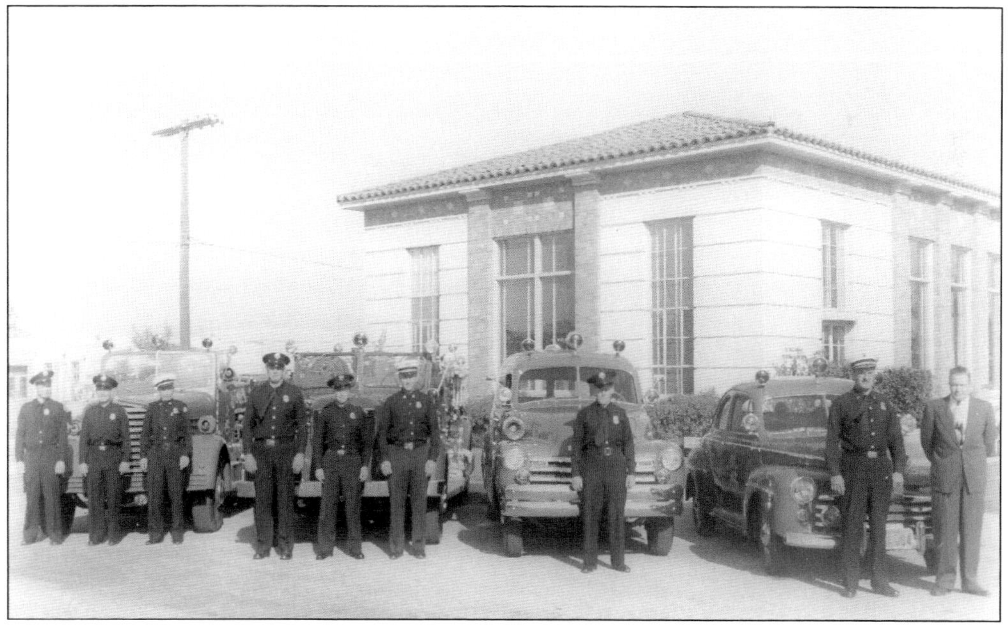

FIRE TRUCKS IN FRONT OF THE LIBRARY, C. 1948. Firemen and their trucks line the Mariposa Avenue side of the new El Segundo Public Library. Bill Coulter is in front of the second truck from the right, and Bruce Clements (left, in uniform) and Mayor Wilburn Baker (right, in suit) are on the far right. The other firemen are unidentified.

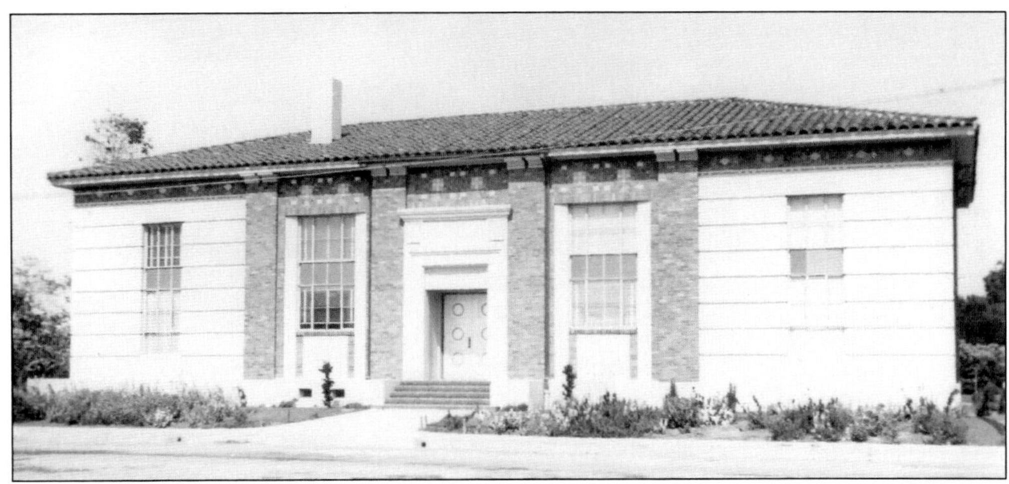

El Segundo Public Library Front Facing Richmond Street, 1948. Although construction of a new public library began in early 1940, it was not completed until after World War II, on August 16, 1948, at a cost of $76,000. At this time, the library's address was 609 Richmond Street, since that was the entrance until the 1960s, when a new wing was added. With the 1960s expansion and remodel, the front door was relocated to 111 West Mariposa Avenue, and this remains the entrance today. Over the door, a sign reads, "El Segundo Public Library / Books contain knowledge – knowledge is power."

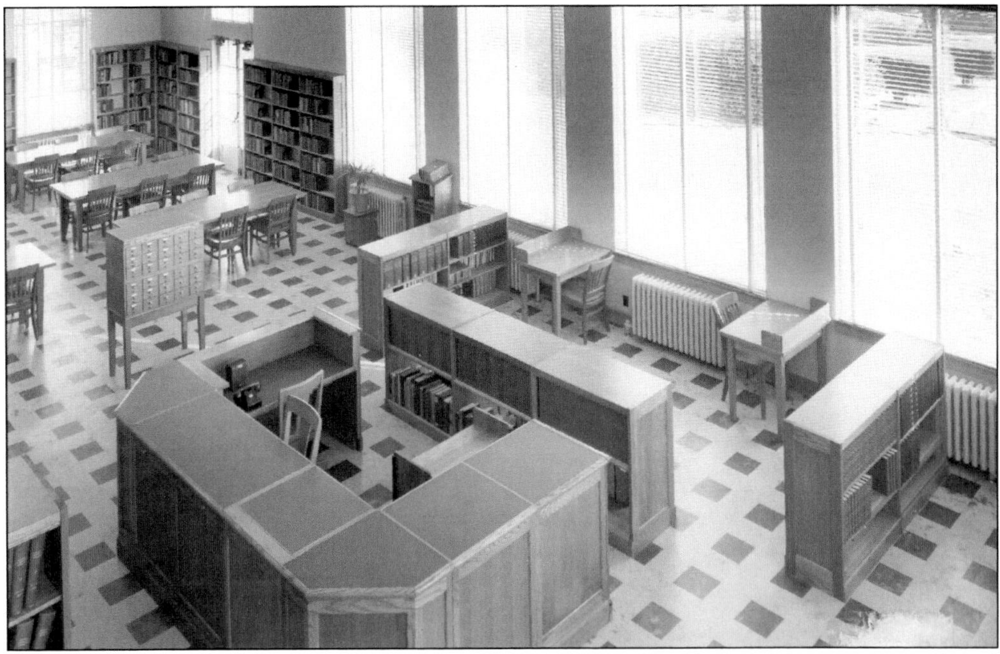

Library Interior View Facing East, 1948. All-wood shelving, tables, and chairs were purchased for the new public library, with a collection size of around 3,000 books. This photograph was taken from upstairs in the mezzanine area looking out the high windows facing Library Park. A new reference desk, card catalog, book stacks, furniture, and heating comprised a modern library facility for that era. Today, the library has expanded into the park, and this area is used for staff offices, a literacy meeting room, and the location for paperbacks, DVDs, and the music collection on CDs.

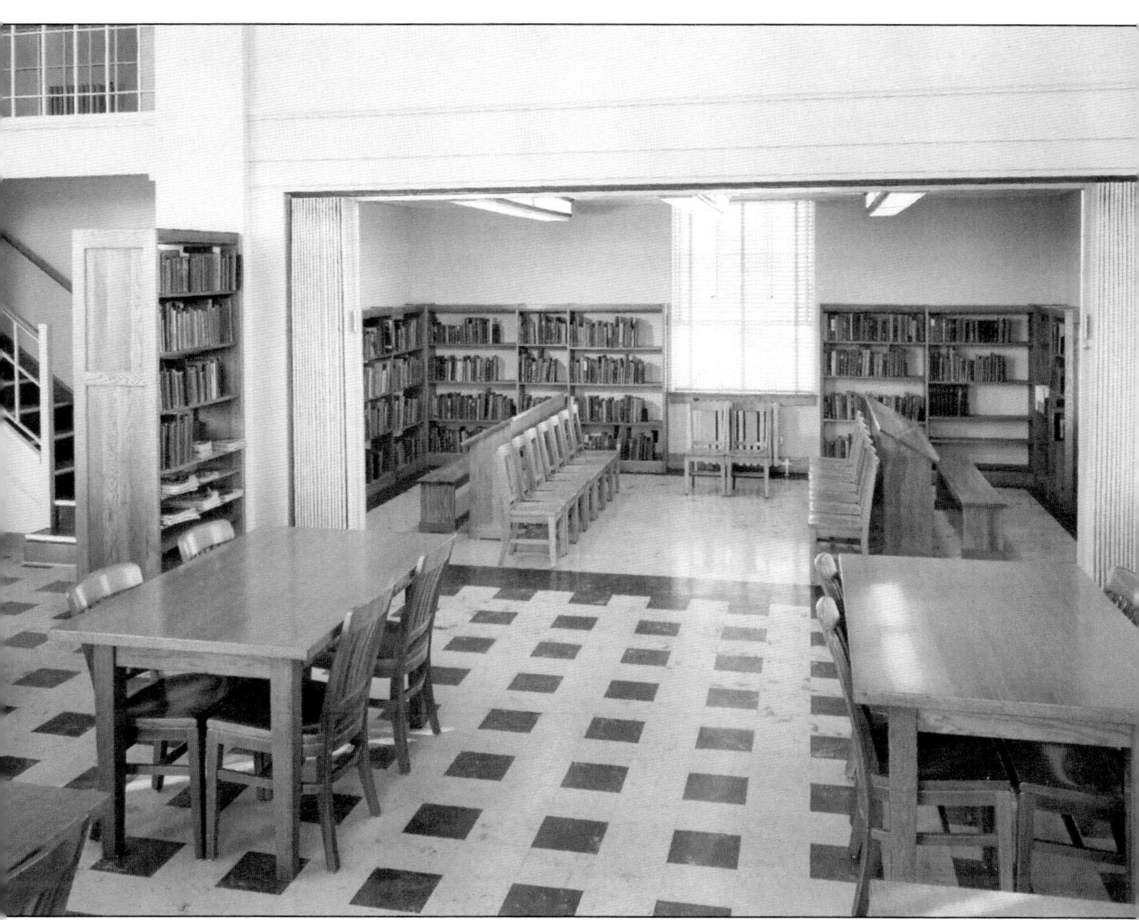

Library Interior View Facing West, 1948. The mezzanine area above the stairway was open to the public at this time, but in later years it was closed off for a staff lounge, restroom, and magazine storage area. Currently, it is used for storage and processing of Friends of the El Segundo Public Library book sale items and as the library's data equipment center.

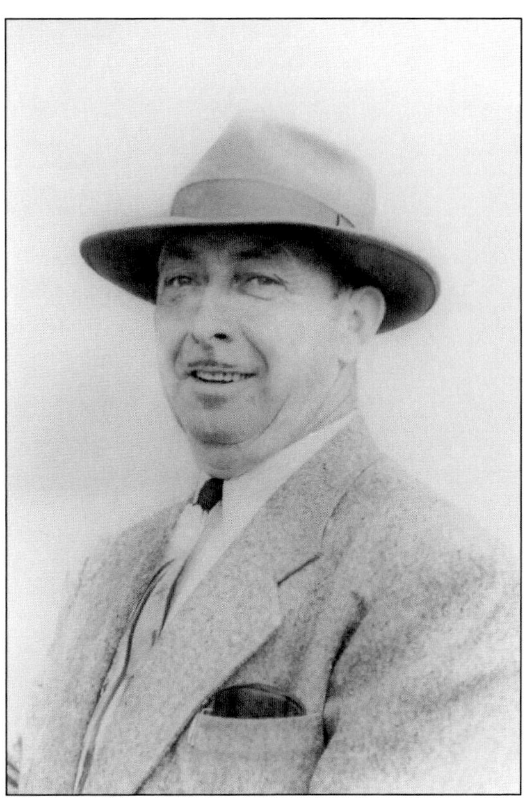

Tom DeBerry, Police Chief. Joining the El Segundo Police Department in 1927, DeBerry succeeded R.T. Hutchins as police chief in 1948. DeBerry remained chief until he retired in 1967. Chief DeBerry was also among the charter members, and later president, of the El Segundo Kiwanis Club, which formed on September 24, 1929.

Collision on El Segundo Boulevard, 1940s. Pictured with his 1947 Ford police car in the background, officer Lee Maxwell is writing an accident report on El Segundo Boulevard. Officer Maxwell was a high school basketball star in 1933, was hired into the police department in 1936, and became acting police chief before retiring in 1971.

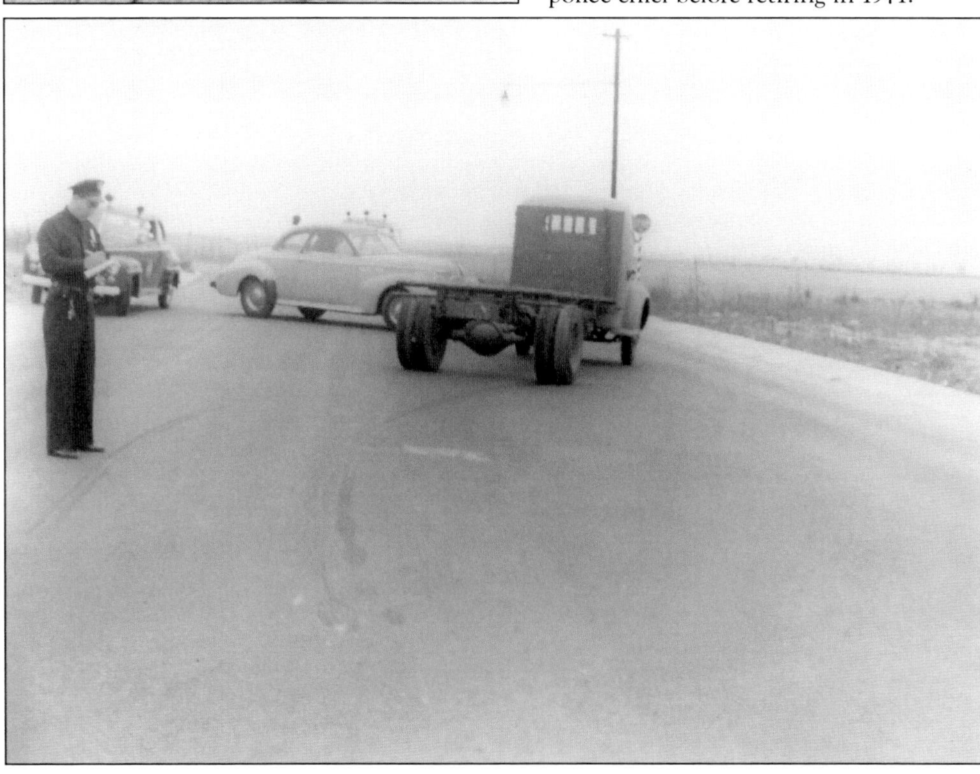

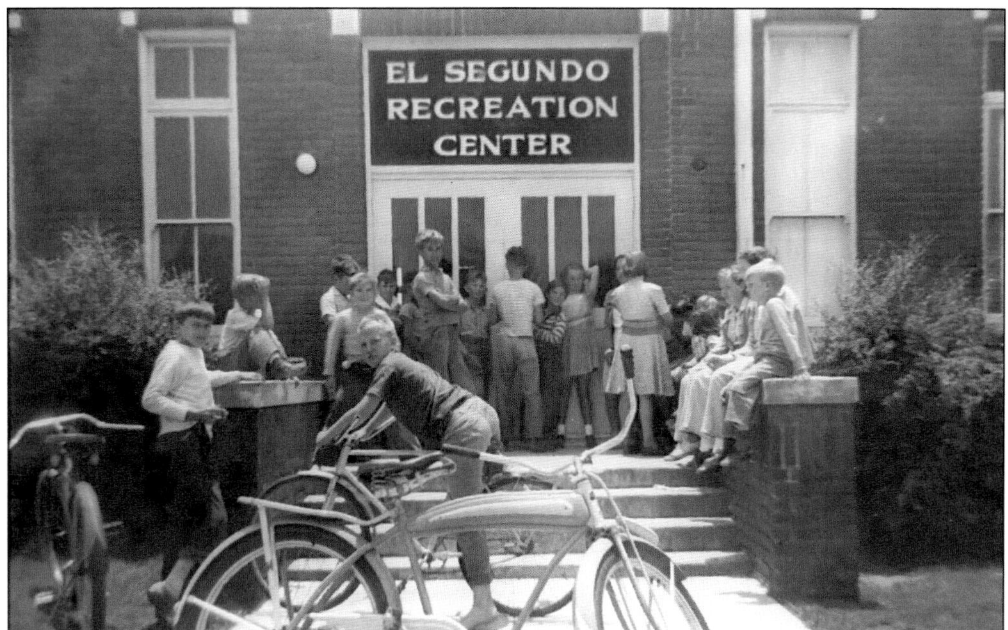

RECREATION DEPARTMENT SUMMER PROGRAM, 1942. Children eagerly wait for the opening of the El Segundo Recreation Center summer program, which ran from June 15 to August 15, 1942. Led by recreation director Maurice E. Ward, the summer activities included a variety of sports, band, drama, a Fourth of July celebration, story hours, dances, crafts, sewing, and a bicycle brigade camping trip.

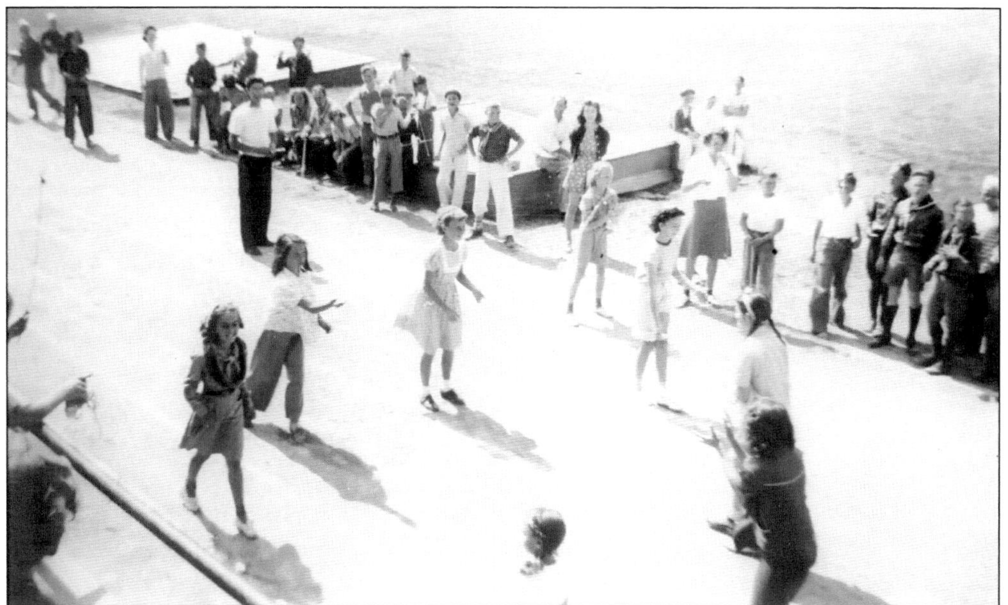

FOURTH OF JULY EGG-THROWING CONTEST, 1942. According to an *El Segundo Herald* article, races and games for children began at 10:00 a.m. on the high school grounds on Independence Day 1942. A baseball game, pony rides, a movie matinee, a fortune-teller, ice cream, balloon darts, and many food concession stands were also all sponsored, like they still are to this day, by various community organizations and businesses.

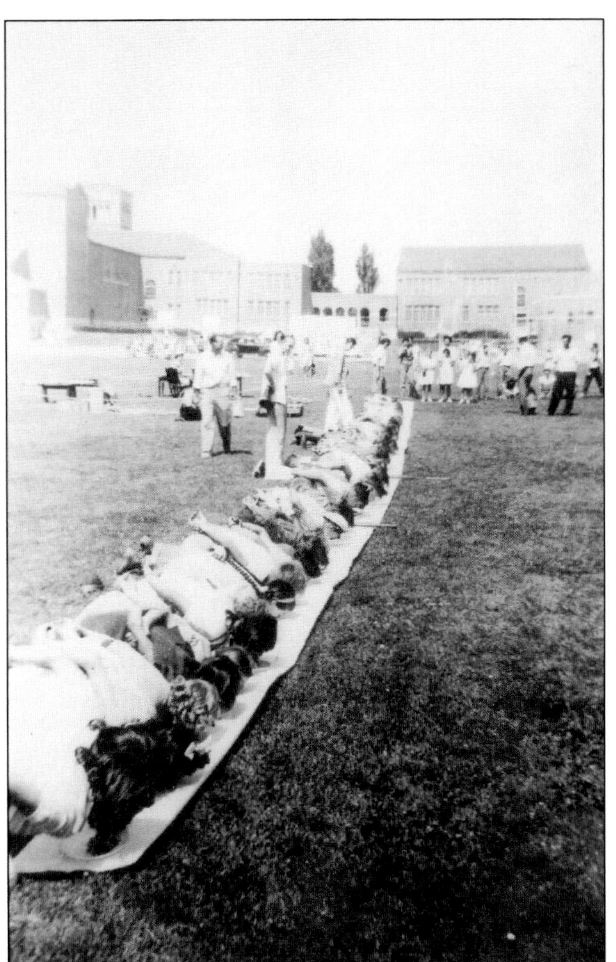

Pie-Eating Contest, 1942. What would a July Fourth picnic be without a pie-eating contest? These contestants are on their knees on the ground with their hands behind their backs behind the high school. Attendance was estimated to be 2,000 that day; 1,150 ice creams were sold, and 750 hot dogs were consumed. Now, a state-of-the-art fireworks display is also part of the anticipated traditions carried out for this special holiday celebration.

Bicycle Brigade Overnight Camp, 1942. Part of the summer program on July 15, 1942, was the bicycle brigade overnight camp. It was held mostly for boys, but there was a half day of bike exercises for girls and small children as well. After passing the required tests, 17 boys out of 80 enjoyed an evening of camp sporting events, including a night ride and eating s'mores on the high school athletic grounds. In the morning, a hotcake breakfast followed a short hike, and camp cleaning and an inspection were the activities before the brigade was dismissed at 9:00 a.m.

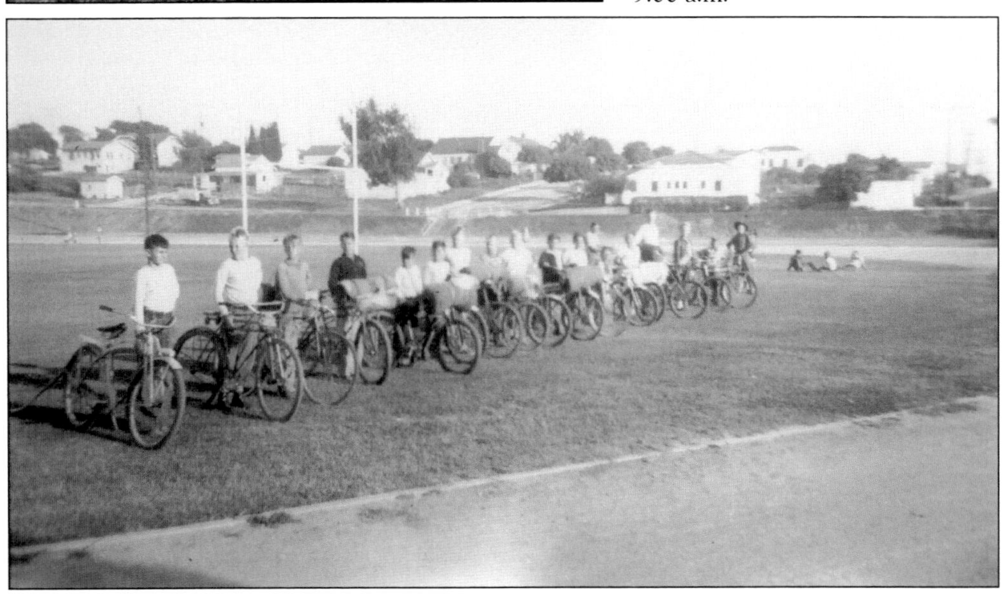

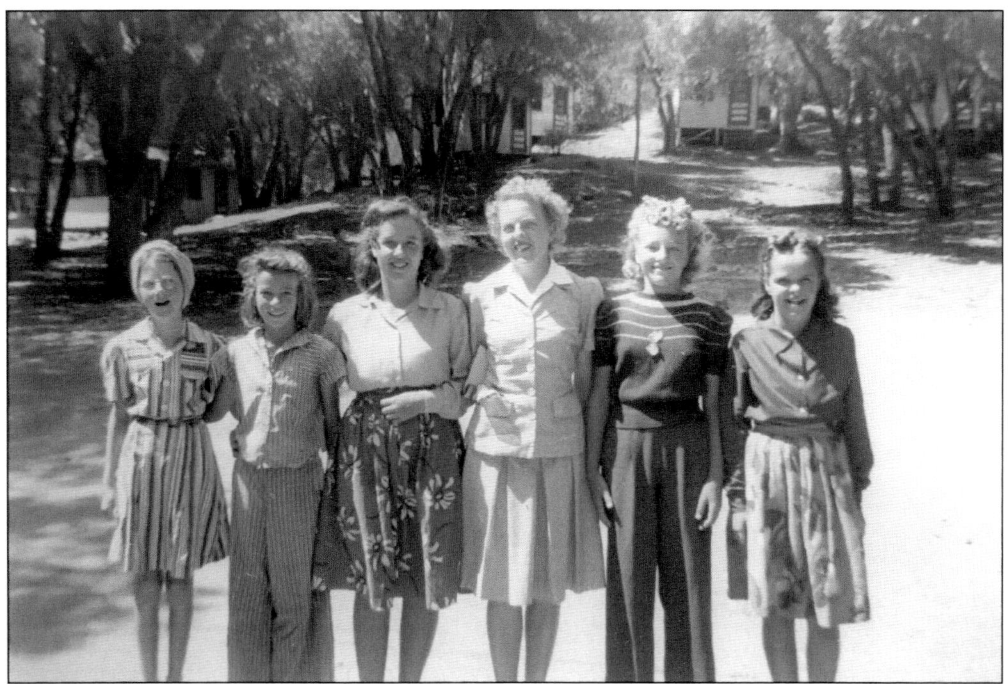

Junior Merrimacs, 1942. A new musical group called the Junior Merrimacs was organized at the recreation center during the summer of 1942. From left to right are Peggy Materna, Dorothy Cline, Audine Campbell, Margaret Mountford (singing director), Ruth Cline, and Geraldine Campbell.

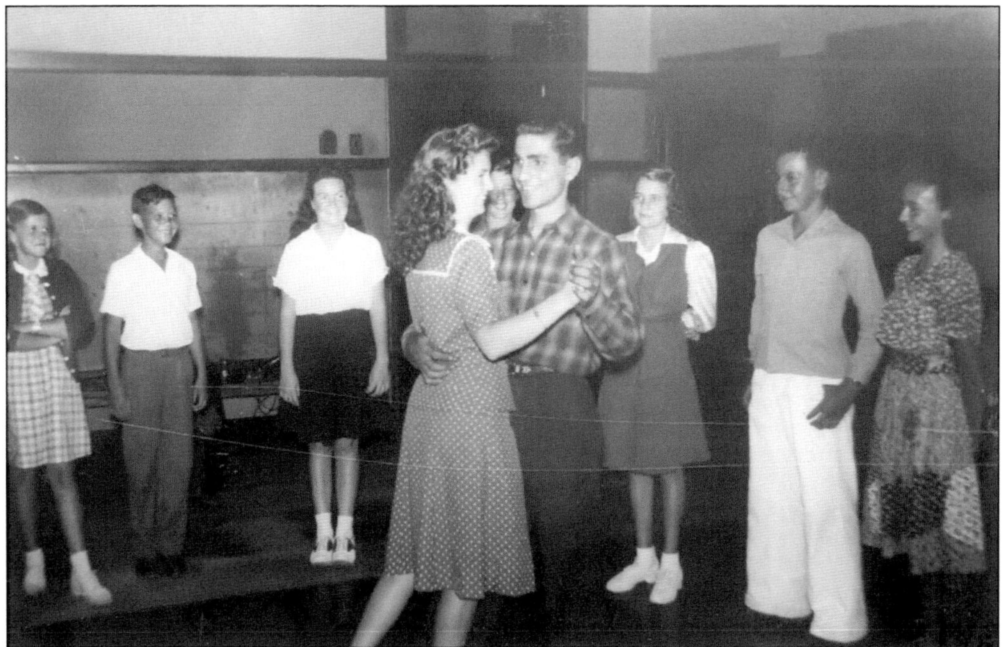

Saturday Dance Night, 1942. Junior boys and girls danced to the music of Dick Griffin and his band at the Woman's Clubhouse. Vaughn Anthony and Mary Donaldson were the chaperones in charge.

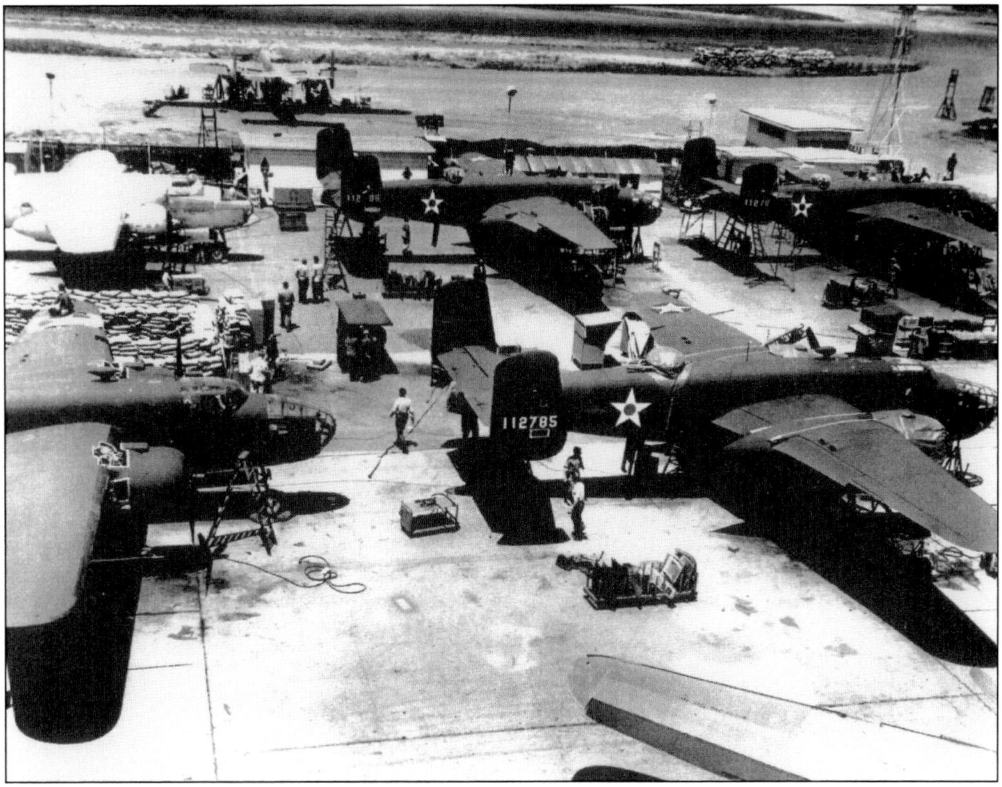

NORTH AMERICAN AVIATION, 1940s. North American came to El Segundo in 1935 and was located on the southeastern corner of Mines Field, what is now Los Angeles International Airport. Pictured are B-25s built between 1940 and 1944.

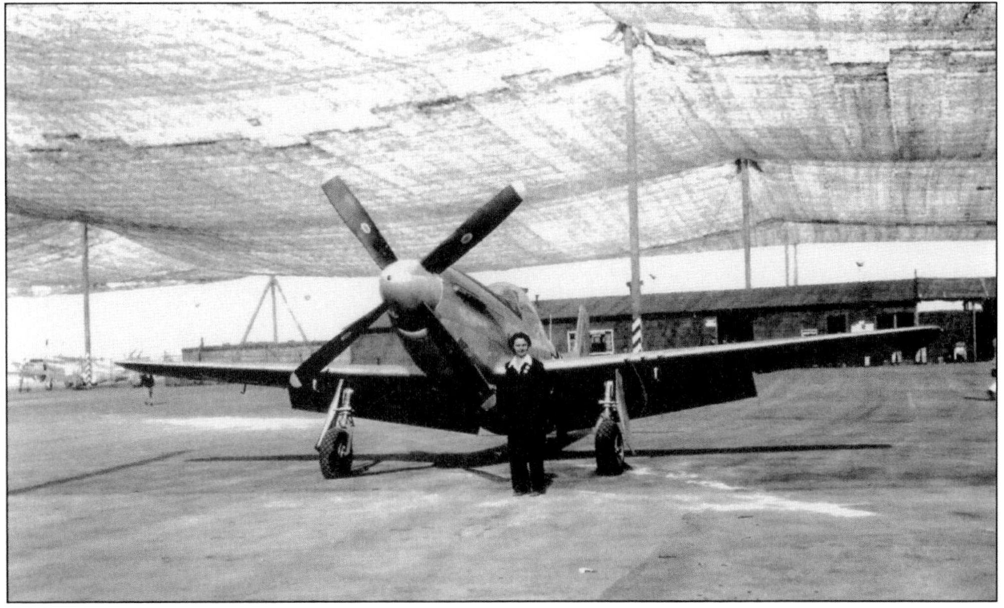

NORTH AMERICAN, 1942. Pauline Keys poses next to a North American P-51 Mustang aircraft in 1942.

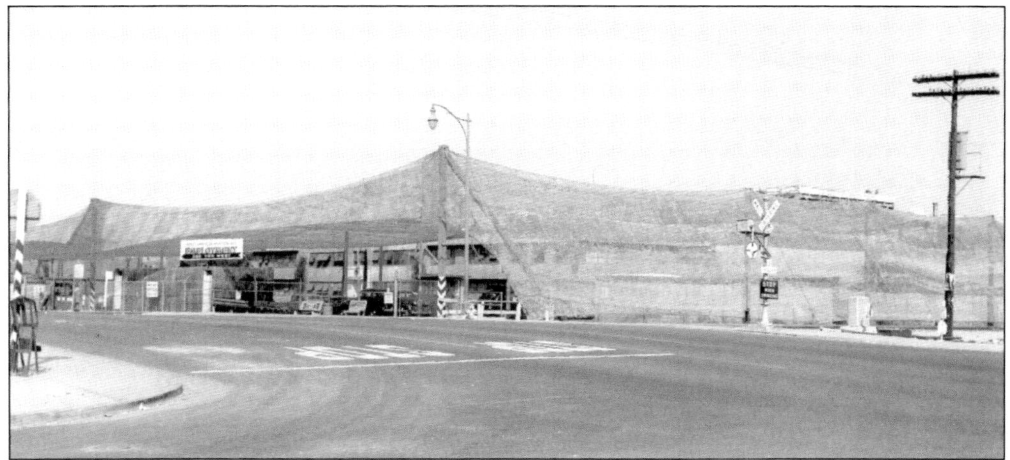

North American under Camouflage, 1942. In this view looking northwest at Aviation Boulevard and Imperial Avenue, the North American plant is covered with camouflage during World War II. After the war, in 1949, North American expanded its property to include facilities at Mariposa Avenue and Nash Street, Imperial Highway, and Lapham Avenue, and built its corporate headquarters on Imperial Avenue just west of Patmar's Drive-In and Sepulveda Boulevard.

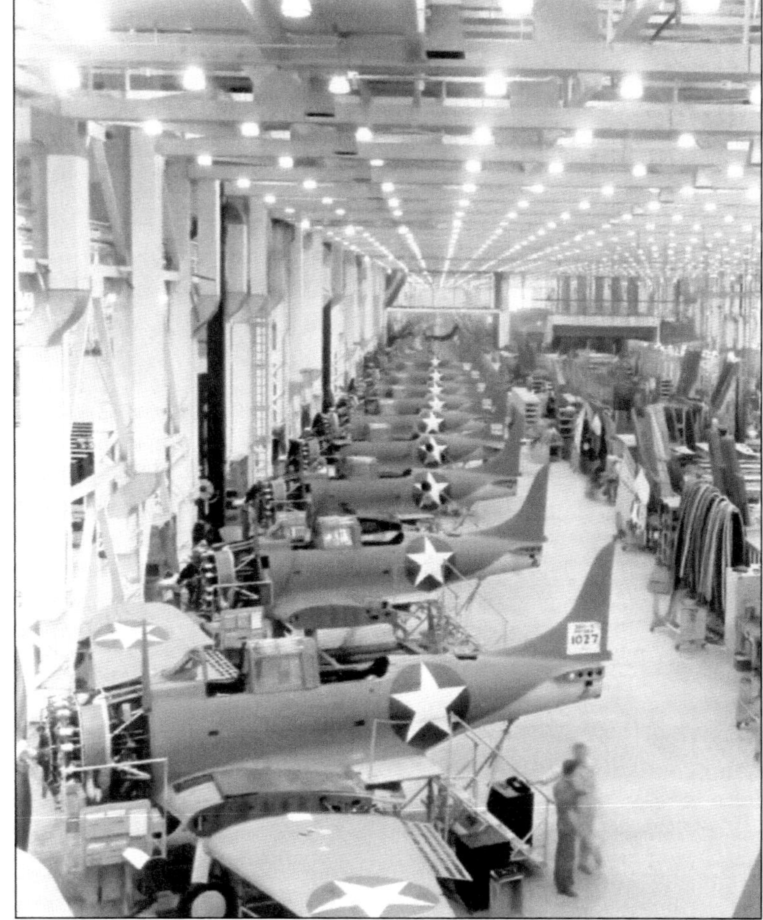

Douglas Aircraft El Segundo, 1943. The Navy dive-bomber SBD Dauntless assembly lines were mainly worked on by women, since most of the working-age men were in the military. They joined six million other women across the nation producing airplanes, ships, vehicles, equipment and ammunition for the war effort. (From *The Douglas Aircraft Plant That Became Los Angeles AFB*, by Robert Mulcahy.)

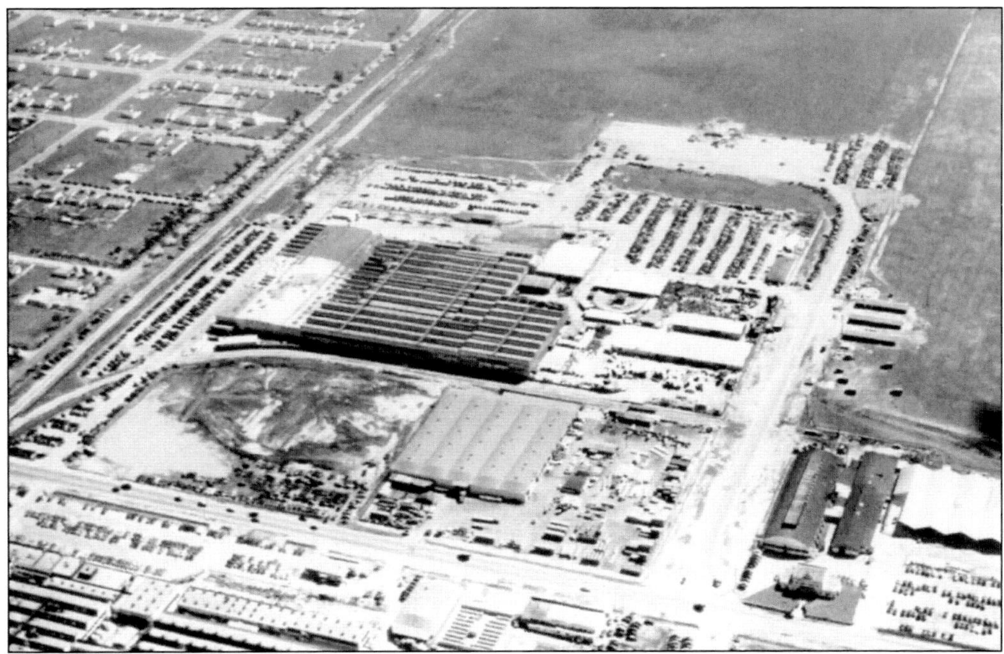

AERIAL OF DOUGLAS AIRCRAFT, 1942. Manufacturing airplanes for 40 years, the El Segundo Division plant was located between Aviation Boulevard (left), Imperial Highway (foreground), and Douglas Street (right). Area B is the undeveloped, open portion of adjacent land south of the plant. (From *The Douglas Aircraft Plant That Became Los Angeles AFB*, by Robert Mulcahy.)

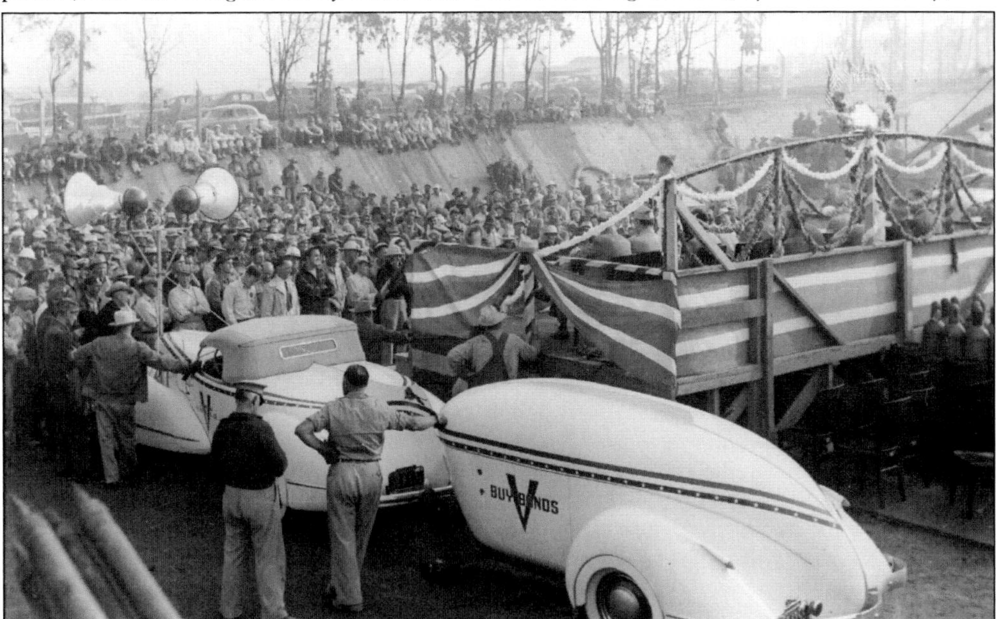

VICTORY BOND DRIVE, 1940s. The Standard Oil Refinery sponsored a Victory bond drive near its butadiene plant, which was a unit of the California synthetic rubber project. The plant manufactured several million tires after it went into operation in 1944. Bond rallies were held throughout the country. Over the course of the war, 85 million Americans purchased bonds totaling approximately $185 billion.

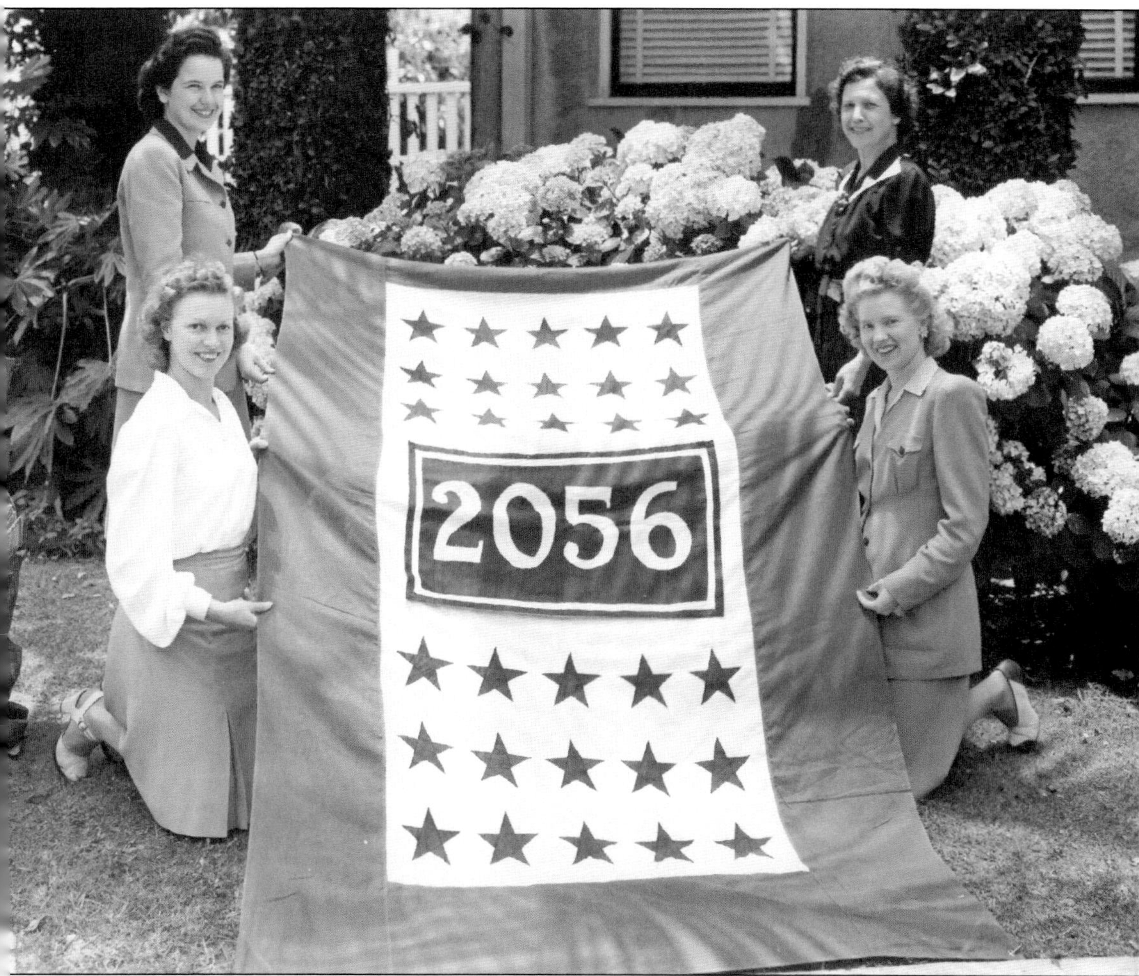

Standard Oil Service Flag, 1942. A total of 2,056 Standard Oil employees had joined the armed services by the summer of 1942. Holding the banner are (in no particular order) Rita Noble, Louise Peterson, Grace West, and Margaret Keenan.

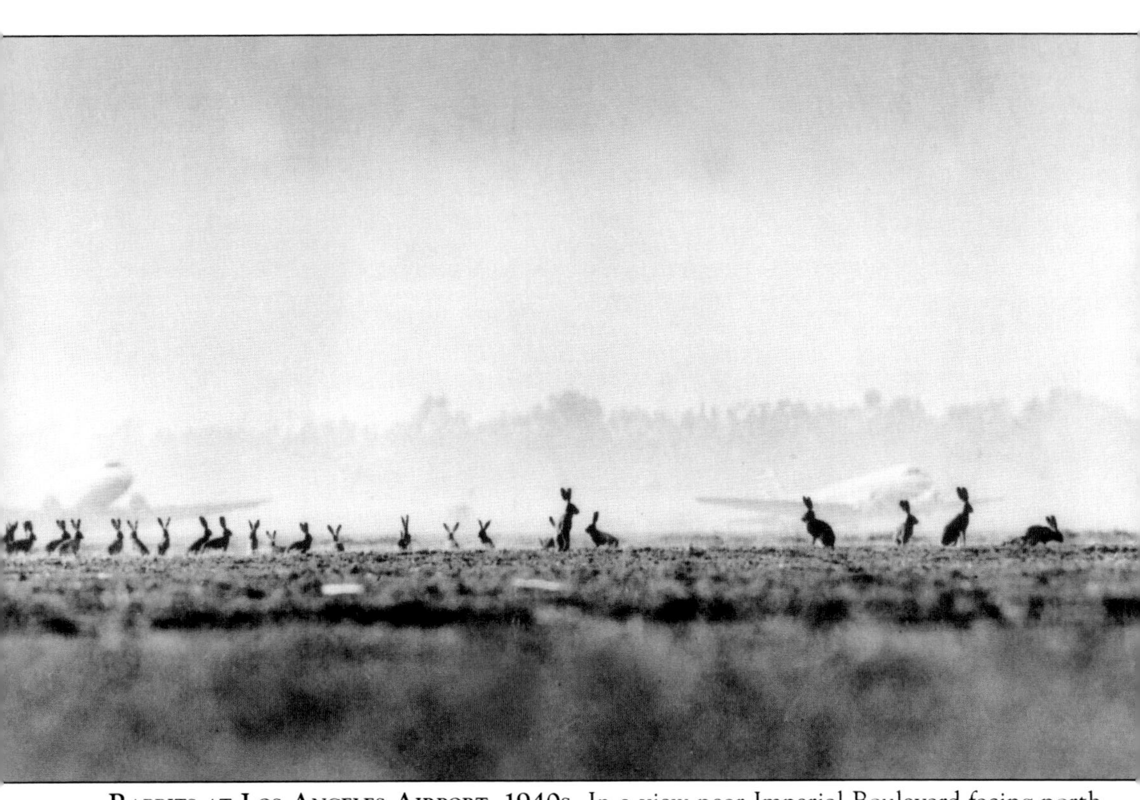

Rabbits at Los Angeles Airport, 1940s. In a view near Imperial Boulevard facing north towards Los Angeles Airport, Passing DC -3 airplanes have caught the rabbits' attention during early-morning landings and takeoffs.

Four

Mid-Century and Aerospace Developments 1950–1969

The 1950s and 1960s were a mixture of expansive civic development, the extension of the aerospace industry on the east side, and further growth of small businesses downtown. Unfortunately, a string of tragedies hit the town during this era, which included a major airplane crash, a fire downtown that consumed a city block, and the shocking murder of two young police offers.

A new city hall complex was completed in the mid-1950s with a city council chamber and adjacent offices. The police department also moved into this complex, and the new Fire Station No. 1 was constructed before the city hall facility on Main Street and Grand Avenue. Later, Fire Station No. 2 was built to protect properties east of Sepulveda Boulevard. Other city projects included a new Recreation Park and Clubhouse, the Joslyn Center, a rededicated Hilltop Park and pool, and an expansion of the 1940s public library.

After World War II, many of the aircraft plants continued to build planes, and they were proud to display them during open houses and events for the public. By the late 1950s and 1960s, however, some of the aircraft companies left the area or merged with other companies or their buildings were moved to make way for further expansion of Los Angeles International Airport.

The first horrendous incident to strike El Segundo during this period was the brutal murders of officers Richard A. Phillips and Milton G. Curtis on July 22, 1957. This was followed by a massive fire on the corner of Richmond Street and Grand Avenue in the early 1960s at a bowling alley complex called the Rose Bowl. The final calamity to occur was on May 10, 1969, when a converted B-26 bomber plane crashed into an apartment building at 335 Eucalyptus Drive, killing six people.

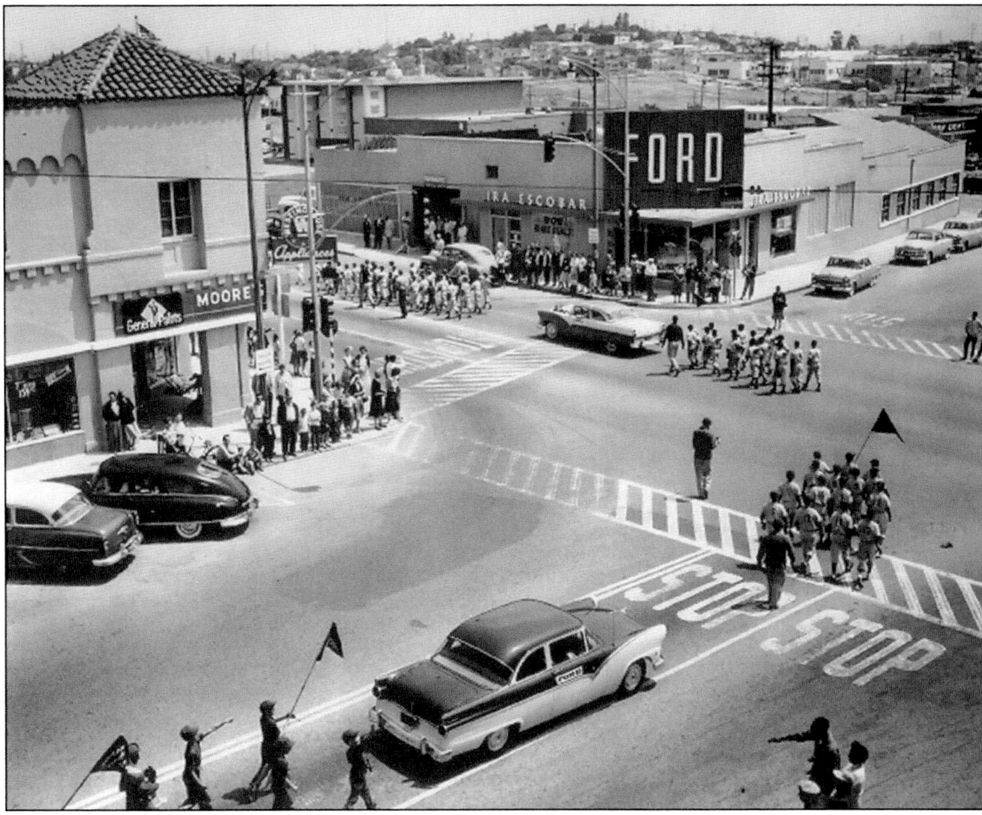

Parade at Grand Avenue and Main Street, c. 1955. This is a good representation of the town in the mid-1950s. In this view looking northeast along Grand Avenue, the parade is turning north onto Main Street. Ira Escobar Ford was at the northeast corner and left the site in the 1960s after more than 25 years of business.

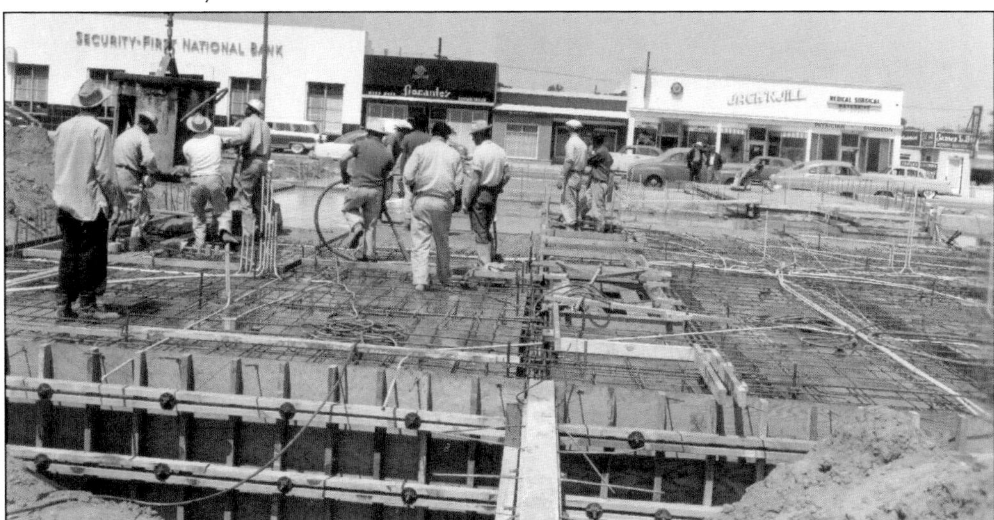

Construction of City Hall on Main Street, 1954. Workers lay a foundation for a new city hall in 1954. The photograph was taken facing west on Main Street and shows a row of retailers including Security-First National Bank, a tailor shop, and a medical surgeon.

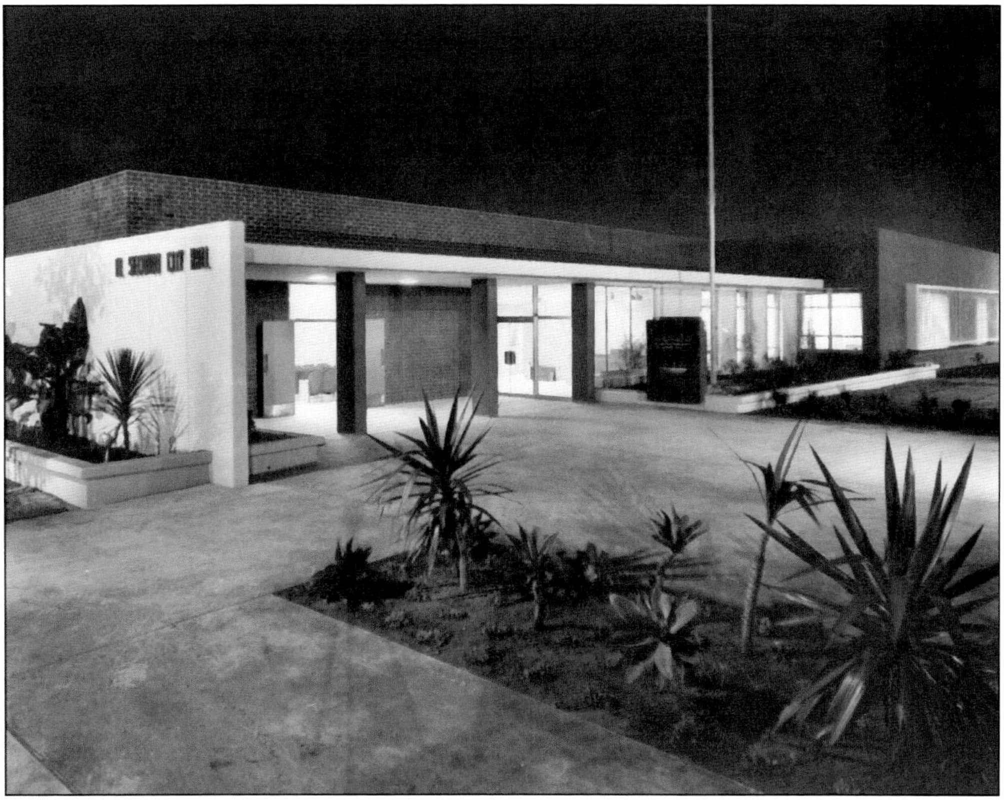

Completed City Hall, 1955. The new city hall is pictured with city council chambers to the immediate left and lighted office buildings to the right. Later, the open area in front of the double doors to the chambers was enclosed.

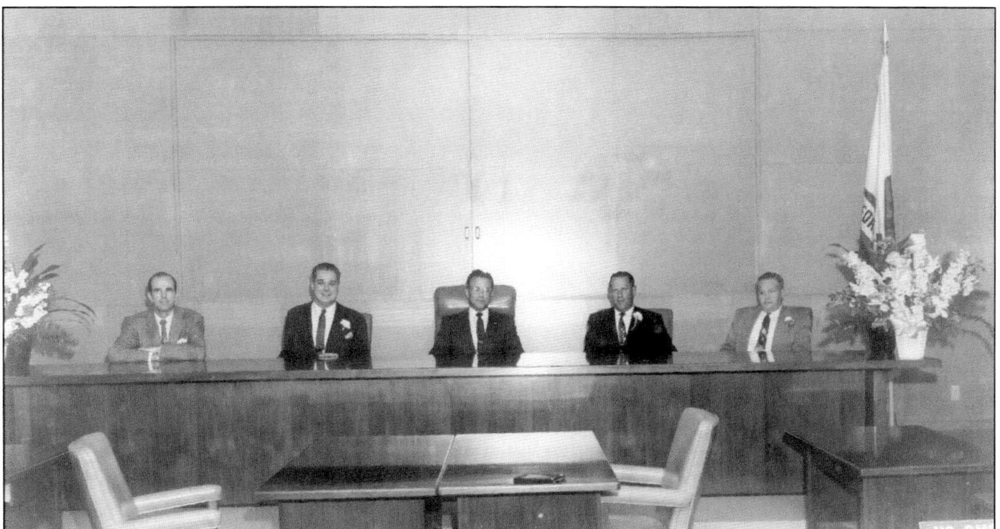

Inside Council Chambers, 1955. Inside the council chambers, the dais and wood-paneled walls created a professional environment for conducting city business. The councilmen seated are, from left to right, Dr. John Meschuk, George E. Gordon (the clubhouse in Recreation Park was renamed in his honor in 1984), Kenneth Benfield, Robert Frederick, and Wilburn Baker.

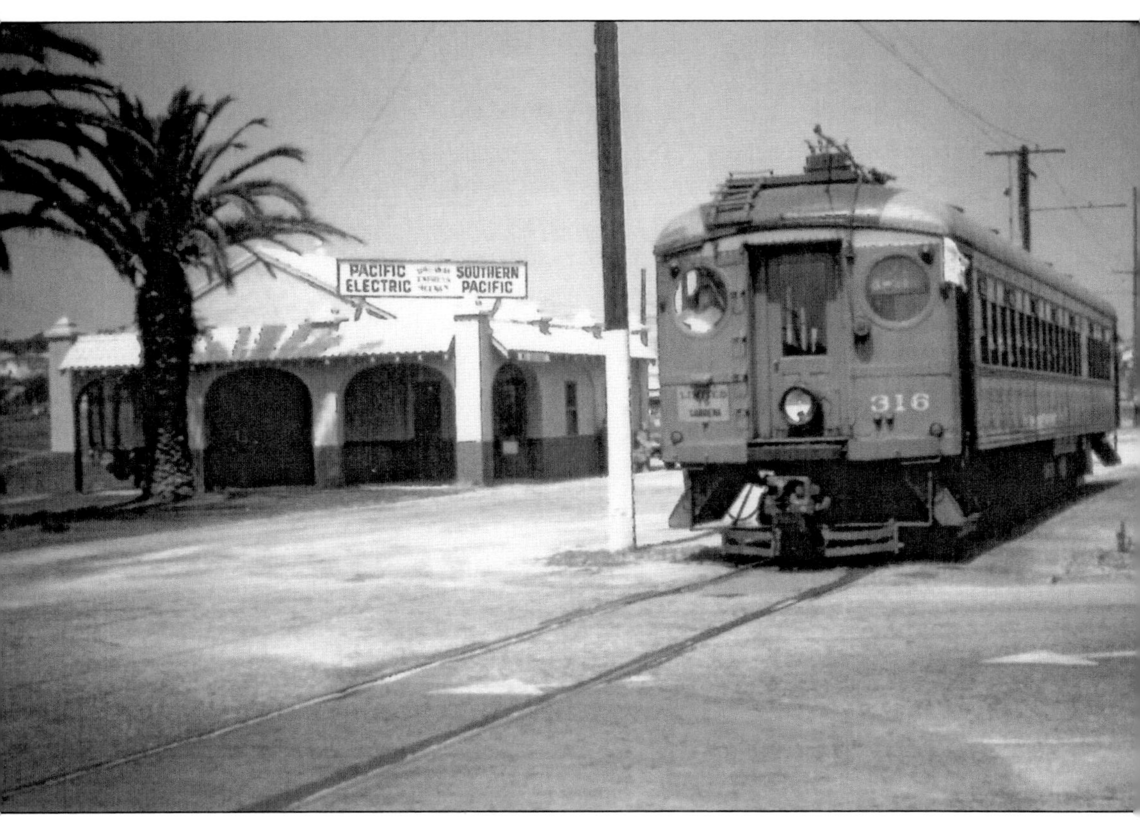

PACIFIC ELECTRIC RED CAR, JULY 26, 1958. On this date, the Pacific Electric Red Car visited El Segundo's Spanish Mission–style station at Grand Avenue and Eucalyptus Street. The station was built in 1914, and passenger rail service was provided to El Segundo from August 10, 1914, to October 31, 1930. The depot was demolished in 1969 after the electric cars fell out of use. That area was turned into a parking lot in 1987 for the Recreation Park facilities above the Joslyn Center.

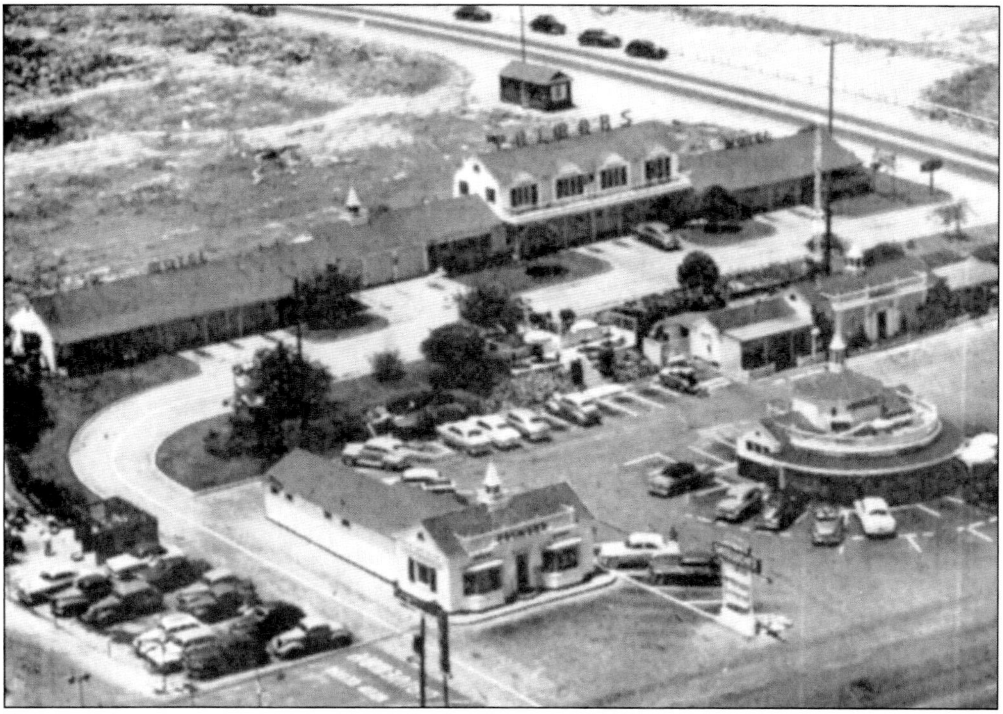

PATMAR'S EXPANSION IN THE 1950S. The famous restaurant with carhops on Imperial Highway and Sepulveda Boulevard, owned by H.B. Patrick and Norman Marsh, continued to expand in the 1950s with a cocktail lounge and motel. This photograph was taken in 1954.

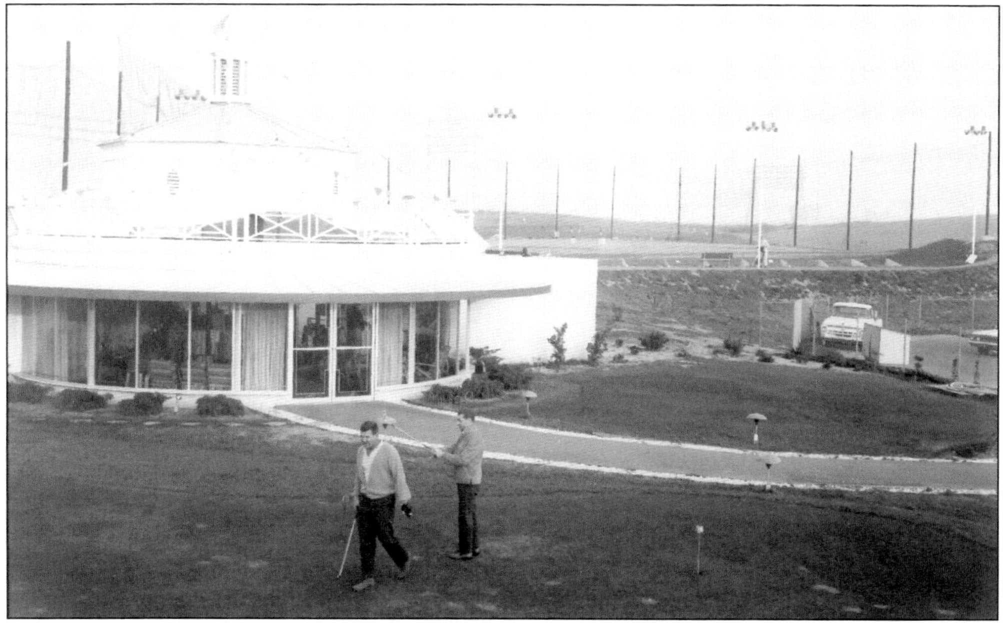

PATMAR'S RELOCATES IN 1959. Patmar's was sold to developers in 1959. Shortly after, Jim Stinnett bought the building for $500 and had it moved to the El Segundo Golf Course at 400 South Sepulveda Boulevard. There, it served as the pro shop until the mid-1990s, when it finally succumbed to termites and was torn down.

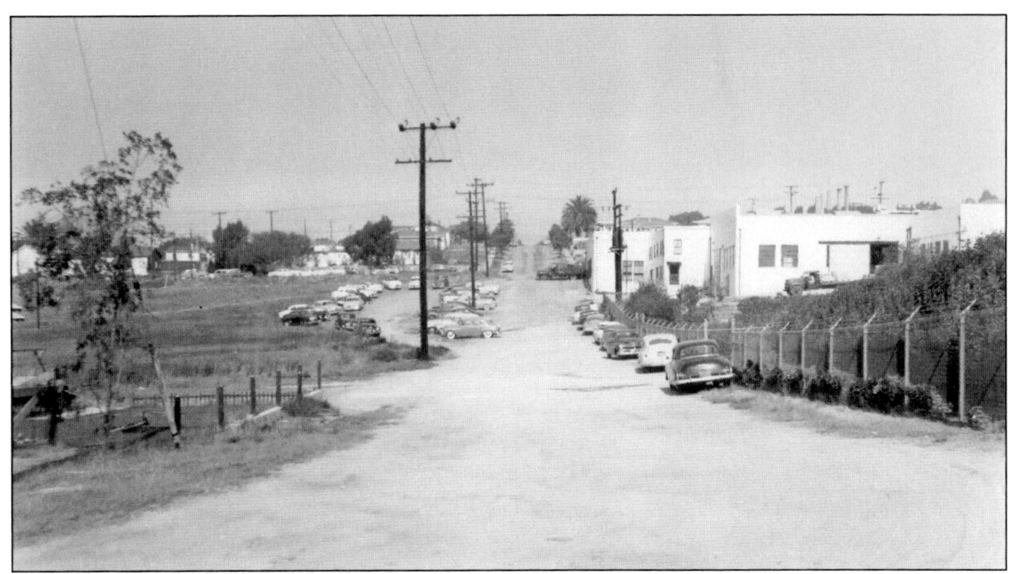

Sheldon Street and General Tile Company, 1950s. Sheldon Street was a dirt road back then, and the large white buildings on the right housed the General Tile Company. Materials for the tiles and the El Segundo Lumber Company (to the right of the tile factory) were brought in by railroad until the tracks were removed in 1975. The area then became a teen hangout and a shortcut to the middle school. After the General Tile Company closed, the city bought the land to expand Recreation Park. It was called Pine Field until 2001, when it was renamed George Brett Field.

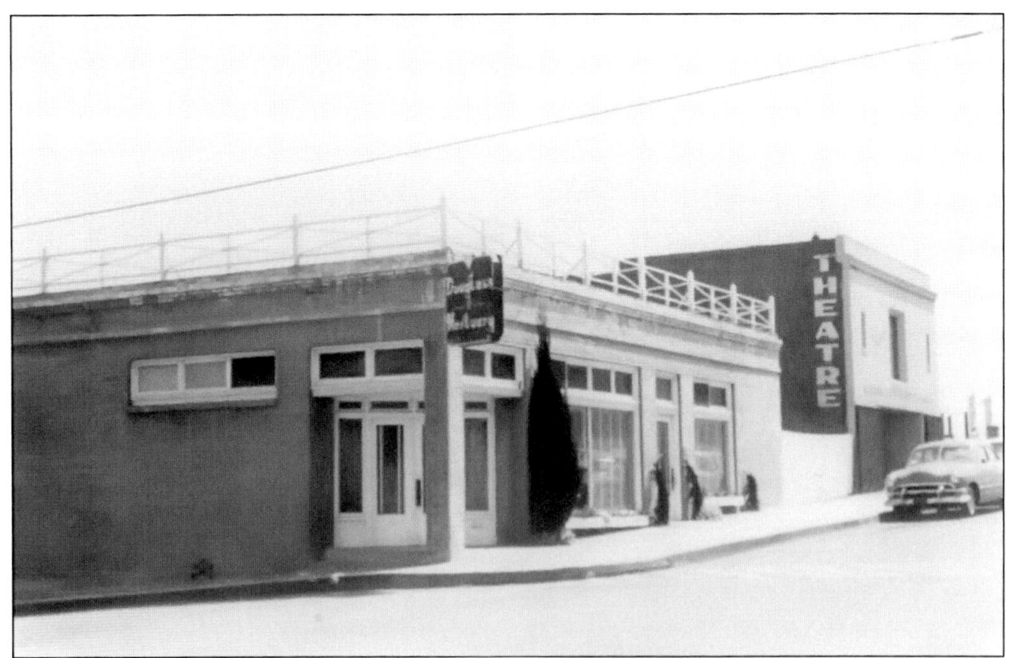

Douglass Mortuary and Theater on Richmond Street, c. 1955. Originally built in the 1920s by T.G. and Nell Ellis as a grocery and post office, the southeast corner of Richmond Street and Franklin Avenue became Douglass Mortuary in 1943, and the theater was later converted to the Old Town Music Hall (see chapter 5). Both buildings are still standing.

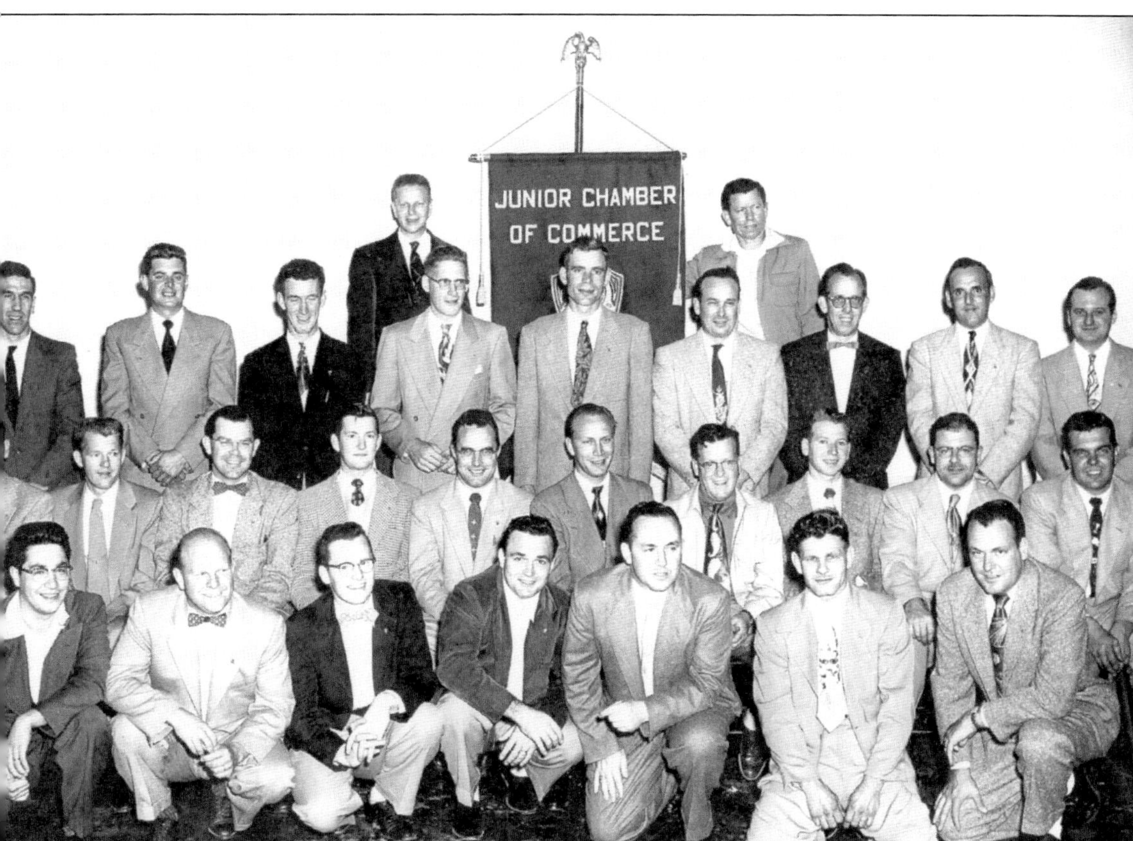

JUNIOR CHAMBER OF COMMERCE, C. 1953. For membership in this organization, also known as the El Segundo Jaycees, the age range was 18 through 35. Unfortunately, the group dwindled after the last members reached the age of 36. They sponsored a Fiesta celebration and a basketball game between Pepperdine and Loyola Universities. From left to right are (first row) Joel McRea, Dick Carr, Jerry Conroy, Gary Wallace, Dick Fitzgerald, Max Vandenberg, and unidentified; (second row) Bill Walker, Paul Biller, Floyd Carr, Sandy Reeves, Gill Goodman, unidentified, Jack Gill, unidentified, Joe Sano, and unidentified; (third row) unidentified, George Laun, Ernie Bowdre, four unidentified, Chuck Morel, and Jack Dawson; (fourth row) Joe Jarczewski and unidentified.

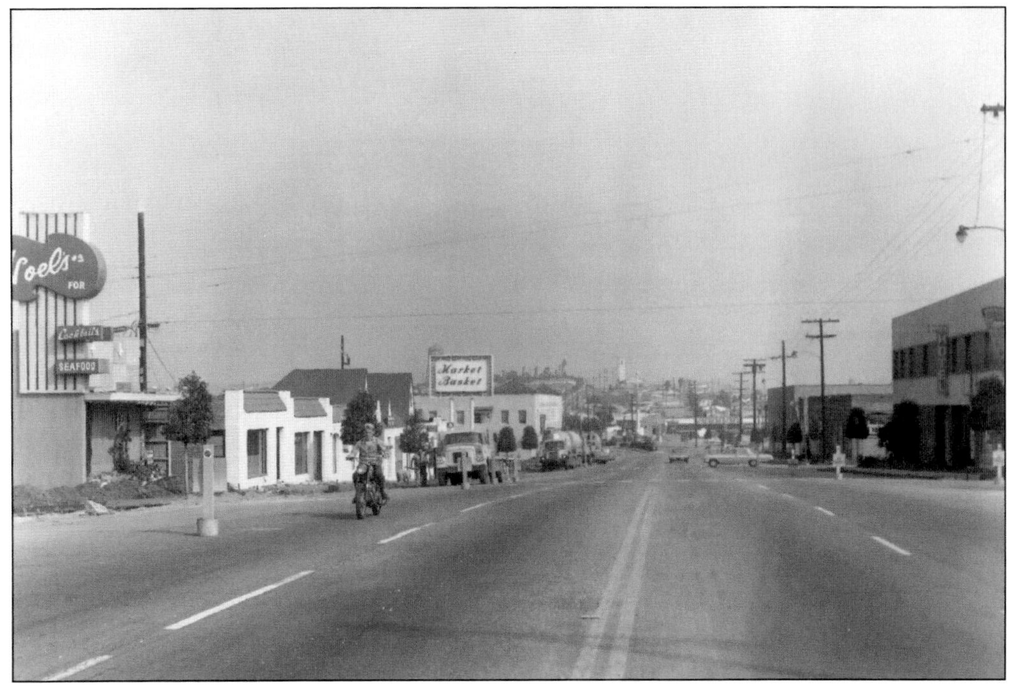

Grand Avenue, 1960s. New concrete sidewalks and curbs are being poured on the north side of Grand Avenue in this view facing east. The Market Basket grocery store was in town for many years after the Rose Bowl burned down, also in the 1960s.

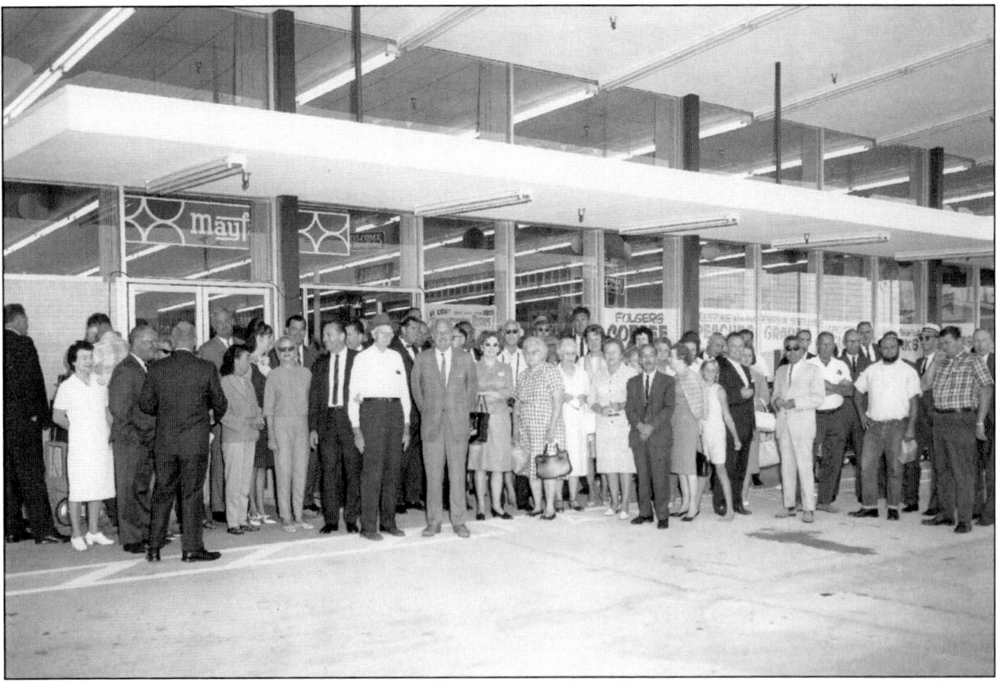

Mayfair Market Grand Opening, 1966. Located at 220 East Grand Avenue, the building has been occupied by a Rite Aid drugstore since 2009. At center in front, next to an older man with a white shirt and hat, is the store manager and later city councilman Marvin Johnson.

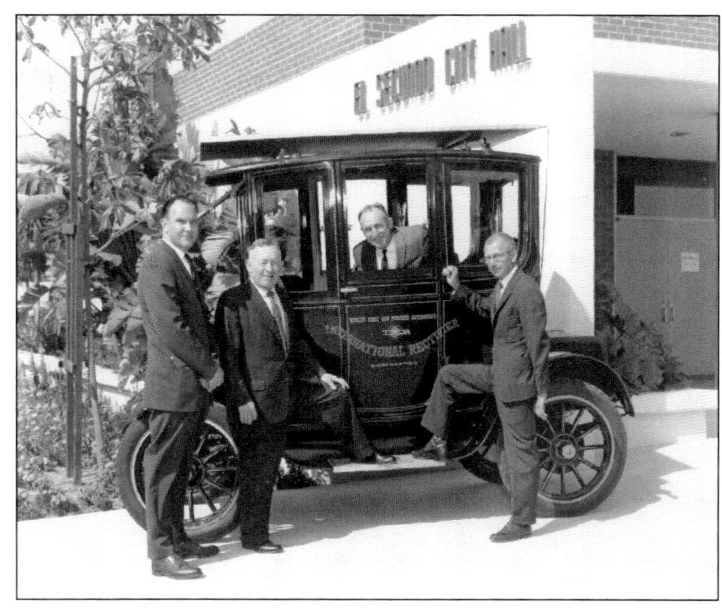

First Solar-Powered Automobile, c. 1960. Produced in El Segundo by International Rectifier Corporation, this vehicle is believed to be the world's first solar-powered automobile. Note the large solar panel on the roof. The car's performance capabilities are unknown. From left to right are unidentified, James Stinnett, Lloyd Ballmer, and Myron Yates.

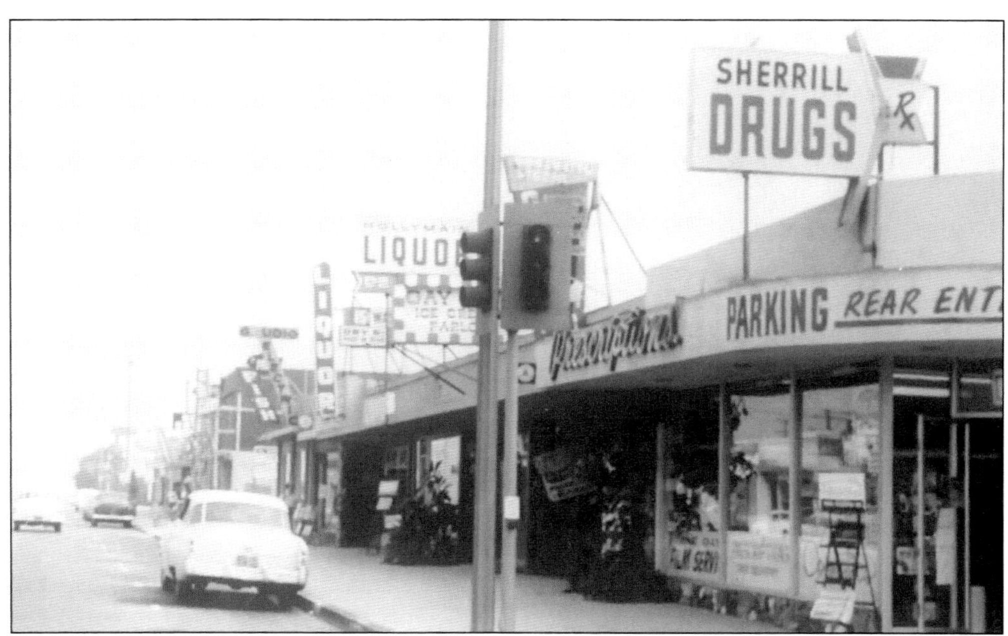

Main Street and Holly Avenue, c. 1965. Sherrill Drugs later moved to the 200 block of East Grand Avenue, and the northeast corner is currently occupied by Stuft Pizza. HollyMain Liquor still remains; however, the Gay Nineties Ice Cream Parlor, Gaudio Electric, a fish market, and a laundromat that charged 15¢ to a wash load and 5¢ to dry have long vacated this popular street corner.

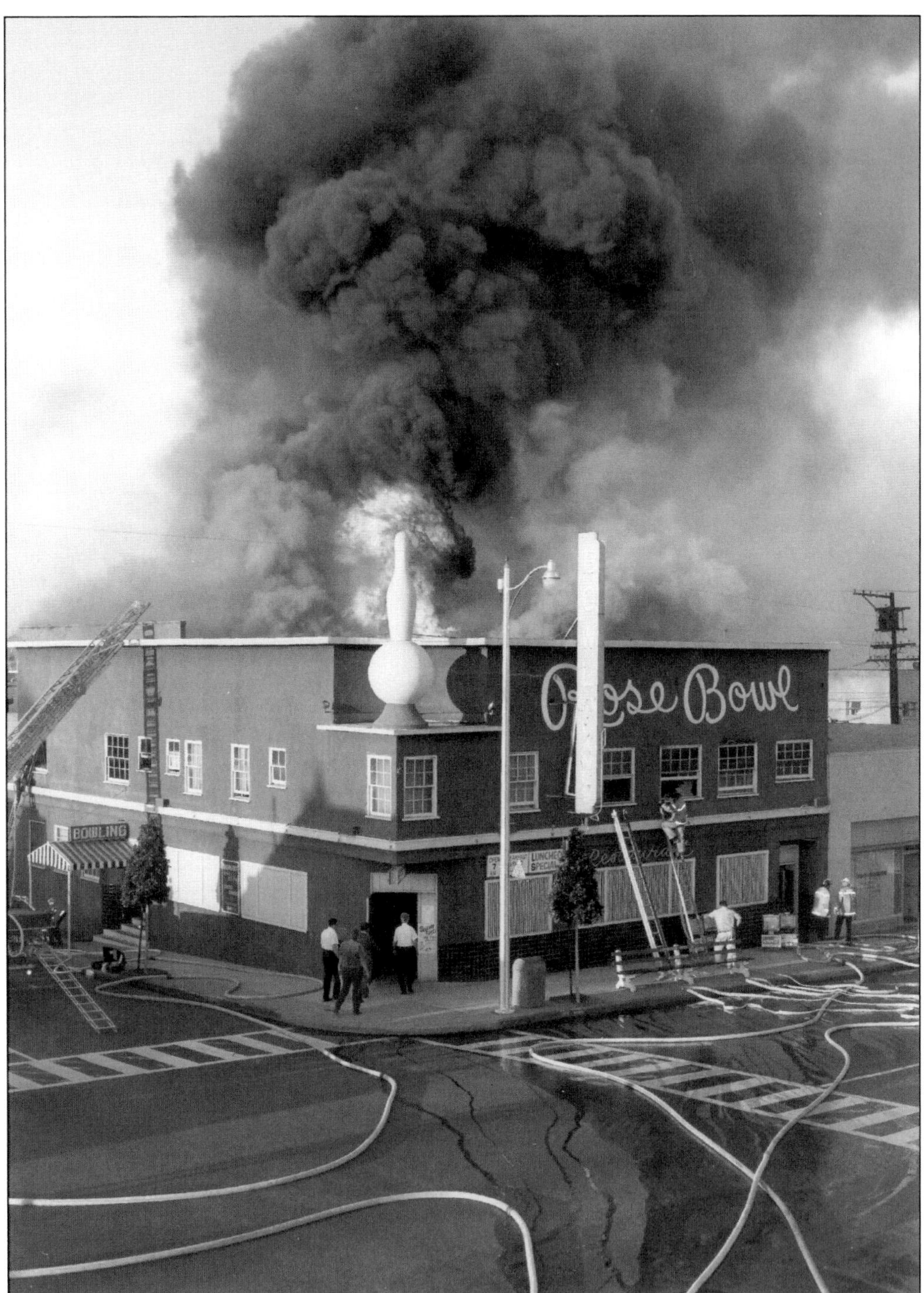

Rose Bowl Fire, c. 1960. This was one of two disasters in El Segundo during the 1960s. The Rose Bowl, a popular bowling center with meeting rooms and a restaurant, which opened in February 1947, caught fire in the early 1960s, and the building was completely leveled. The Market Basket took over that lot shortly after. Today, the site has a 99¢ store, restaurants, and a multilevel parking garage.

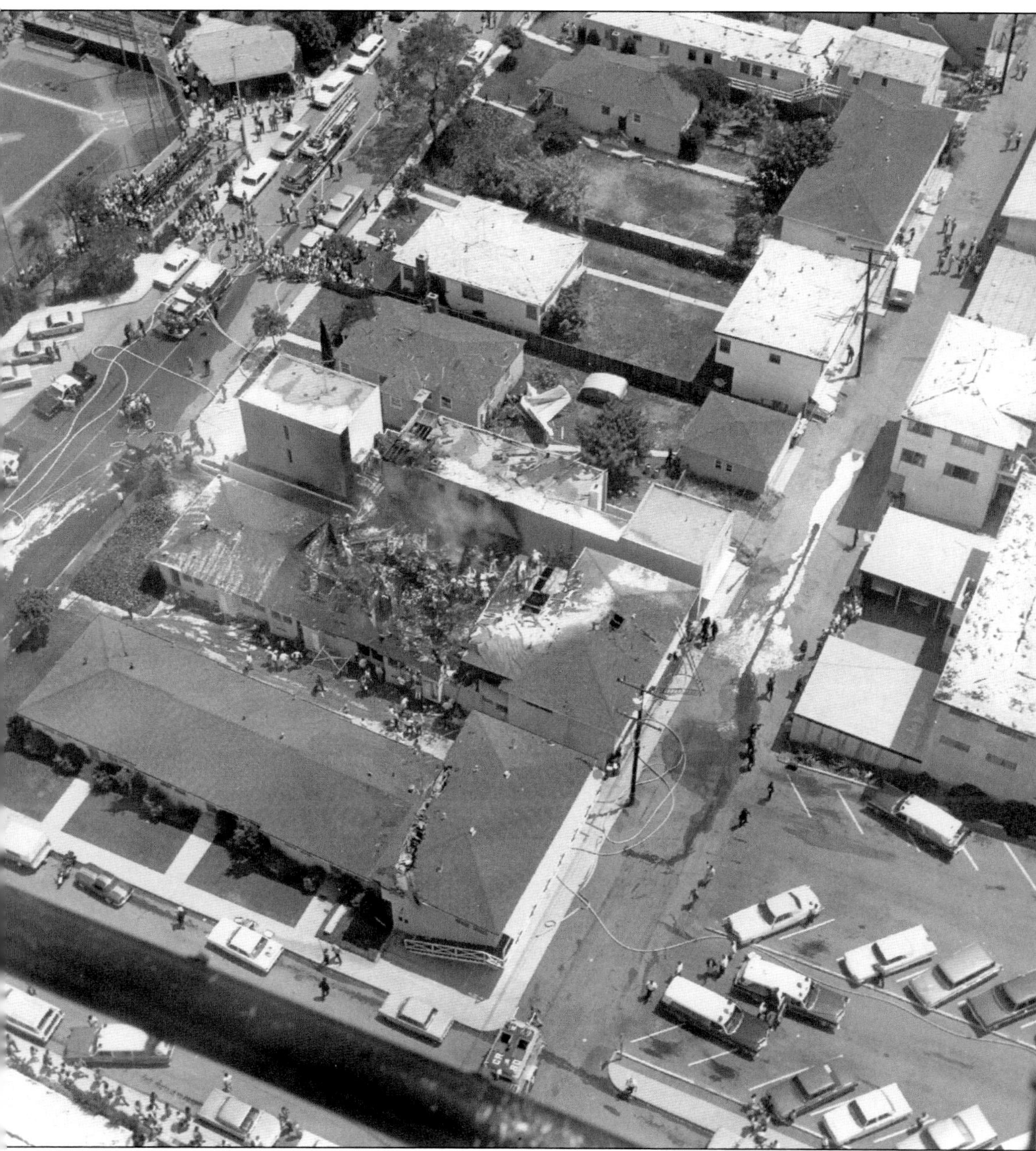

AIRPLANE CRASH, MAY 10, 1969. The second major disaster was the crash of a converted B-26 bomber at 335 Eucalyptus Drive in El Segundo. The plane was taking off for its second flight of the day testing equipment when, at 12:15 p.m., pilot Marvin Easton reported engine problems. Although six people were killed, including all four in the plane and two from the apartments (Donna Ryerson and a Mr. Hood), the accident could have been much worse. The heroic pilot veered the plane at the last moment before it would have crashed into a baseball park full of youngsters and families at a carnival in Recreation Park.

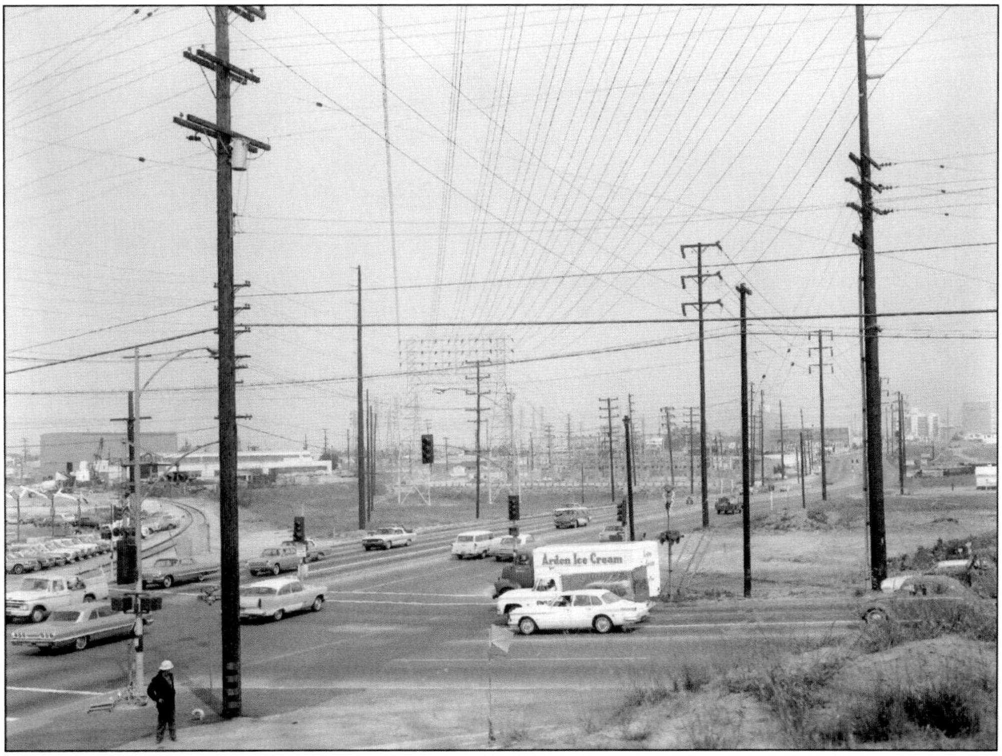

SEPULVEDA BOULEVARD AND EL SEGUNDO AVENUE, LATE 1950S. In the late 1950s, before high-rise buildings occupied this expensive tract of real estate, high wires, telephone poles, and train tracks make up most of the landscape at a very busy intersection. This view is looking northwest at Sepulveda Boulevard and El Segundo Avenue towards Los Angeles International Airport.

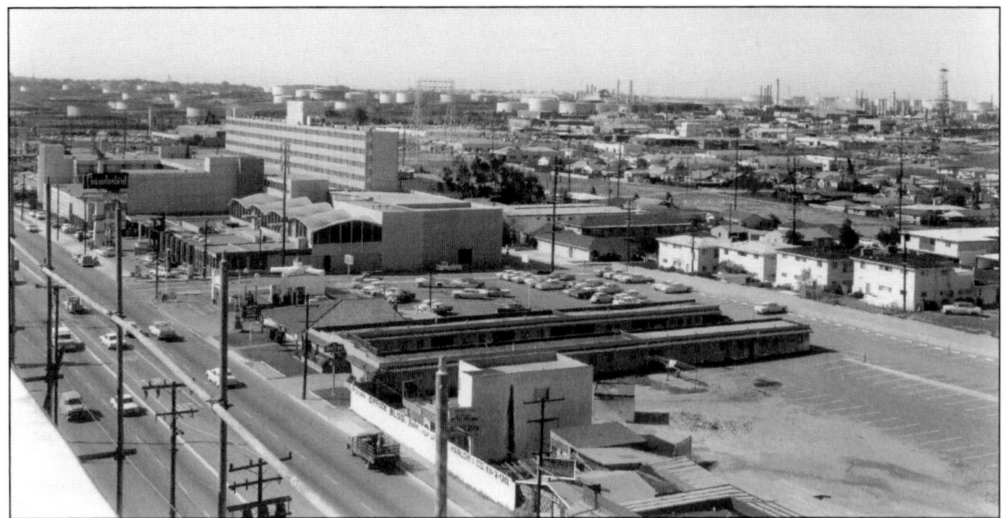

SEPULVEDA BOULEVARD AND MARIPOSA AVENUE, 1960S. The opposite view a few years later looks southwest, with the Chevron Refinery in the background. Before it was called the Hacienda Hotel at the corner of Sepulveda Boulevard and Mariposa Avenue, it was named the Thunderbird Hotel. The parking lot off Mariposa Avenue still exists, and a major renovation of the hotel was also in progress in 2015.

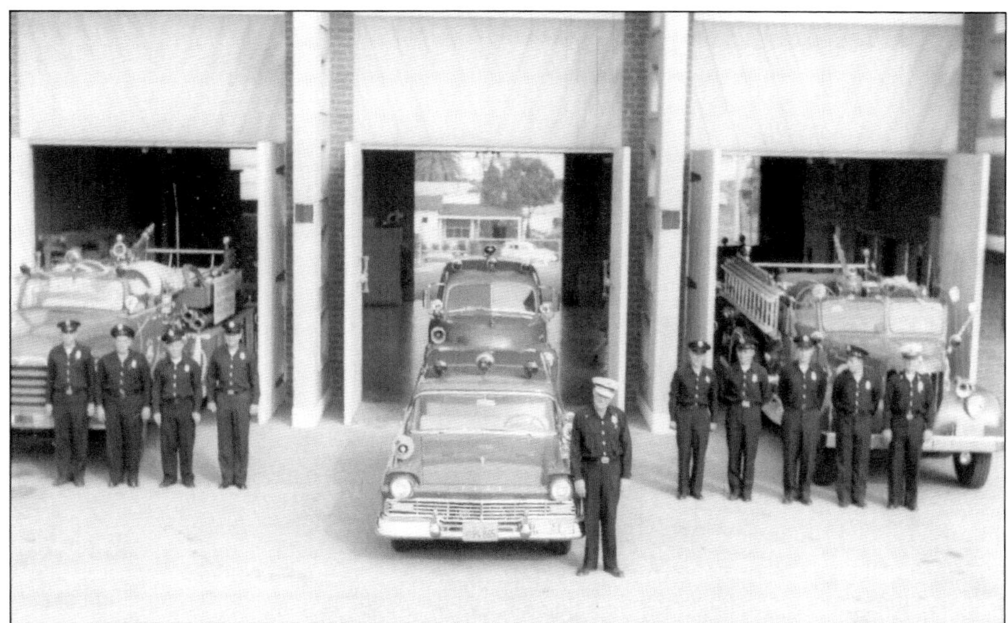

Fire Station No. 1, 1951. After completion of Fire Station Number No. 1 in March 1951, the adjacent city hall complex, with a new police station, was finished in 1955. In October 1950, Capt. Leo Freedman was promoted to chief, and he held that position until 1959. This photograph may show one of the fire department's Fire Service Days, which began under Chief Freedman and served as open houses for the public to tour the facilities and equipment.

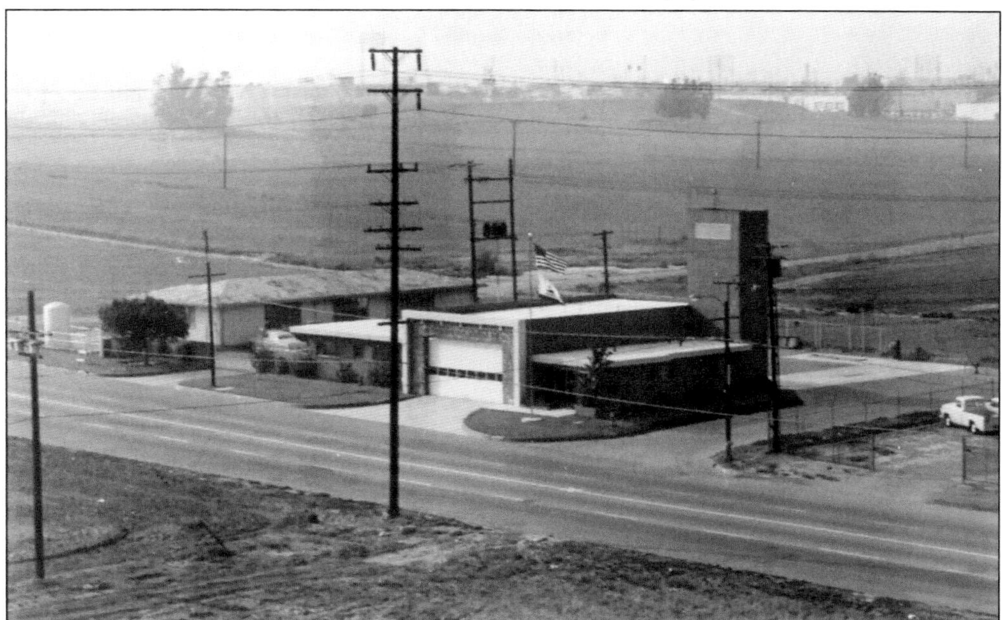

Fire Station No. 2, c. 1958. In 1957, the city council decided that the increased demands for protecting businesses east of Sepulveda Boulevard warranted a second fire station. The council selected the design of architect Marion J. Varner and Associates, which cost $80,000 to build. In the early 2010s, this site at El Segundo Boulevard and Nash Street was converted to a shopping center after a new Fire Station No. 2 was constructed at 2261 Mariposa Avenue in 2009.

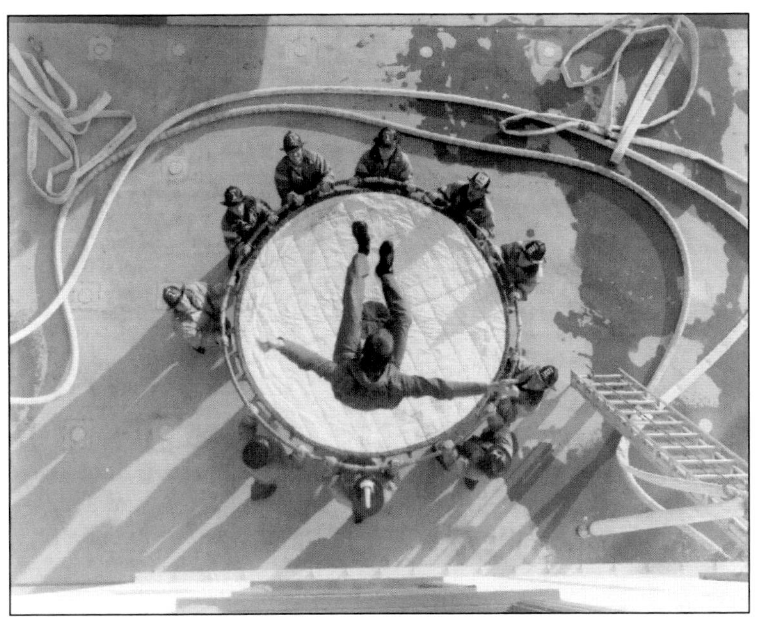

TRAINING AT FIRE STATION NO. 2, DECEMBER 13, 1965. By 1965, the fire department had 40 firemen, who used a four-story tower to practice techniques for dealing with fires in high-rise buildings. The tower contained a sprinkler system, an enclosed stairway, window openings, and a basement pit for practicing pumping operations.

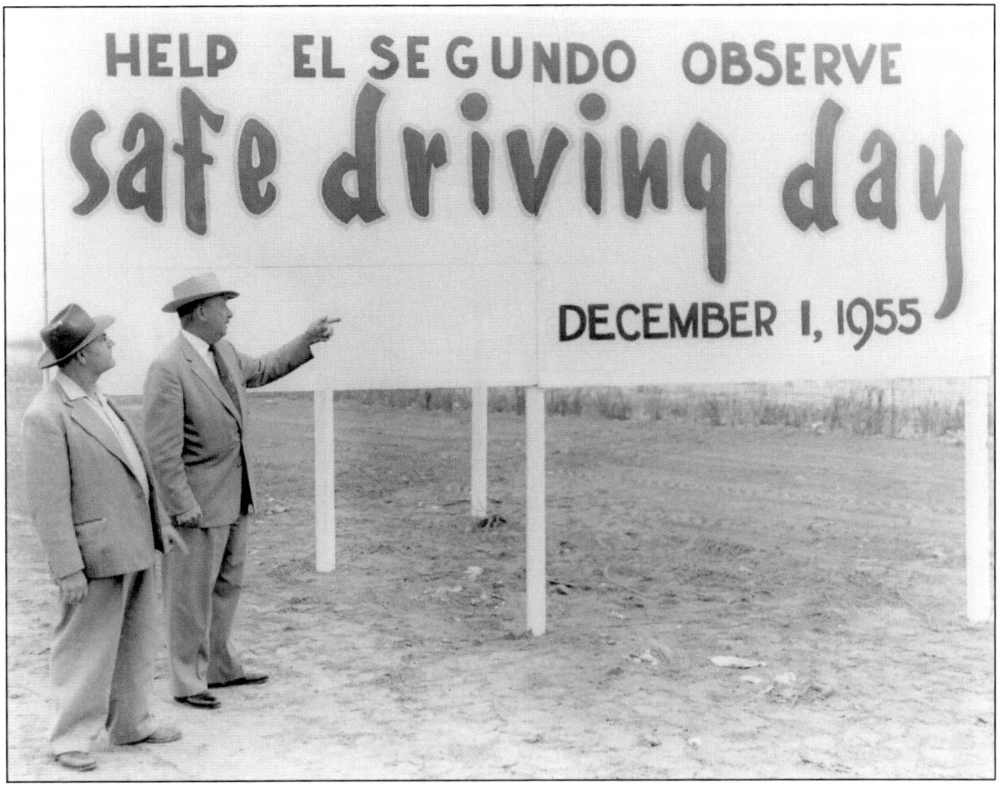

SAFE DRIVING DAY, DECEMBER 1, 1955. Chief DeBerry points to a sign that reminds motorists to "Help El Segundo Observe Save Driving Day." The gentleman beside him is unidentified.

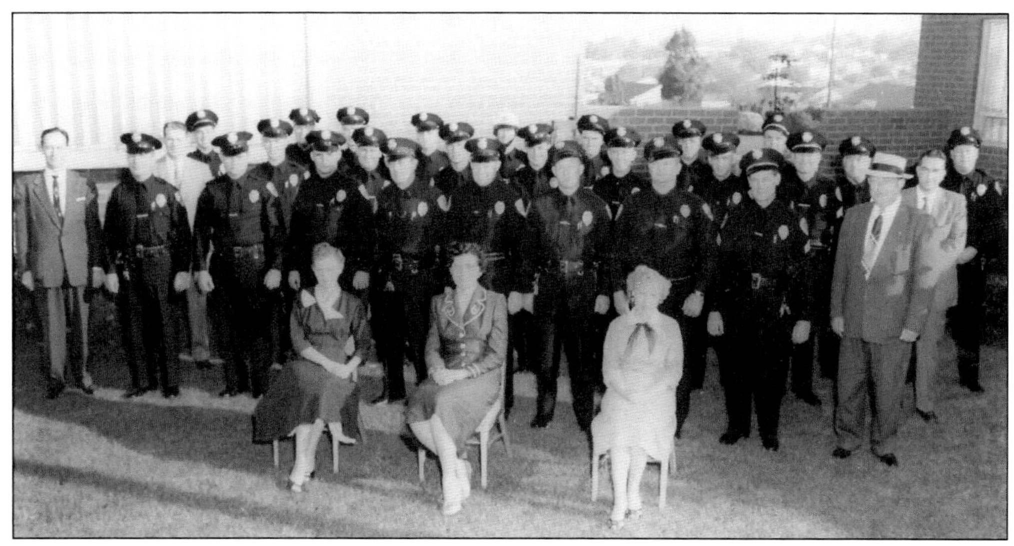

El Segundo Police Department, December 1956. From left to right are (ladies) Phyllis Flanagan, Marcella Bracy, and unidentified; (first row) Vern Wood, Charles Porter, James Johnson, Ken Newman, Kent Annis, Ollen Roach, John Booterbaugh, Andy DeJong, Boyd Coulter, and T.B. DeBerry; (second row) Ed Hora, John Nagy, R. Whitley, Keith Platt, Bernie Bangasser, Jerry Stephens, Glen Rose, Ed Flowers, and Lee Maxwell; (third row) Jack Partlow, Ted Gilbert, R.C. Phillips, Ken Schmidt, Don Webb, Lee Clements, J.C. Devilbiss, Frank Berkline, Ken Searles, and Roy Spear.

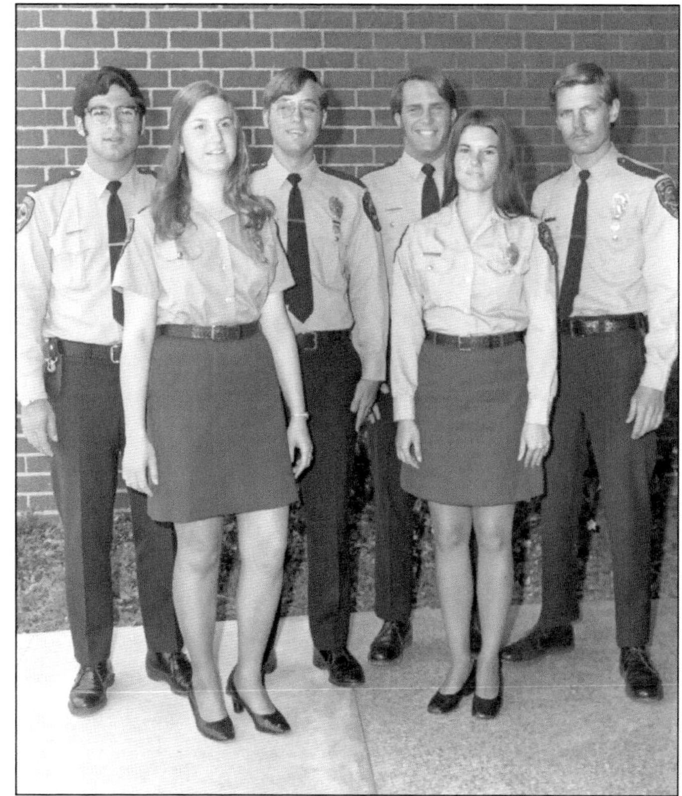

Police Cadets, 1967. The cadet program started in 1967 and is aimed at young people between the ages of 18 and 22 who may be considering a career in law enforcement. Duties may include clerical tasks, front desk interaction with the public, processing licenses, assisting in educational and public awareness programs, directing traffic, and issuing citations to vehicles in violation of city parking restrictions. From left to right are Tim Brunner, Loretta Brock, Scott Armstrong, Steve Martin, Christine Lizzi, and Tim Friel.

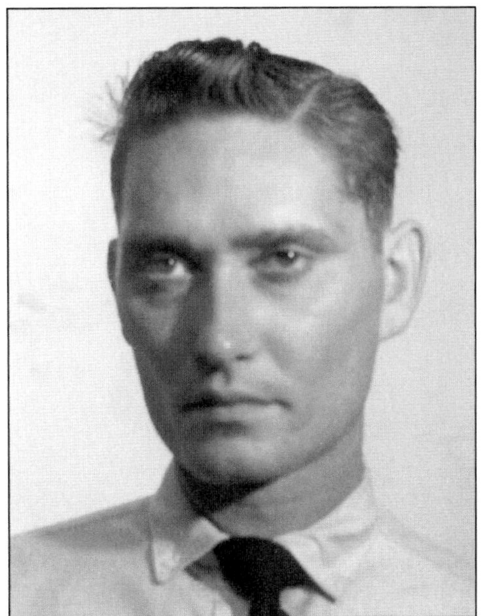

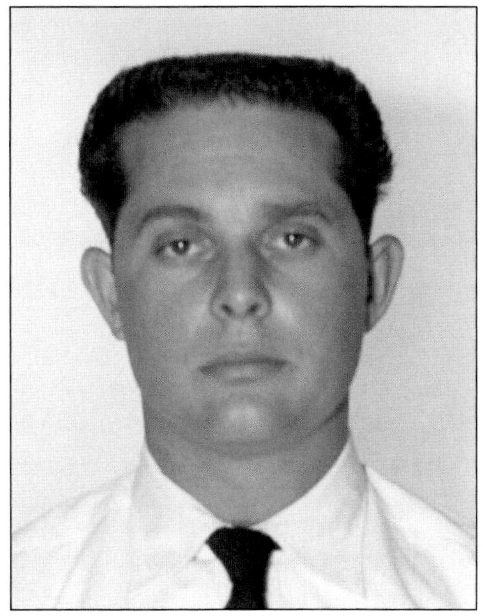

Slain Officers Richard Allen Phillips (left) and Milton Gus Curtis, July 22, 1957. At 1:24 a.m. on July 22, 1957, officers Phillips (28) and Curtis (25) observed a car running a red light at Rosecrans Avenue and Sepulveda Boulevard. Unknown to the officers, the car was stolen and the suspect had just robbed two couples at gunpoint and raped a teenage girl. The suspect ended up killing both officers and then disappeared.

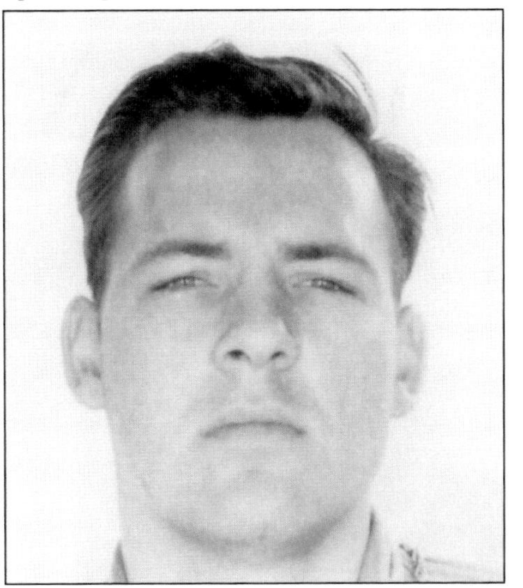

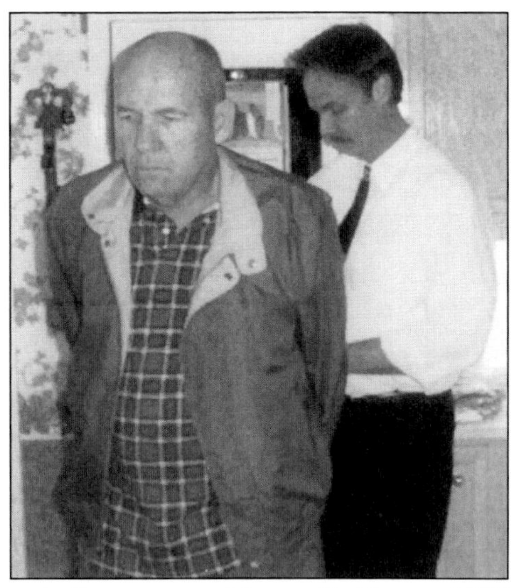

Gerald F. Mason, Murderer of Officers Richard A. Phillips and Milton G. Curtis, 1957 and 2003. In September 2002, fingerprints taken at the crime scene in 1957 were entered into the Federal Bureau of Investigation's database, which led investigators to Mason, who had been arrested for burglary in 1956. That was the only record the FBI had of him on file. On January 29, 2003, Gerald F. Mason, 68, was arrested in South Carolina and finally pleaded guilty in Los Angeles County Court. He was sentenced to two consecutive life terms. Det. Craig Clearly, pictured in 2003, was the arresting officer. Further information can be found on the city's website: www.elsegundo.org/depts/police under "Fallen Brothers."

Police Facility, 1966. As part of the City Hall Plaza complex, this driveway was the Standard Street entrance to the plaza and police department in the 1960s. Today, the building is where the planning and public works departments are located. The police department is now housed southwest of this driveway, which is now a pedestrian stairway into the plaza.

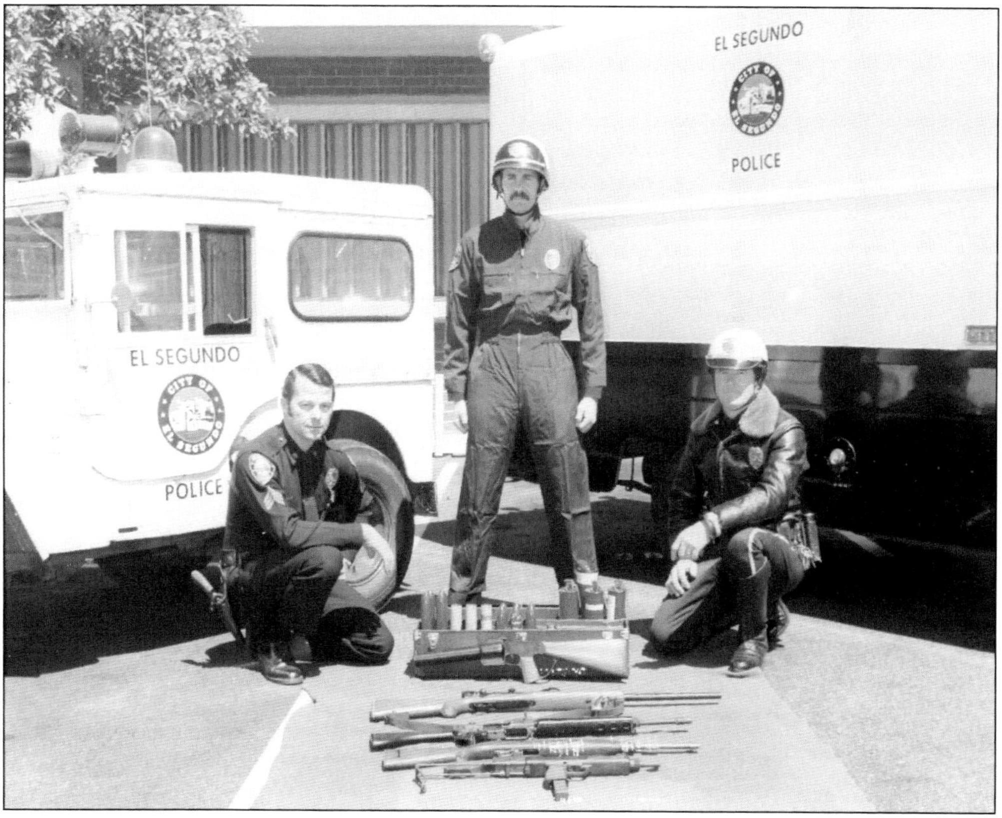

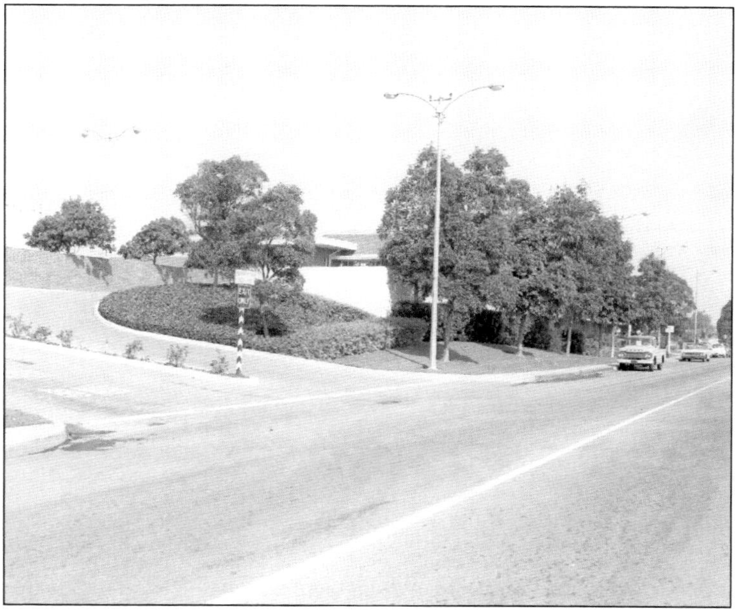

Police Weapon Display, 1960s. Officers display an array of weapons and chemical agents in front of the 1960s police department and vehicles. From left to right are Sgt. Charles Harworth, officer John "Jack" Wayt (police chief and city manager in the 2000s), and motor officer Newland "Duke" Hingley.

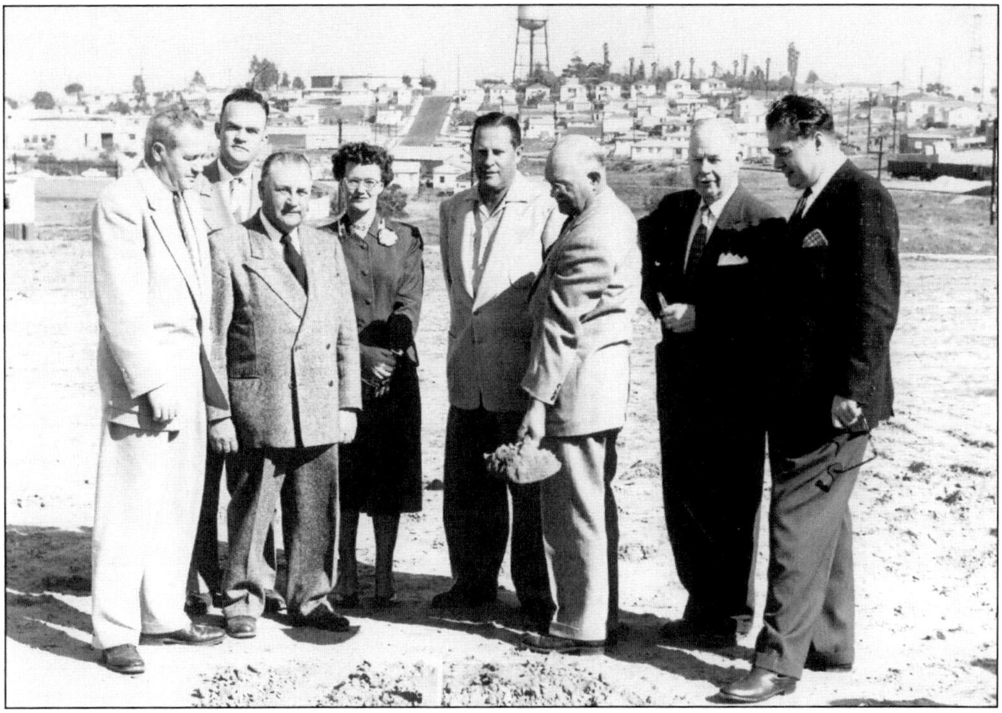

RECREATION PARK GROUND BREAKING, 1954. City council members and staff break ground for the new Recreation Park and facilities. From left to right are Wilburn Baker, councilman; Earl Udall, city manager; Walter Swanson, councilman; Ruth Hopp, treasurer; Robert Fredericks, councilman; Roy Selby, mayor; unidentified; and George Gordon, councilman.

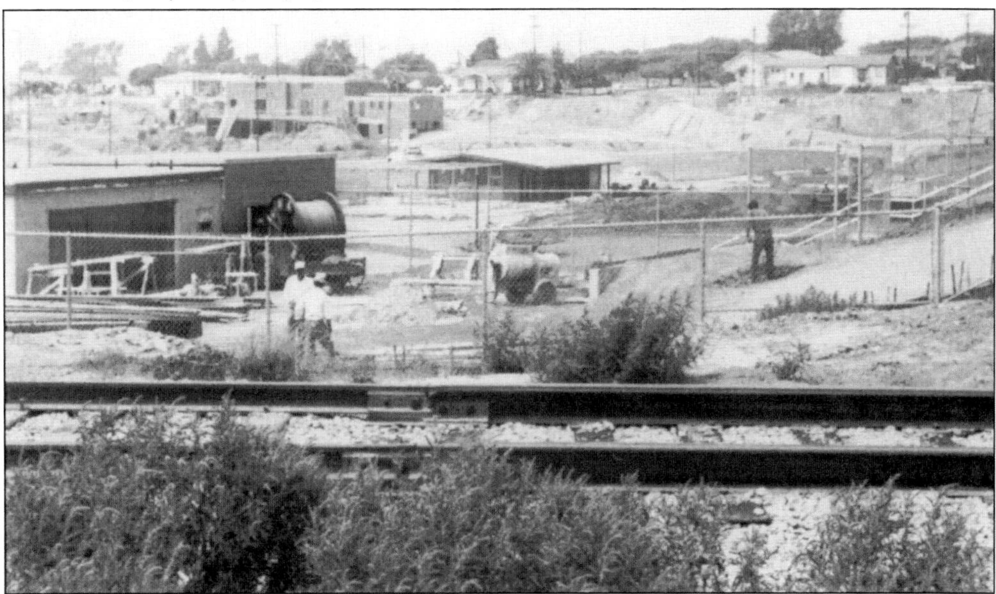

CONSTRUCTION OF RECREATION PARK, 1956. In this view facing northwest, workers build Recreation Park facilities, including the George E. Gordon Clubhouse in the background. In the foreground are the checkout building and a main track of the Pacific Railway that delivered materials to the El Segundo Station on Eucalyptus Drive.

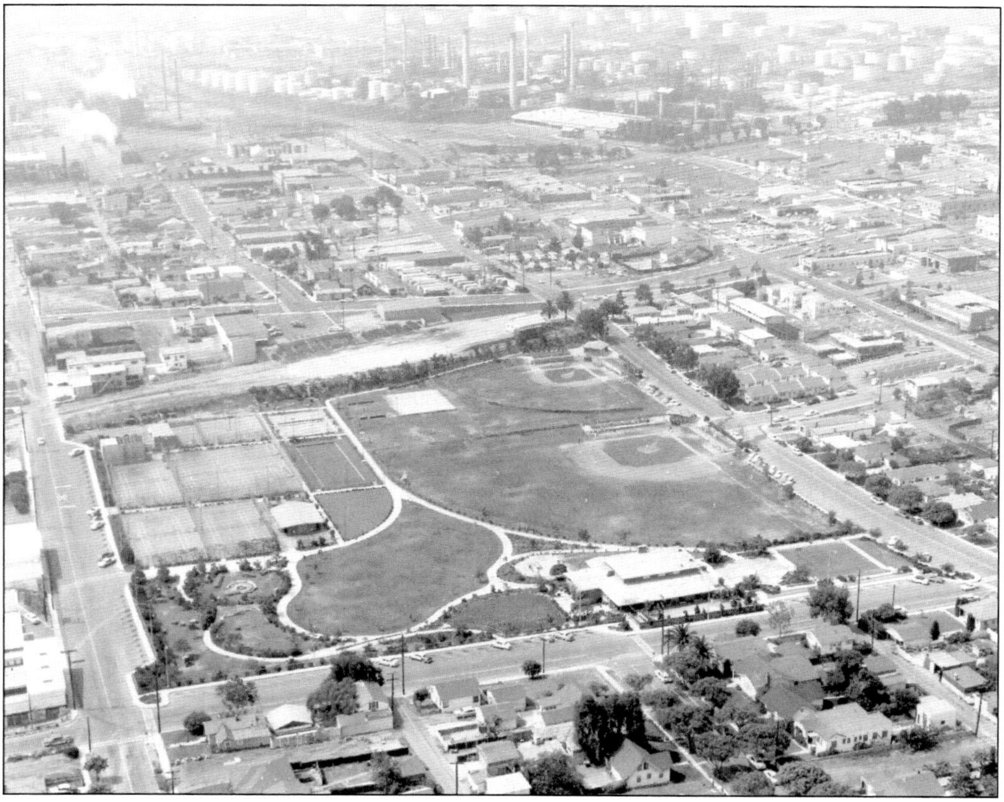

COMPLETED RECREATION PARK, 1960S. This aerial photograph shows the newly completed Recreation Park with baseball diamonds, tennis courts, picnic area, walking paths, and the George E. Gordon Clubhouse in the foreground. The surrounding downtown and Standard Oil Refinery are seen in the upper right corner and background.

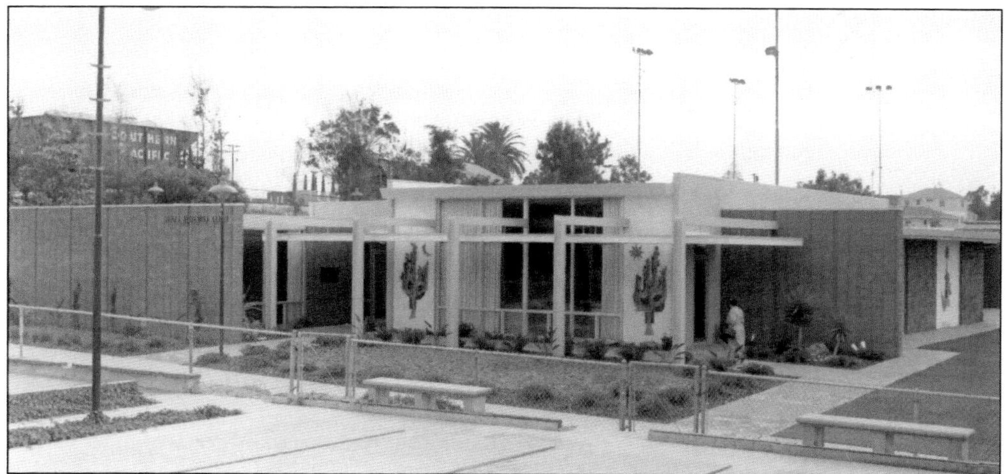

JOSLYN CENTER, 1966. The Joslyn Center was dedicated in the spring of 1966. Located in the southwest corner of Recreation Park, it was built for use by adults and older citizens in the community. In the far left corner is a Southern Pacific railcar, which delivered materials for the General Tile Company. As noted previously, the rail lines were abandoned in 1969 and demolished in 1987.

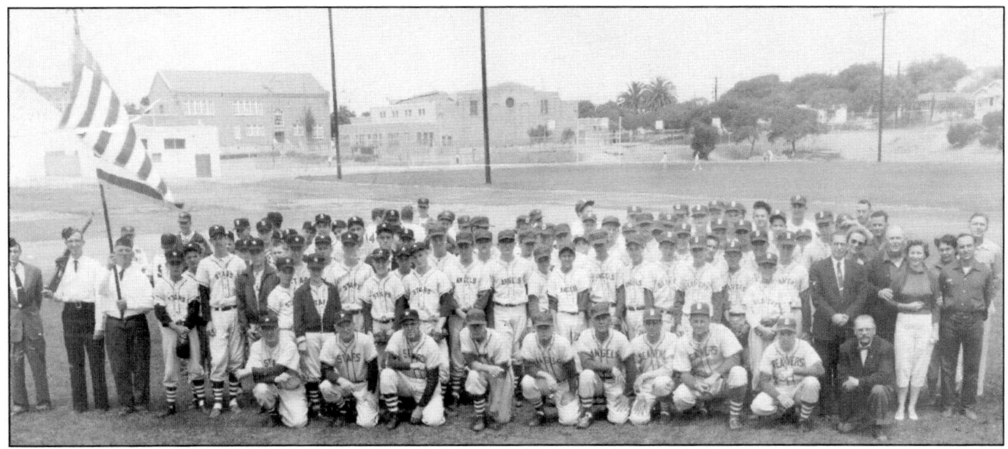

Babe Ruth Baseball, 1954. The first-year teams of Babe Ruth Baseball in El Segundo were the Stars: manager Joe Vinson, Coach Whipple, Coach Fike, Roy Fuke, Tim Whipple, Pete Beathard, Bill Law, Charlie Malock, John Rightmire, and Jack Searman; the Seals: manager Steve Coscarart, Gary Coscarart, Mike Hunley, and Swift "Speedy" Torrance; the Angels: Manager Hamrick, coach Billy Floyd, Dick King, Ray Sanchez, Danny Marks, and Stephen Cramlett; the Beavers: Tommy Atchison, Larry Tesdahl, Dick Miller, Gary Osterberg, Mike Millen, Coach Callahan, and Tom Callahan; the Oaks: manager Hal Chamberlain, Ron Ranson, Bob Flynn, Ken Wayatt, and George Whitney; and the Padres: Jerry Cox. Others are Joe Dubie, Pres. Walt Swanson, Mrs. Miller, Ed Eddington, Mrs. Whipple, and Santo Prete.

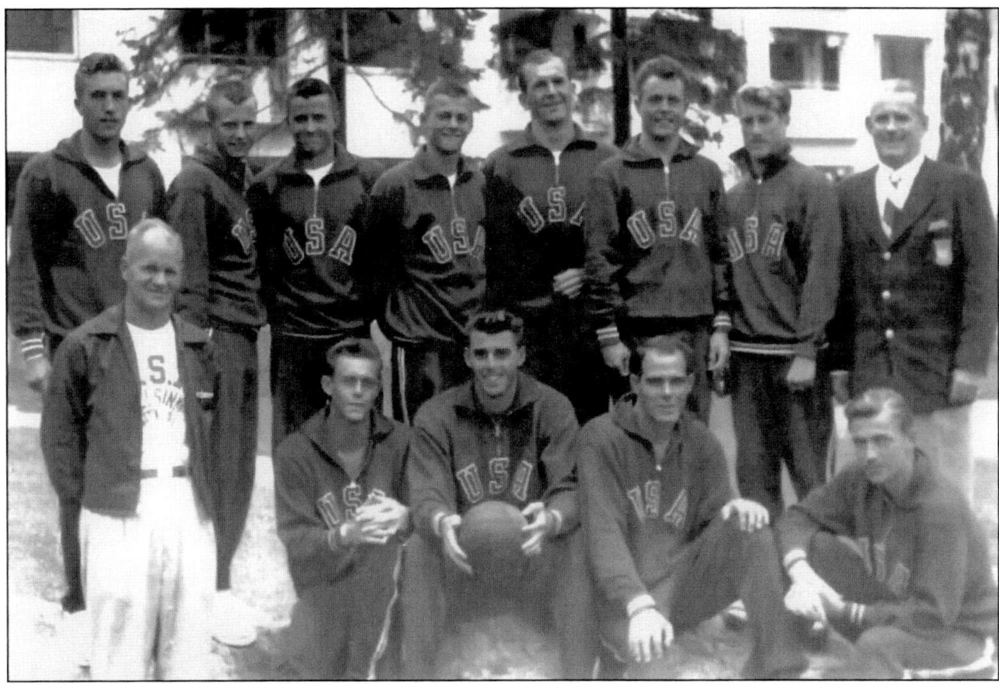

US Water Polo Team, 1952. The El Segundo water polo team, led by coach Urho Saari, won fourth place in the 1952 Olympic Games in Helsinki, Finland. From left to right are (first row) coach Urho Saari, Harry Bisbey, Marvin Burns, Bob Hughes, and Ed Gowaski (Illinois Athletic Club); (second row) Jim Norris, Bill Lake, Jack Spargo, Bob Koebler and Bill Koostra (New York Athletic Club), Bill Dornblaser, Pete Stange, and team manager John Curren.

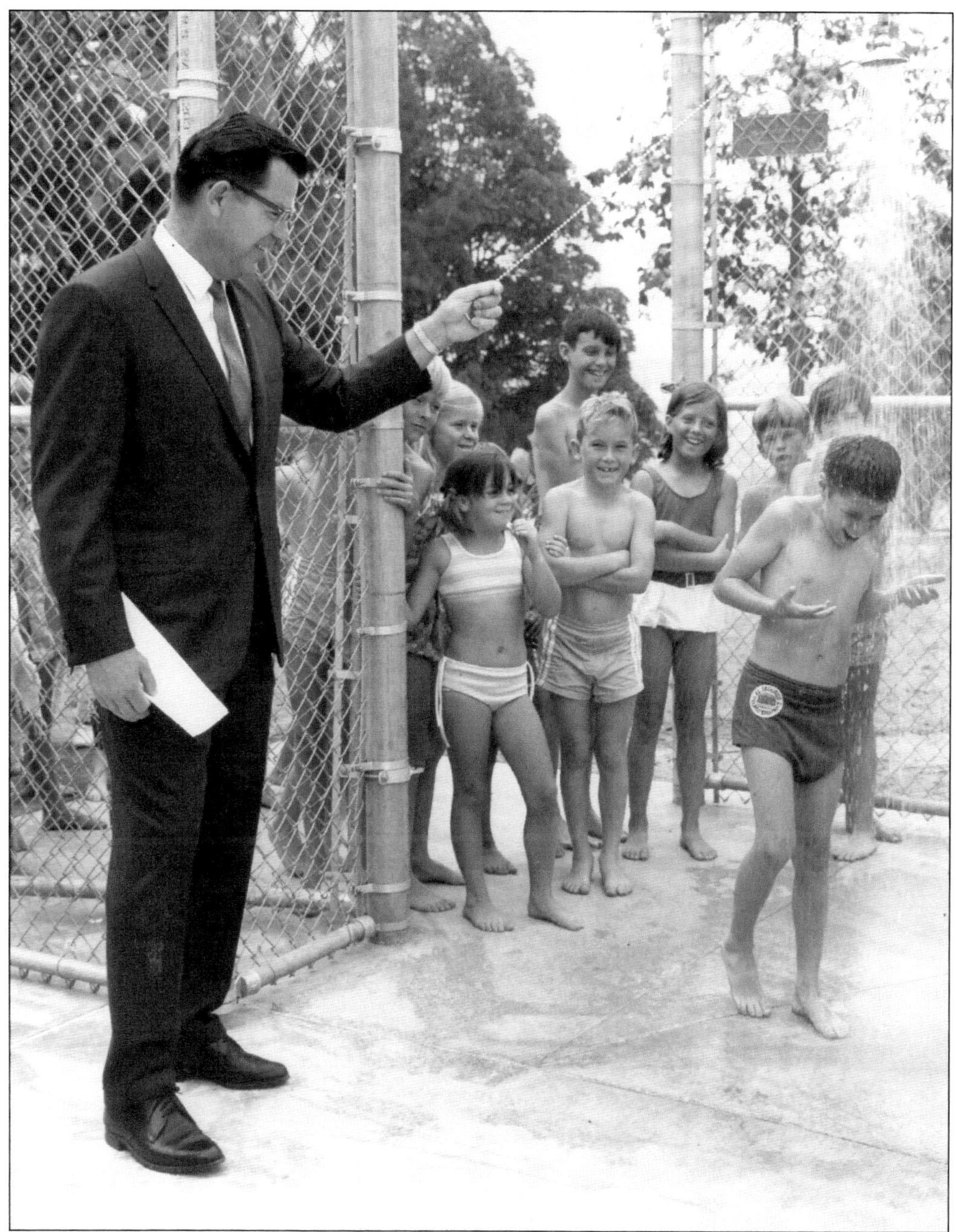

REDEDICATION OF HILLTOP PARK, 1969. Some smiling but soon to be very drenched children experience the new shower operated by Mayor Floyd Carr at Hilltop Park on Grand Avenue.

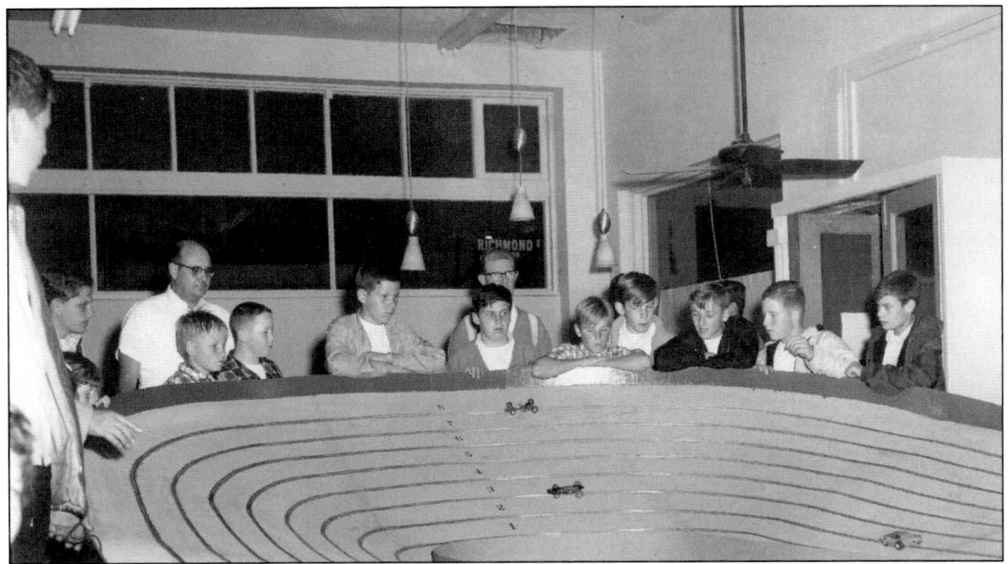

SLOT CAR RACING, JANUARY 1965. Held at the southeast corner of 130 Grand Avenue and Richmond Street, slot car racing was popular in the 1960s among teens. Seated closest to the table are, from left to right, Craig Cousins, two unidentified, Keith Wise, Mark Muio, two unidentified, Barry Bullock, Lenny Roscito, and David Marikos; the others are unidentified.

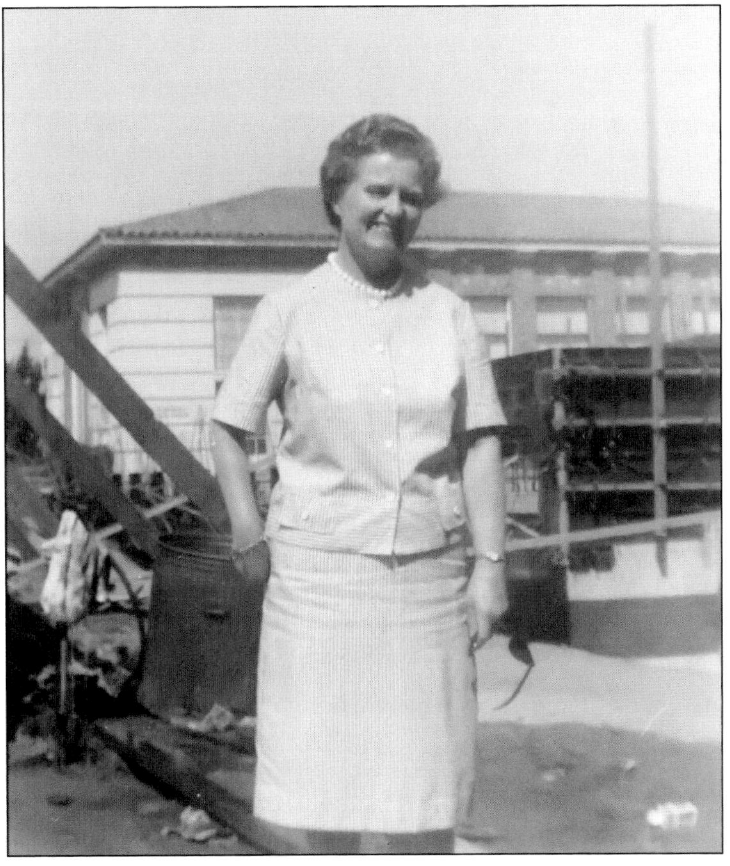

DOROTHEA FITZGERALD OVERSEEING THE LIBRARY EXPANSION, 1964. Dorothea is pictured in chapter 1 as one of the youngest residents in town in 1916. She started working at the El Segundo Public Library on February 17, 1934, and became chief librarian in May 1954. She retired on July 1, 1978, and was succeeded by Barbara Kirby.

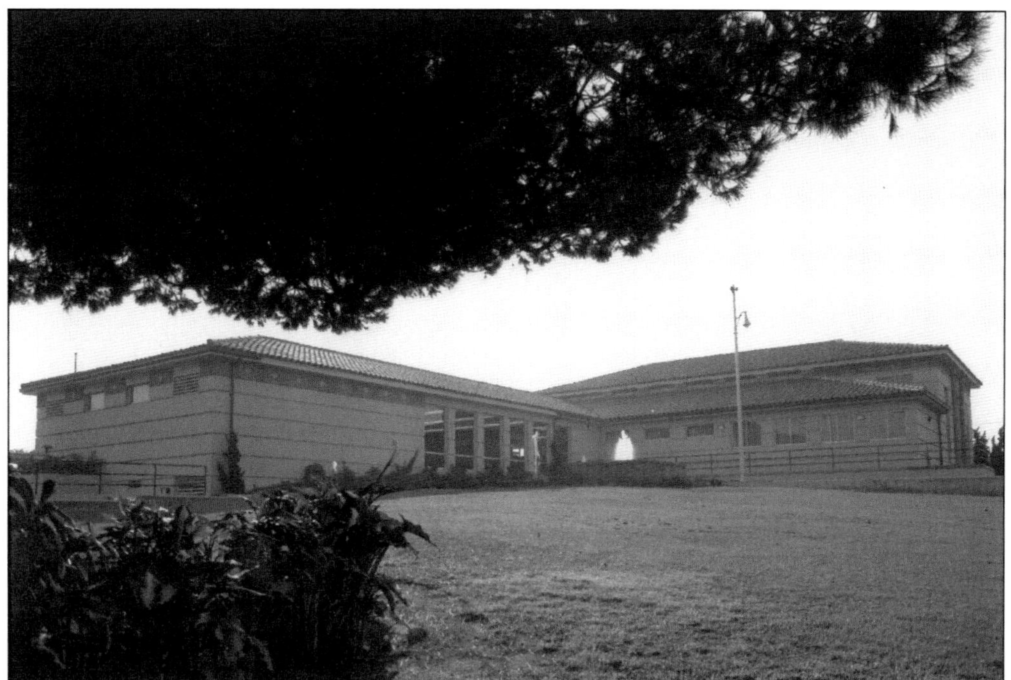

EXTERIOR OF COMPLETED LIBRARY EXPANSION, 1964. The El Segundo Public Library expanded by 8,000 additional square feet southeast into Library Park.

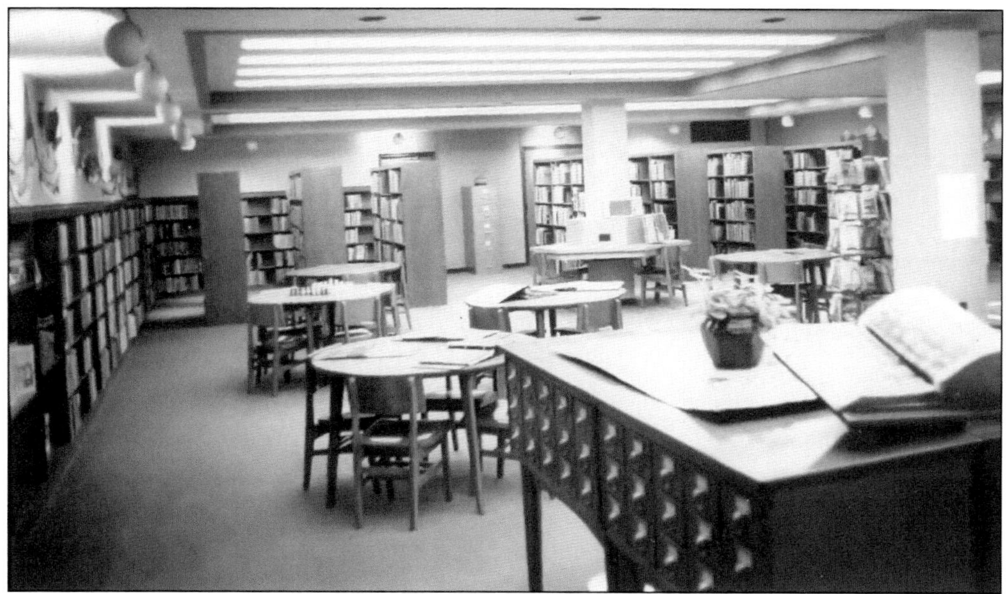

INTERIOR OF LIBRARY EXPANSION, APRIL 1964. Ready for the open house on April 12, 1964, the El Segundo Public Library had 4,000 cardholders and a book collection of 3,400 books. Here, wooden tables for sitting and the newly expanded library shelving are set to accommodate the library's numerous visitors and volumes until the 1970s, when a new children's wing would be added. In the early 1990s, the library was at full capacity again for both seating and books, plus it had a large audio-video collection, so another expansion was completed in 1992.

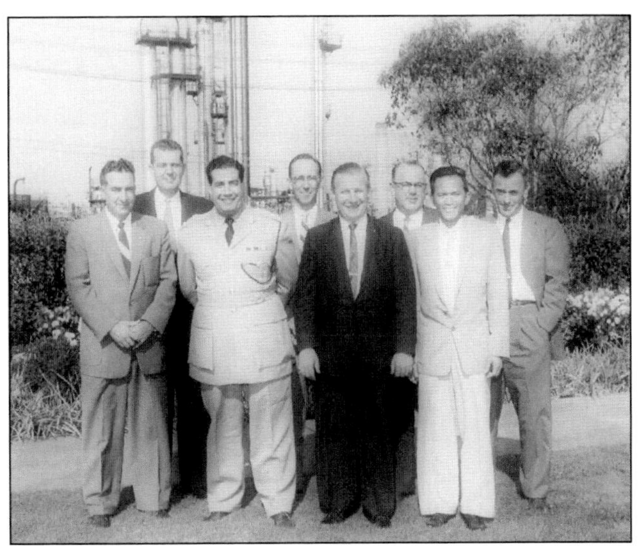

Another Visit to Standard Oil Company, October 30, 1958. Several members of the El Segundo Police Department (ESPD) and two representatives from international police forces visit Standard Oil Company (SOC) in El Segundo during 1958. From left to right are (first row) Lee Maxwell, chief, ESPD; Lt. Al-Jadon, Iraqi National Police; Charles D. Porter, ESPD; and Major Saroso, National Police Force, Indonesia; (second row) Ray Atherton, SOC; Vern Wood, deputy chief, ESPD; Clayton Williams, SOC; and Chuck Barker, SOC.

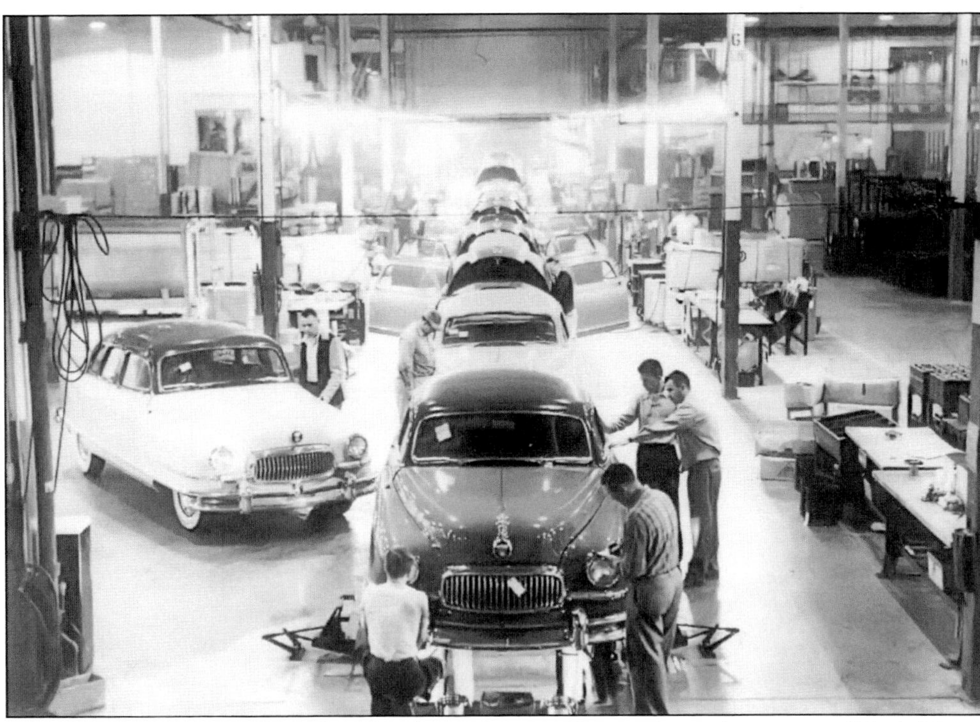

Nash Motors, 1950s. This photograph is an extremely popular and rare one of Nash Motors' assembly plant at Imperial Highway, east of Sepulveda Boulevard. Production of Nash cars started in 1948, but the plant was purchased by Hughes Aircraft Company in 1955, when Nash and several other independent auto manufacturers merged with American Motors.

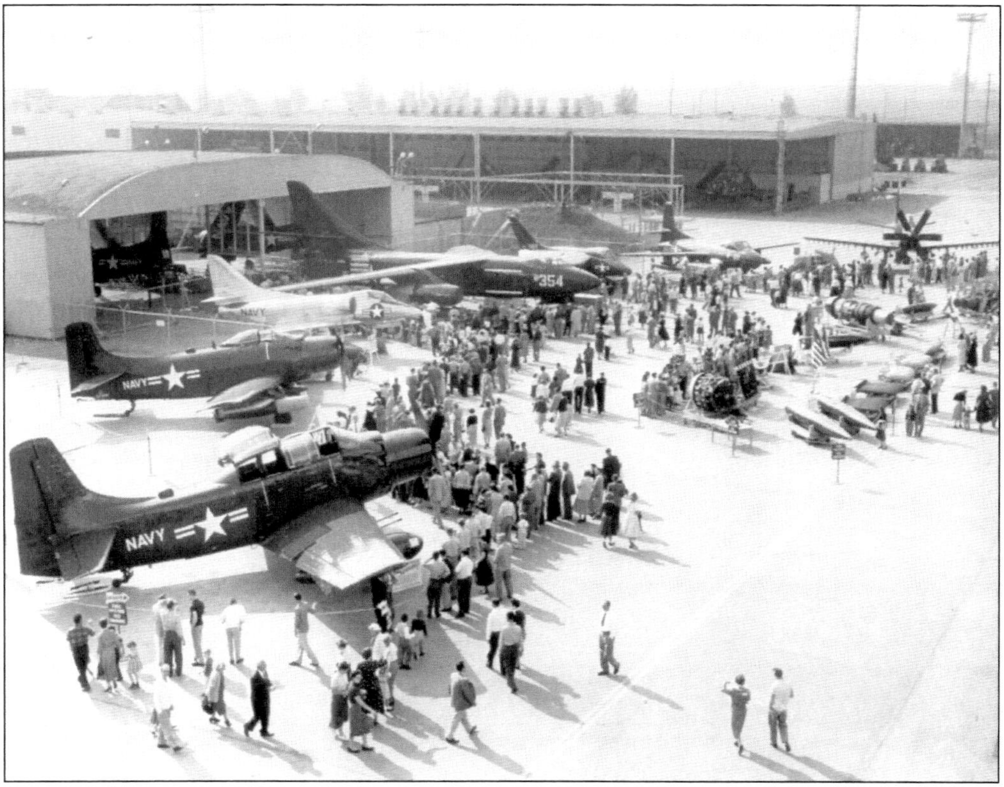

DOUGLAS AIRCRAFT, EL SEGUNDO DIVISION, NOVEMBER 14, 1954. Pictured during an open house at Douglas Aircraft, the buildings include, from left to right, the aircraft gunnery range, the aircraft paint booth, and the modification building. The airplanes on display are the AD-5 Skyraider, AD-6 Skyraider, A-4D Skyhawk, A-3D Skywarrior, F4D Skyray, F3D Skyknight, and the A2D Skyshark. (From *The Douglas Aircraft Plant That Became Los Angeles AFB*, by Robert Mulcahy.)

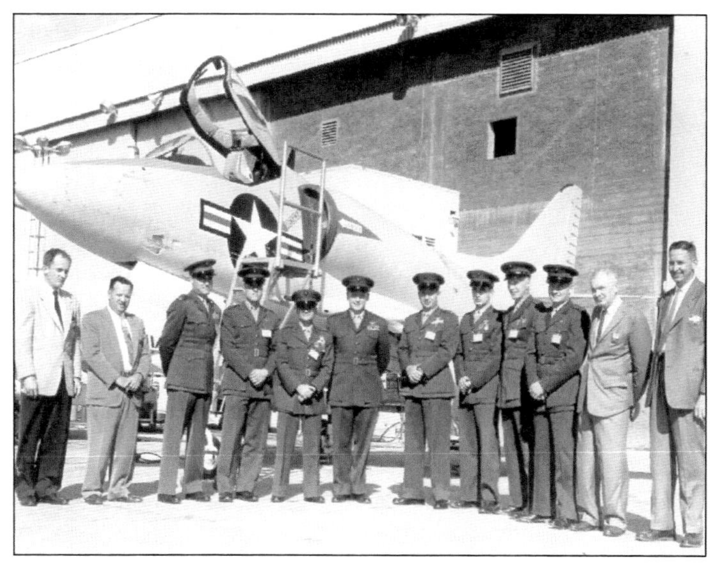

MARINE CORPS PILOTS, MARCH 20, 1958. Pilots from El Toro Marine Corps Air Station visited the El Segundo Division of Douglas Aircraft in March 1958. By 1962, Douglas Aircraft had left El Segundo, and the Navy had transferred the Naval Weapons Industrial Reserve Plant to the Air Force. The site was later designated as Area B by the Air Force. (From *The Douglas Aircraft Plant That Became Los Angeles AFB*, by Robert Mulcahy.)

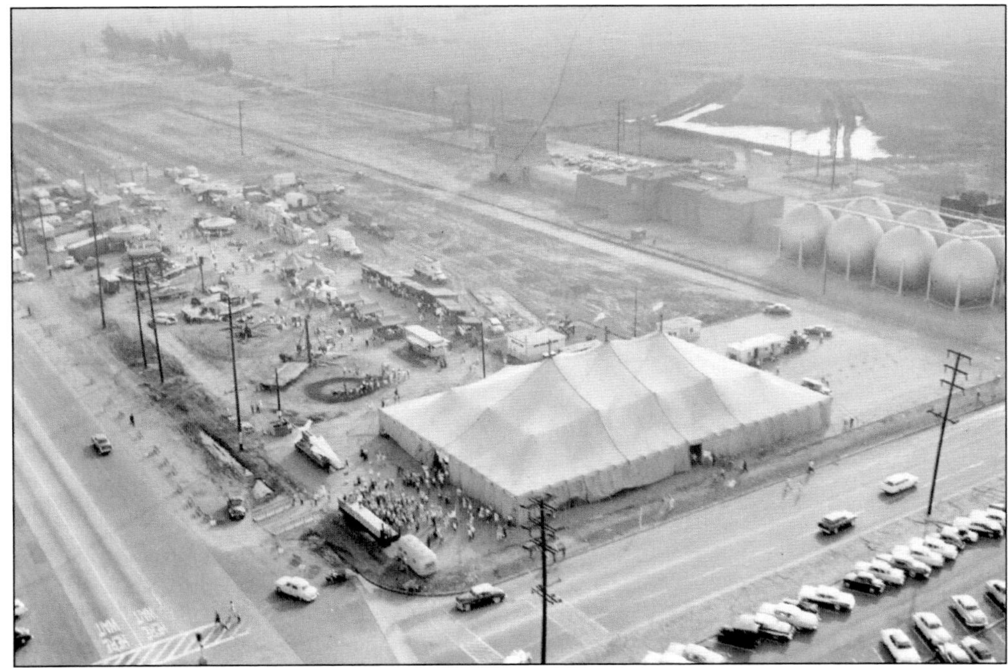

Fiesta at Douglas Aircraft, c. 1959. In the late 1950s, Douglas Aircraft Company hosted a fiesta with rides, booths, and a tent with aircraft, presumably, on display. The fiesta was held at the corner of Mariposa Avenue and Nash Street. A sonic wind tunnel for testing is in the background, to the left of the round tanks.

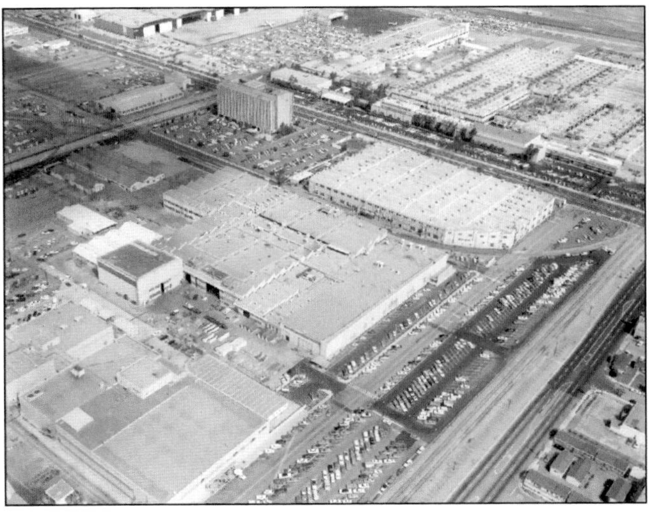

Aerial Taken with a View Looking Northwest near Los Angeles International Airport, August 20, 1968. North American Aviation and Douglas Aircraft Company occupy the area between Aviation Boulevard in the lower right corner, Imperial Highway in the upper right corner, and Douglas Street in the upper left corner. A few years after this photograph was made, the North American buildings were demolished and replaced with air cargo facilities.

Five

Approaching a New Century 1970–1999

As the 20th century came to a close, a few major transportation projects were also nearing completion. In the early 1970s, Grand Avenue was extended past Sepulveda Boulevard, which encouraged more economic growth on the east side of town. The Continental Grand Plaza on Continental Boulevard opened in 1986. And in 1991, Mattel built a 14-story corporate headquarters at Continental Boulevard and Grand Avenue. Other expansion projects in that vicinity included the Aerospace Corporation in 1981 and Computer Sciences Corporation in 1985. Finally, in the 1990s, the 105 Freeway and the Metro Green Line were completed. The 105 Freeway ends and merges onto Imperial Highway near the northwest section of town. The Metro Green Line has stops at the Mariposa Avenue, Nash Street, and Douglas Street stations in El Segundo.

Speaking of expansions, it was during this period that the El Segundo Public Library underwent two more addition and remodeling projects. In 1975, the children's library was enlarged to accommodate more young reader bookshelves and a story time area. By the 1990s, the public library had outgrown the 1960s footprint and needed more room. In 1992, a $4 million expansion project almost doubled the size of the library to 26,000 square feet, allowing more seating areas, meeting rooms, a history room, an expanded children's room, a new online catalog, a reference area, and more shelving space for magazines, music and books on CD, and DVDs (called videos back then).

Before the new millennium was ushered in, two other major developments were completed: the Park Vista Senior Housing Project and the Embassy Suites hotel. The new Park Vista opened in 1987 with 97 units on Holly Avenue. It is still administered by the recreation and parks department, and a senior housing board is selected by the city council to oversee operations. Near the city's greenbelt, south of Imperial Highway, a new Embassy Suites hotel was constructed in 1987. Significant community events during this time included the construction of a grand gazebo in Library Park, Fire Safety Days, a paramedic program, donations of fire trucks to El Segundo's sister city of Guaymas, Mexico, the start of Student Government Day, and a K-9 dog program through the police department in the 1970s and 1980s.

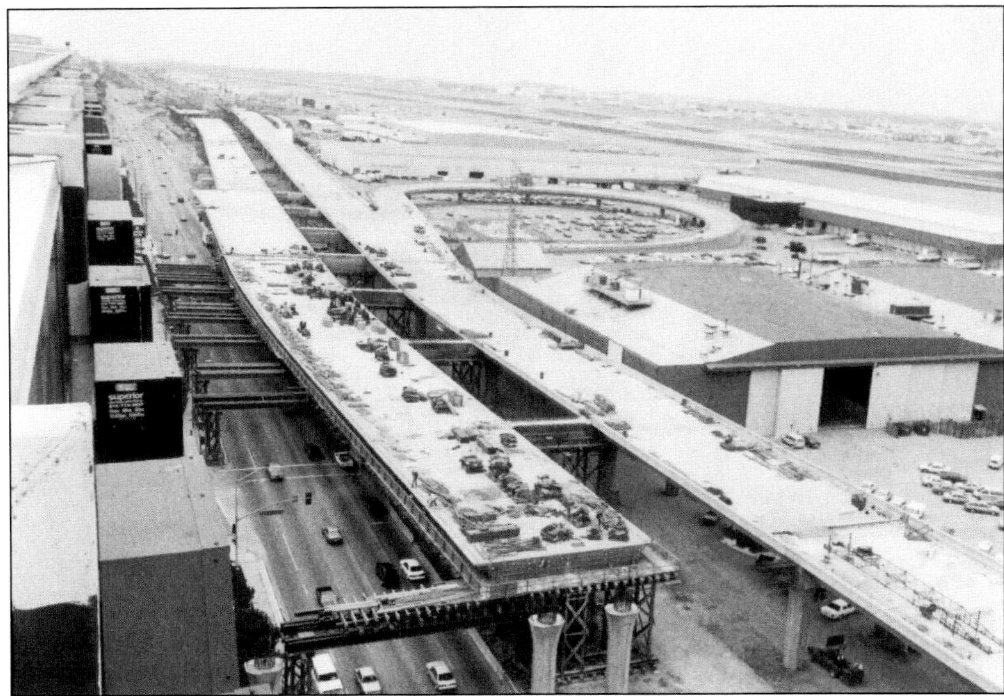

Construction of the 105 Freeway, 1990s. The 105 Freeway runs east-west from the Interstate 605 Freeway in Norwalk, California, to Sepulveda Boulevard in El Segundo. It is officially known as the Glenn Anderson Freeway, after the California politician who advocated its construction. The length of the freeway is 18.82 miles, and it is maintained by Caltrans. At a cost of $2.5 billion, construction started in 1982, and it opened in 1993.

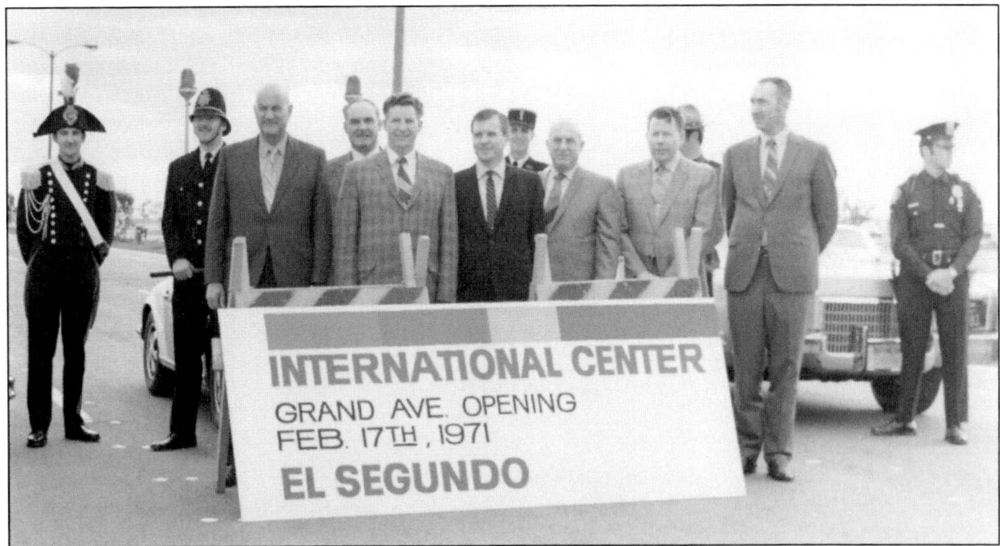

Grand Avenue Ceremony, February 12, 1971. A photograph shows the Grand Avenue extension opening east of Sepulveda Boulevard. The officials are, from left to right, Councilman Les Balmer, chamber of commerce manager Wesley Bush, Mayor Gordon Stephens, chamber president Tom Longsden, banker Lloyd Ballmer, Councilman Herman McGill, and Councilman Richard Nagel. The police officers are unidentified.

Retired Fire Truck Demonstration, c. 1970. During Fire Prevention Week, representatives from Guaymas, Mexico, El Segundo's sister city, view a ladder truck being presented to them. The *bomberos*, or firefighters, will drive the truck south of the border to Guaymas for use during their fire emergency services.

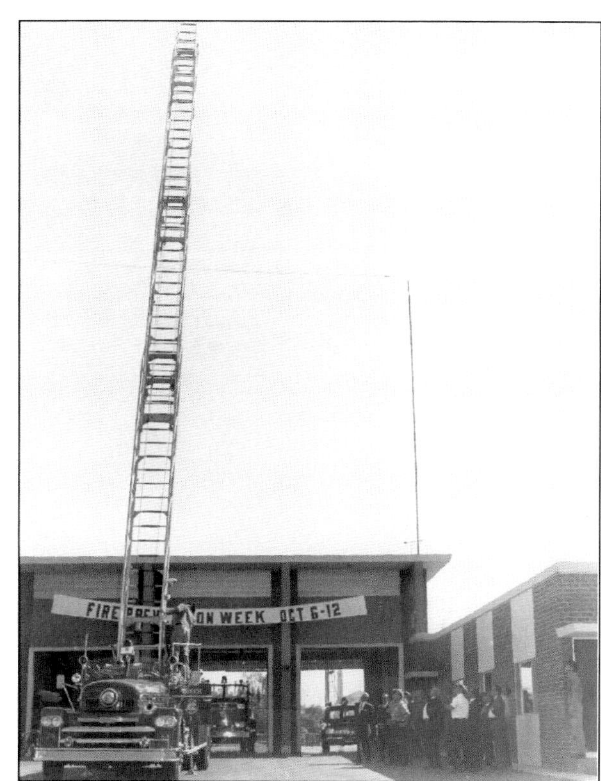

Another Fire Truck Presented to Guaymas, c. 1975. Former fire chief Harry Gates, on the left, presents the keys to another retired fire engine to the unidentified *jefe de bomberos* (fire chief) of Guaymas, Mexico (center). On the right is an unidentified fire captain.

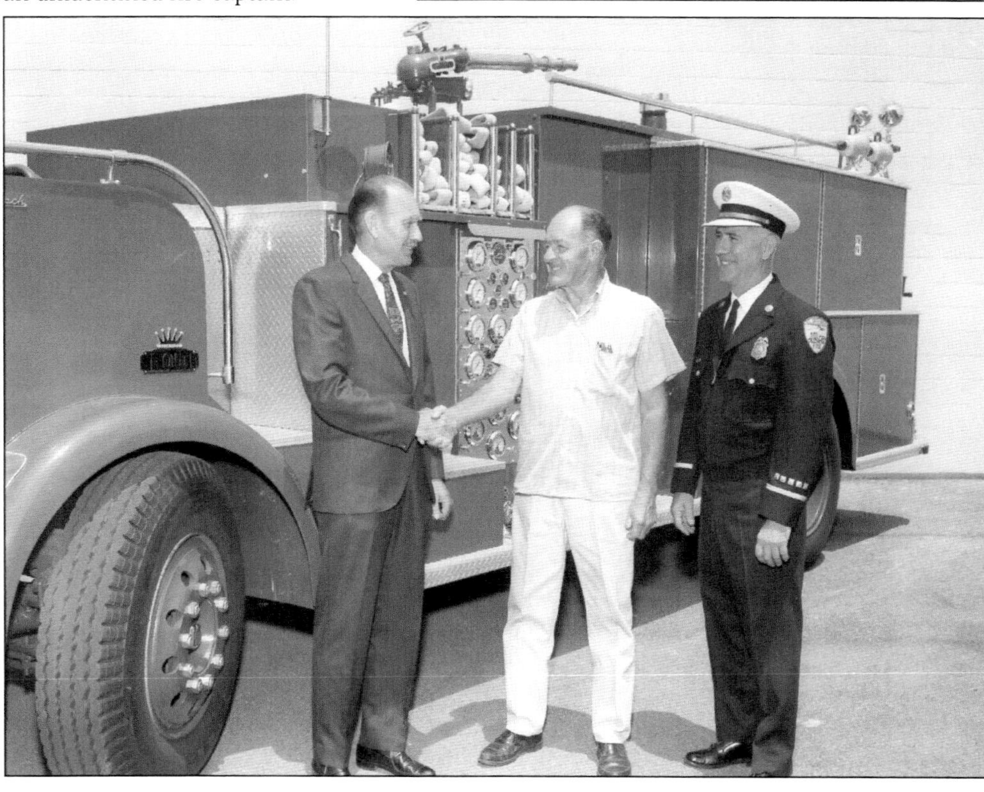

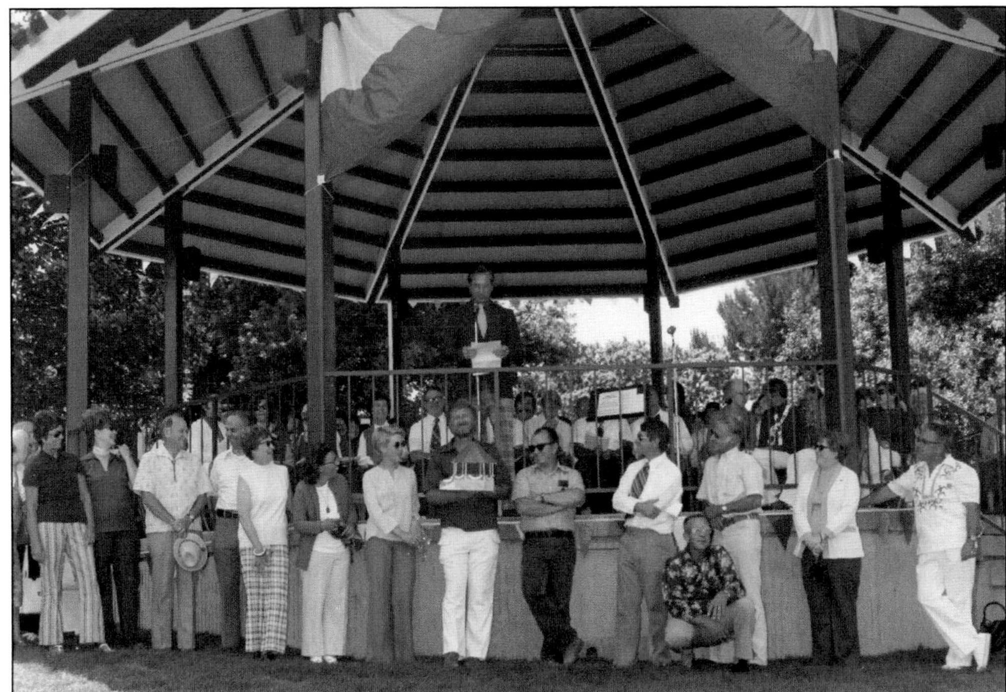

LIBRARY PARK GAZEBO DEDICATION, JULY 3, 1976. Designer Norman Bell holds a model of the new gazebo, dedicated during the country's bicentennial celebration. Councilman Dick Nagel is at the microphone with members of the bicentennial committee around the gazebo. Concerts, weddings, graduations, summer camps, and the Home Town Fair are still held in the park with the gazebo as a prominent feature. The local library even has a meeting room facing the park called the Gazebo Room.

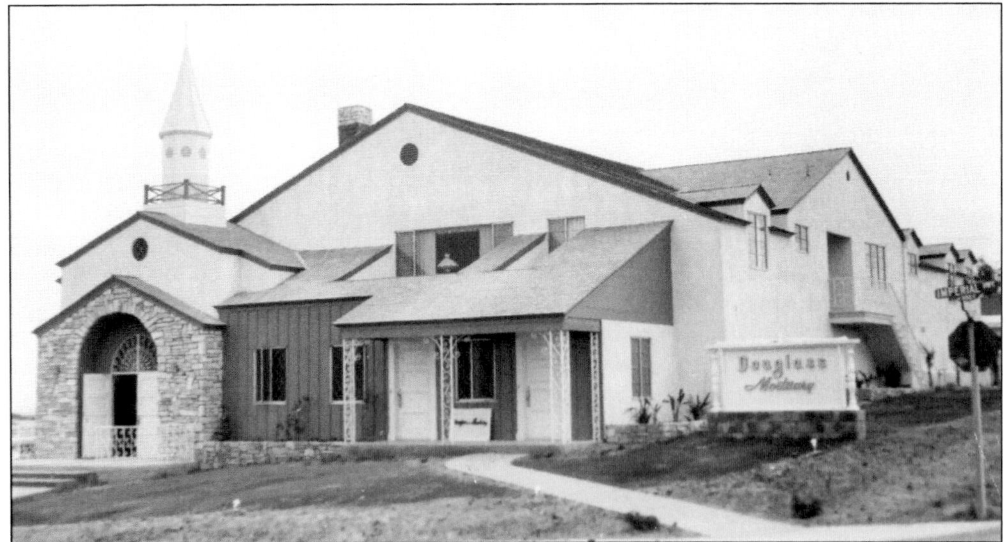

DOUGLASS MORTUARY, 1970s. The extended family business was started in the late 1920s. Sam Douglass Sr. and his wife, Cravens, purchased a storefront on Richmond Street in 1943, then they constructed and moved in 1958 to the current site of Douglass Mortuary at 500 East Imperial Avenue.

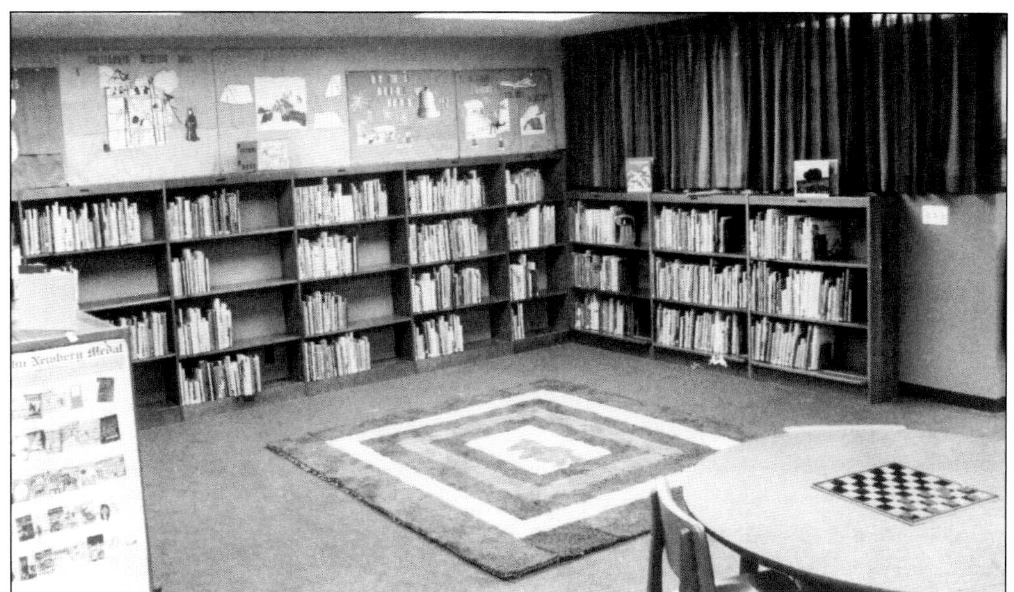

Library Children's Room Remodel, 1975. Formerly a storage area and bomb shelter and built as part of the 1960s expansion, this area was converted to enhance the children's library in 1975. Along with more room for books to check out, children could also play games and puzzles and use the story time rug for reading, which is still a popular feature in the young people's library today.

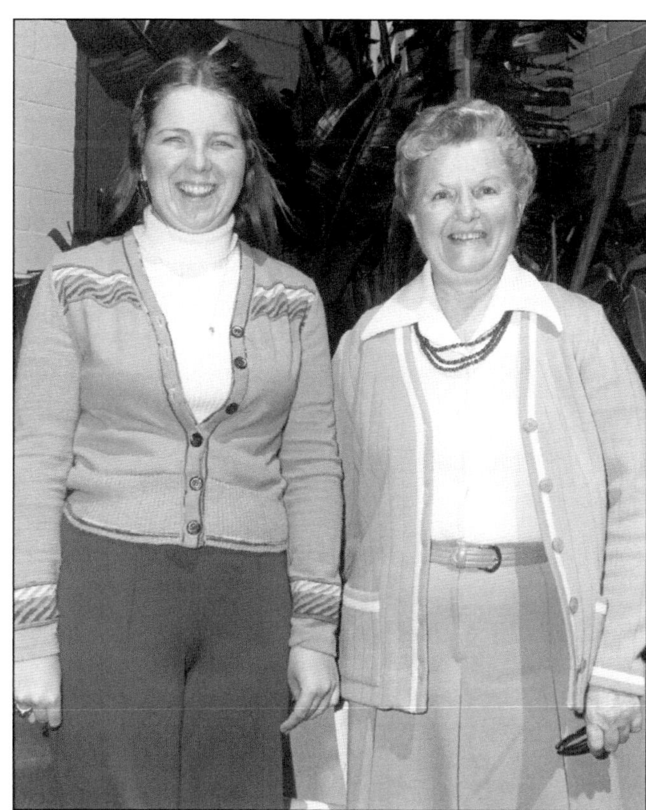

Student Government Day, March 13, 1975. It was popular in the 1970s and 1980s for local high school students to spend a day shadowing city department heads and officials in order to learn how the city operated. Pictured are student and possible future librarian Chris Thorne along with chief librarian Dorothea Fitzgerald.

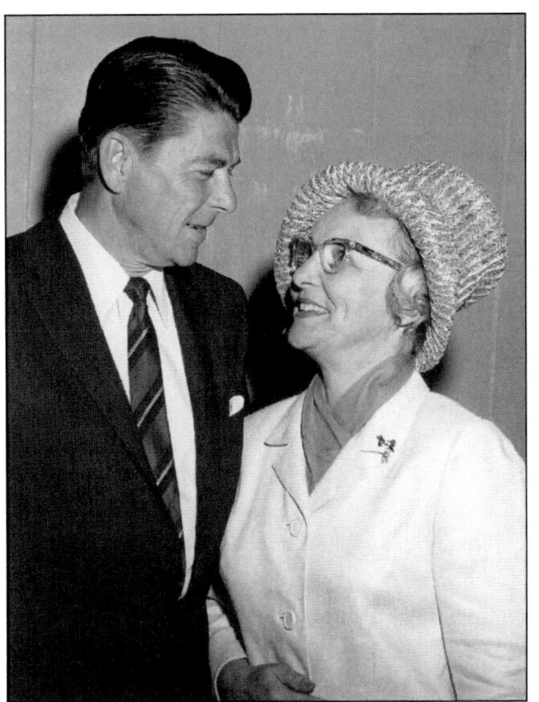

Olga Benson with Gov. Ronald Reagan, 1970. Olga Benson was a longtime realtor in El Segundo. She was fortunate to meet Governor Reagan at Los Angeles International Airport during one of his stops and have this photograph taken. The library's History Room was fortunate that she donated it to the collection.

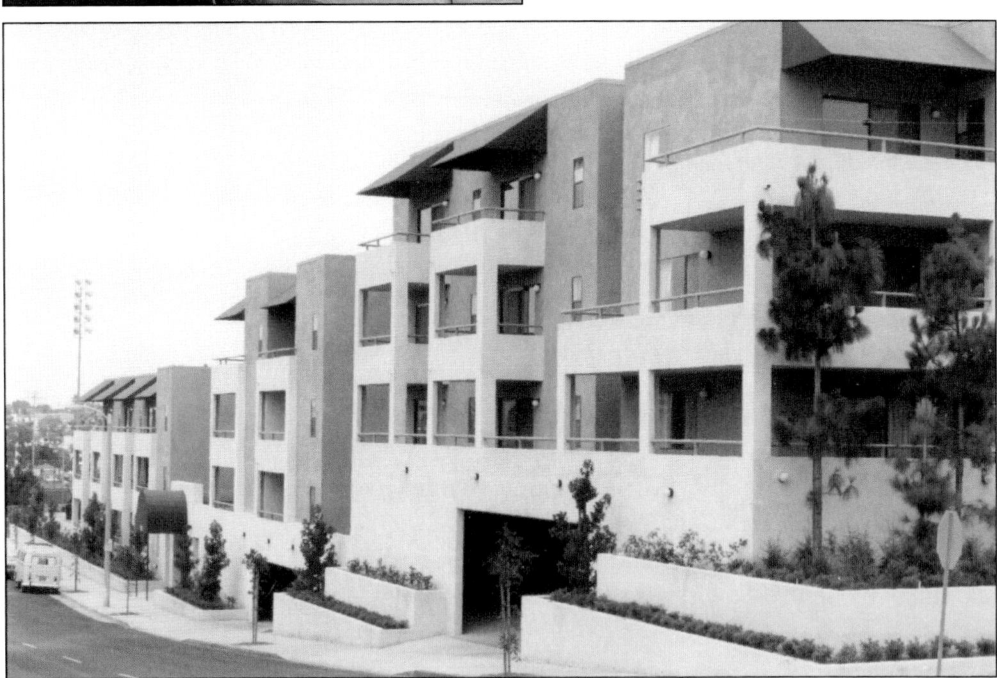

Park Vista, El Segundo's Senior Housing Project, 1987. On December 13, 1985, a groundbreaking ceremony took place at 615 East Holly Avenue. Two years later, the new Park Vista opened on August 6, 1987. Owned and operated by the City of El Segundo, Park Vista has three floor plans and a total of 97 units, all one-bedroom apartments with private patios, bathrooms, and kitchen facilities. It is administered by a senior housing board under the recreation and parks department, and the city still maintains this community residential center for seniors.

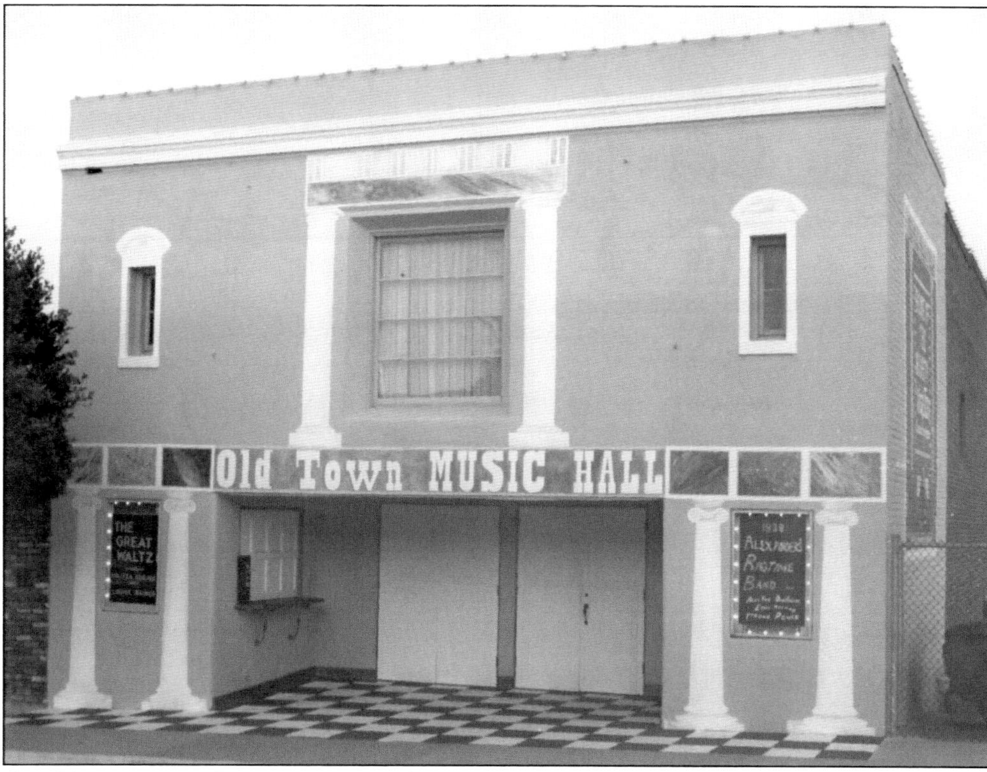

OLD TOWN MUSIC HALL, C. 1980. Built in 1919 as the State Theater, this building is located at 140 Richmond Street. Starting in 1978, silent films were shown here at the Old Town Music Hall to the accompaniment of a 1925 Wurlitzer pipe organ, which is still played today.

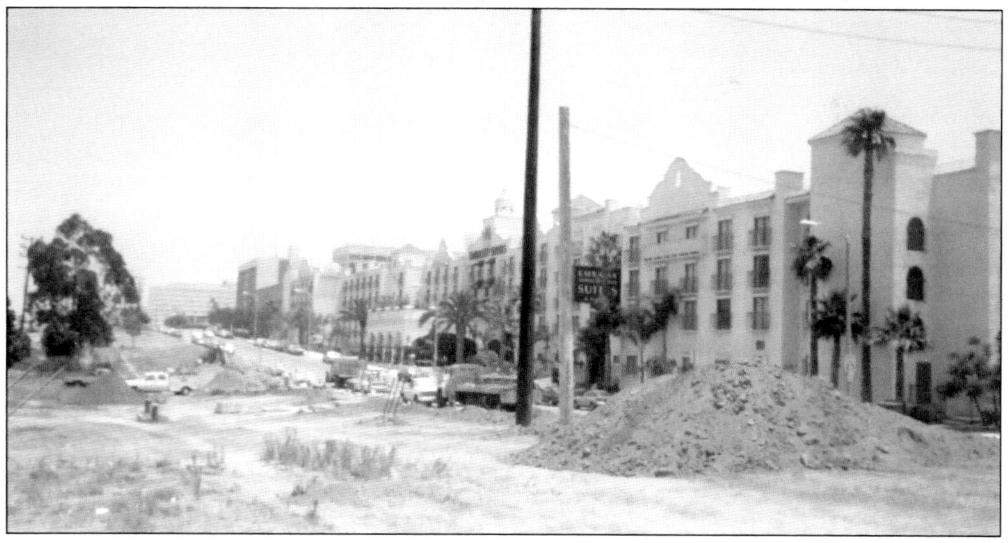

EMBASSY SUITES, 1987. Located at 1440 East Imperial Avenue, the hotel is now the Embassy Suites Los Angeles International Airport South Hotel. After the construction of the hotel in 1987, the greenbelt median that separates Imperial Avenue from Imperial Highway was improved. The hotel sits opposite Los Angeles International Airport and has approximately 350 guest rooms, an indoor pool, meeting rooms, and a central atrium court for the restaurant, bar, and lobby area.

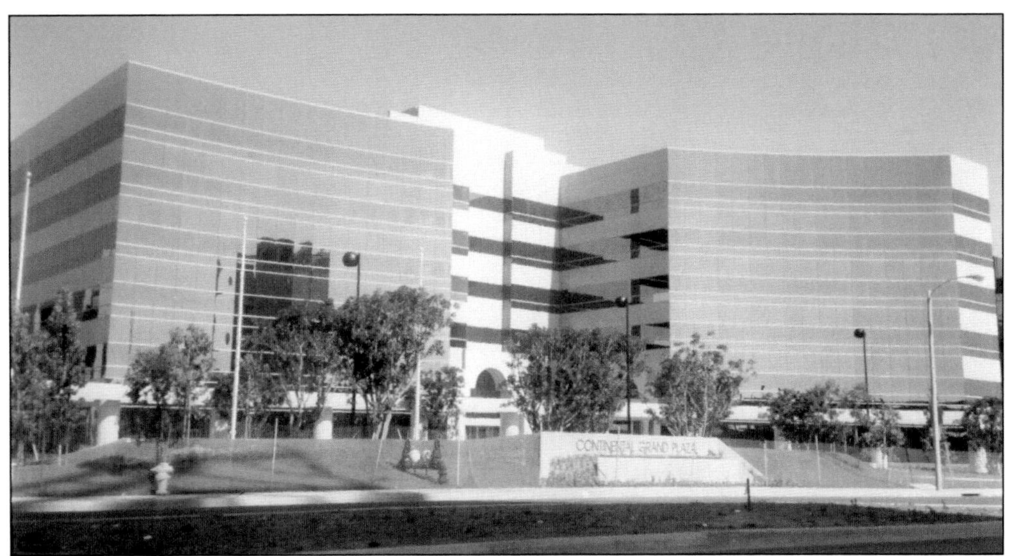

CONTINENTAL GRAND PLAZA, JULY 1986. The first Continental building was a six-story commercial office structure at 300 North Continental Boulevard. Grand Plaza II was added in 1999 at 400 Continental Boulevard. Today, Continental Park, at 2041 Rosecrans Avenue in El Segundo, is the latest business complex to be added to the Continental Development Corporation locations.

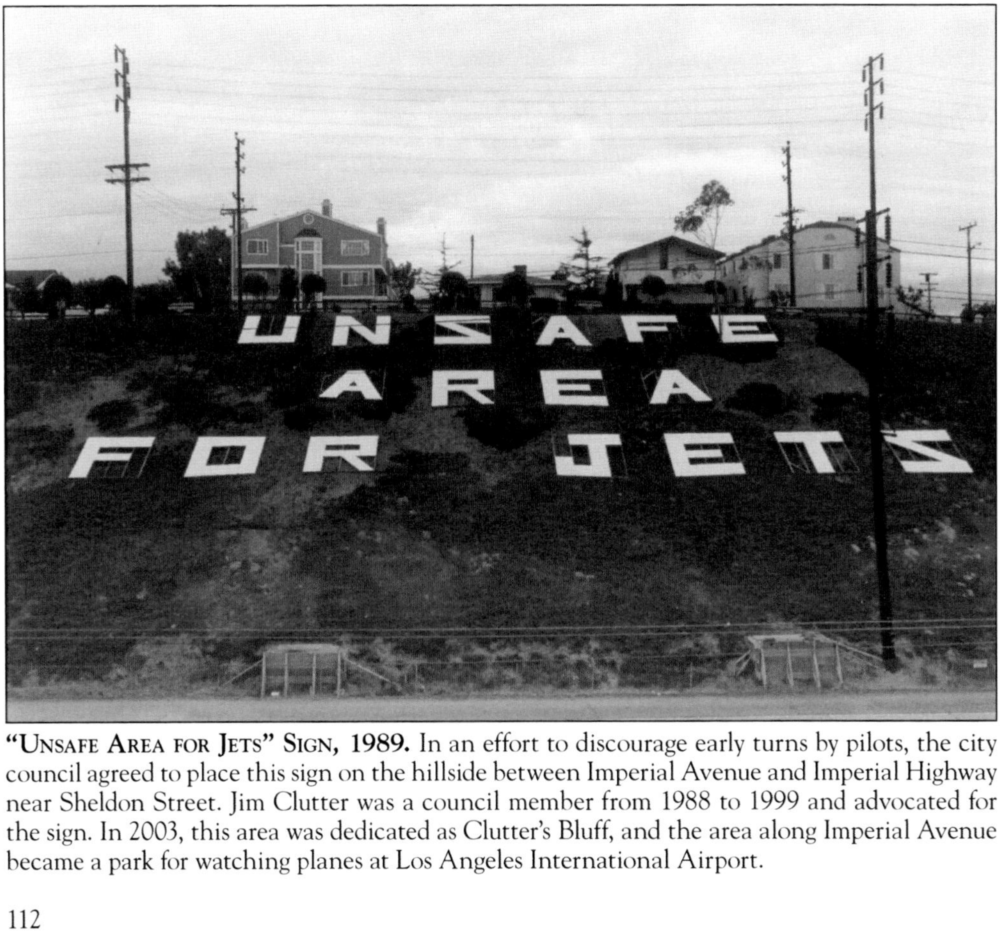

"UNSAFE AREA FOR JETS" SIGN, 1989. In an effort to discourage early turns by pilots, the city council agreed to place this sign on the hillside between Imperial Avenue and Imperial Highway near Sheldon Street. Jim Clutter was a council member from 1988 to 1999 and advocated for the sign. In 2003, this area was dedicated as Clutter's Bluff, and the area along Imperial Avenue became a park for watching planes at Los Angeles International Airport.

The Aerospace Corporation, 1981. The Aerospace Corporation was formed as nonprofit on June 3, 1960, to provide noncompetitive and objective technical assistance to American military operations in space. It performs engineering, planning, analysis, and research for space systems. This 1981 aerial photograph with a view looking southeast shows the Ivan A. Getting Laboratories in the foreground, the James H. Doolittle Facility and general offices in the center, and the headquarters of the Air Force Space Division in the upper right corner.

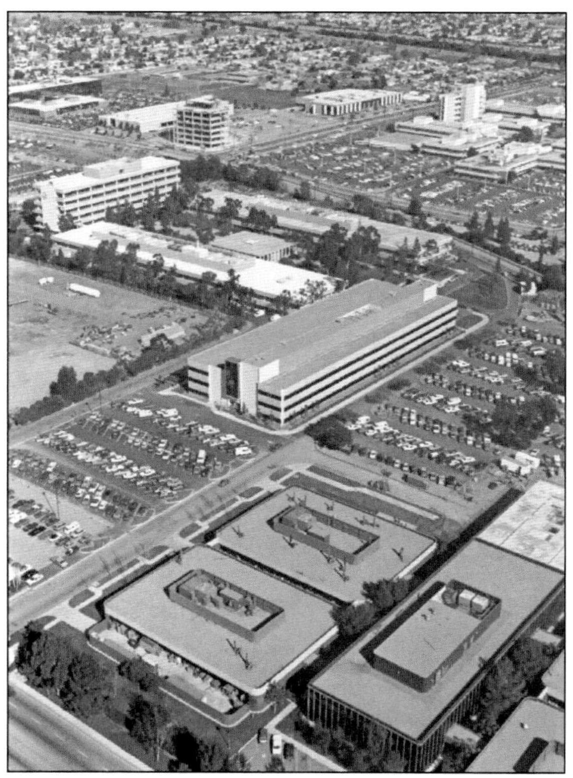

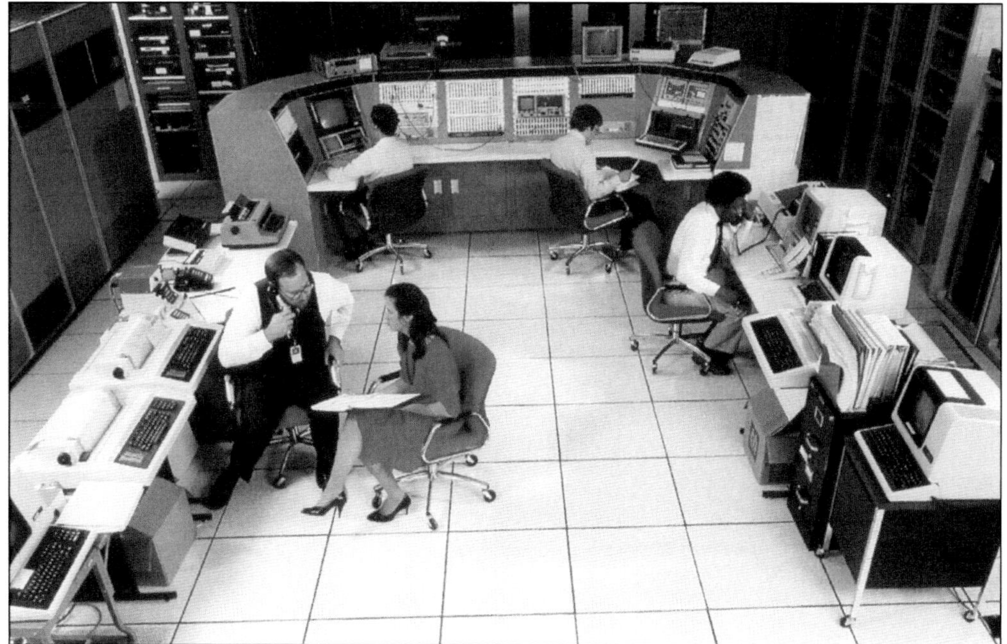

Computer Sciences Corporation, 1985. Founded in 1959, the Computer Sciences Corporation was located at 2100 East Grand Avenue for many years until it moved its headquarters to Falls Church, Virginia, in 2008. This photograph was taken at its INFONET data communication center in El Segundo.

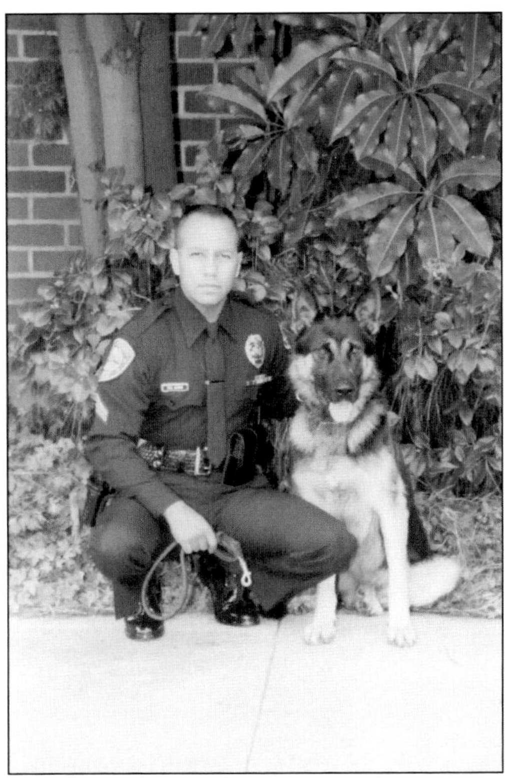

POLICE DEPARTMENT K-9 PROGRAM, 1990s. Officer Ray Garcia and his dog, Dako, were part of the K-9 program using highly trained police dogs in the detection and apprehension of dangerous suspects, narcotics, and evidence. It began in 1980 and still runs today, with officers selected to be dog handlers undergoing a lengthy training course before they begin patrolling duties. Patrol cars are modified specifically for the dogs, and officers take their dogs home at the end of each shift so that the dogs become part of the family.

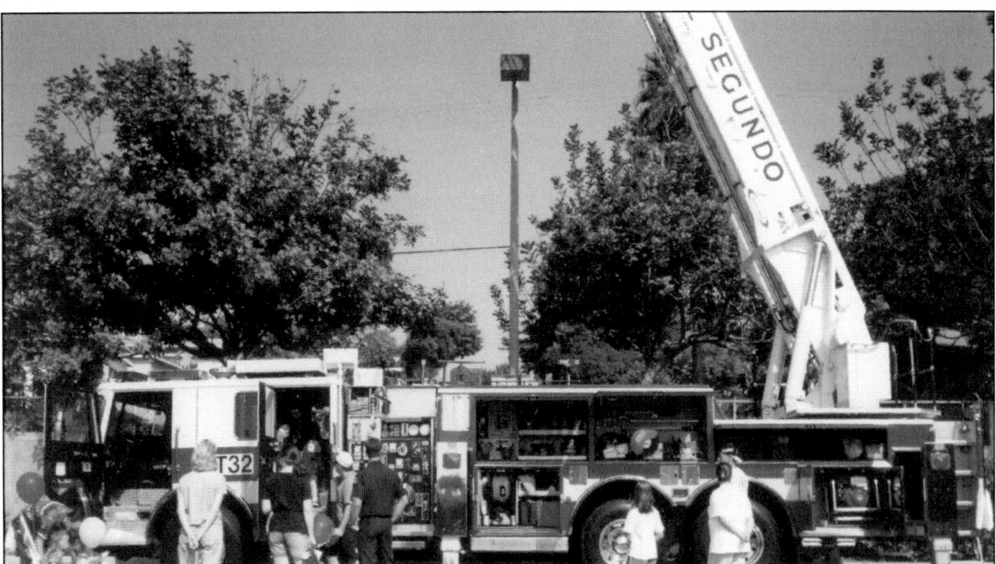

FIRE SAFETY, 1997. The fire department presented a fire safety event for the community with demonstrations of its ladder truck, a Yogi Bear "school house," a fire hose exercise, and a "stop, drop, and roll" drill for children to teach them what to do in case of a fire emergency. Today, besides conducting open house tours of the two fire stations, the department does many community outreach programs, including the promotion of smoke alarm safety in the home, offering CPR classes, conducting 9/11 memorial services, and assisting local charities with a pancake breakfast and Spark of Love Toy Dive.

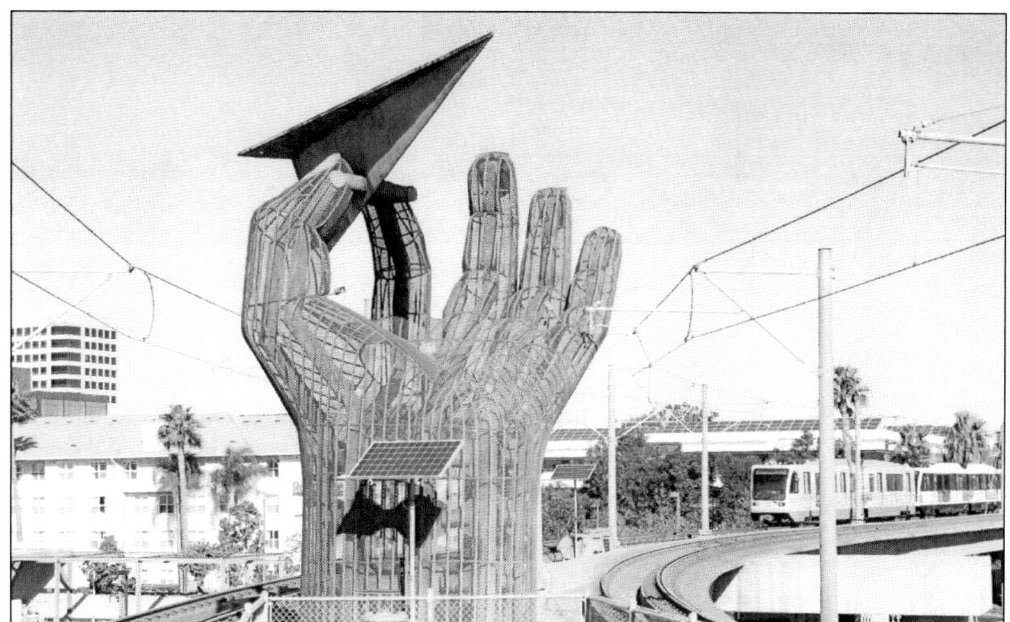

METRO GREEN LINE STOP IN EL SEGUNDO, 1995. The Metro Green Line was constructed with 14 stations over 17 miles of tracks, beginning at the I-605 Freeway in Norwalk, California, and ending at Marine Avenue in Redondo Beach, California. The cost was $717.8 million and was paid with state and local funds. Pictured here is the Nash Street station in El Segundo with the landmark 30-foot wire mesh paper-airplane art by Daniel Martinez.

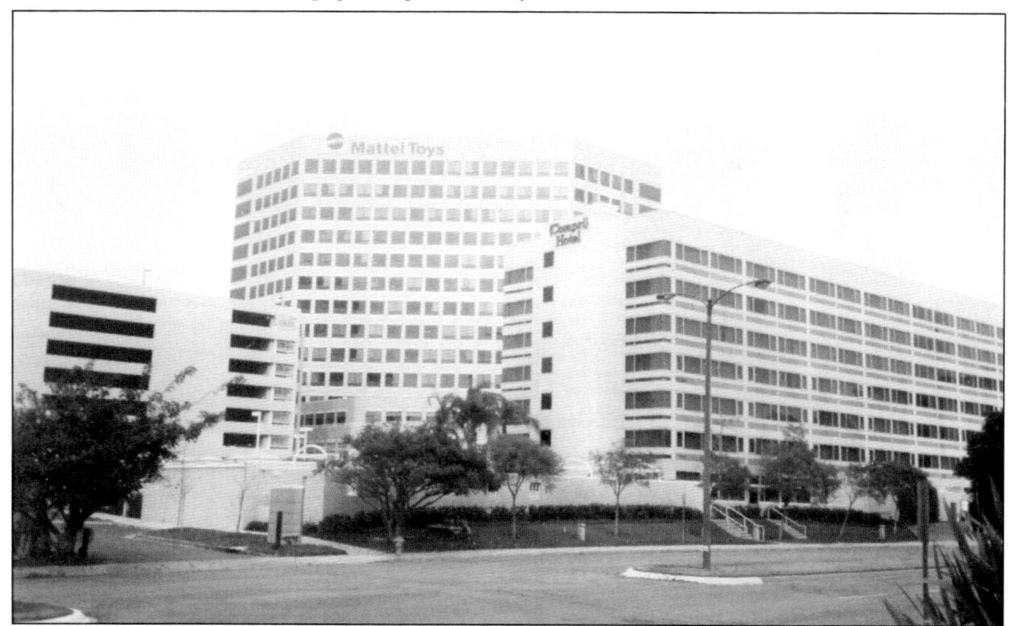

MATTEL TOYS, 1991. Founded in 1945 by Harold Matson and Elliot Handler, Mattel, Inc., built its 14-story corporate headquarters in El Segundo in 1987 at 333 Continental Boulevard. Its most popular doll, Barbie, was created in 1959, followed by the talking doll Chatty Cathy a year later. Mattel's products now include Fisher-Price, Barbie dolls, American Girl dolls, Monster High dolls, Hot Wheels, Matchbox toys, and Masters of the Universe.

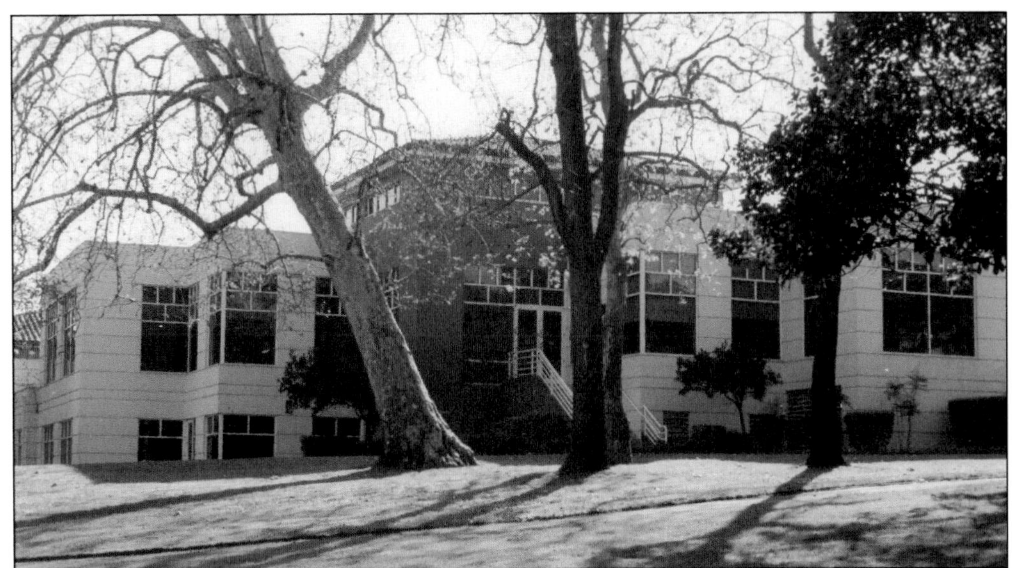

LIBRARY EXPANSION AND RENOVATION PROJECT, 1992. The $4 million public library expansion project, designed by Charles Walton & Associates, added approximately 16,000 square feet to the existing north and east sides of the building and doubled the seating and book shelving capacity. A new children's library with a saltwater aquarium, a historical archives room, literacy program room, large meeting room, computer room, and small study rooms were all furnished by over $100,000 in donations from a campaign lead by the Friends of the El Segundo Public Library.

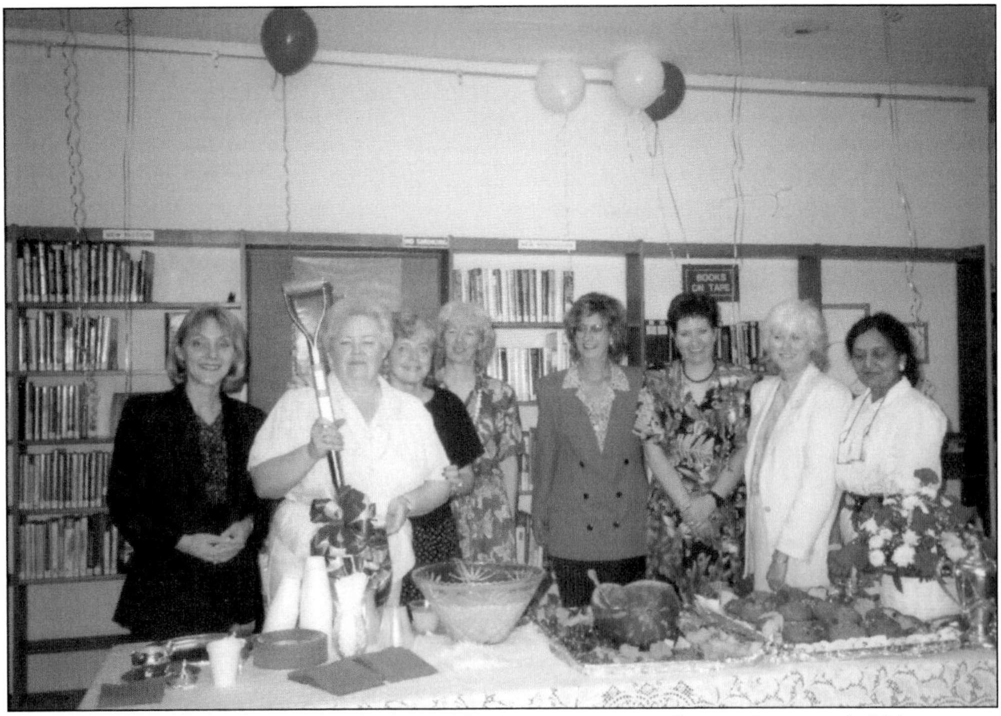

STAFF AT OPEN HOUSE, MARCH 15, 1992. Greeting visitors to the newly expanded library are, from left to right, staff members, Carey Rowan, Esther Oakleaf, Barbara Anderson, Kathleen Schweiger, director Barbara Pearson, Denise Dumars, Karen Stone, and Renuka Rami.

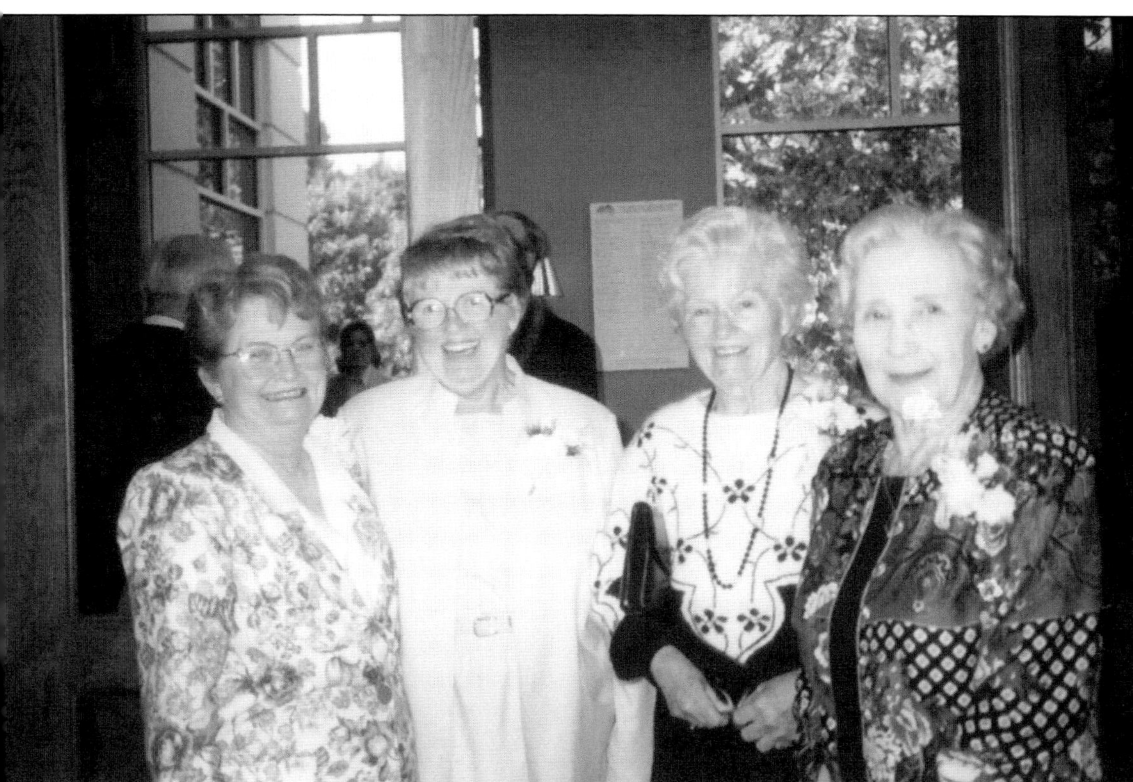

Former Library Directors in front of History Room, March 15, 1992. This very determined group of ladies greatly improved services and devoted many years to the El Segundo Public Library. From left to right are former president of the Friends of the El Segundo Public Library Sue Carter; former library director Barbara Kirby; former library director Dorothea Fitzgerald; and former assistant director Nina McCoy.

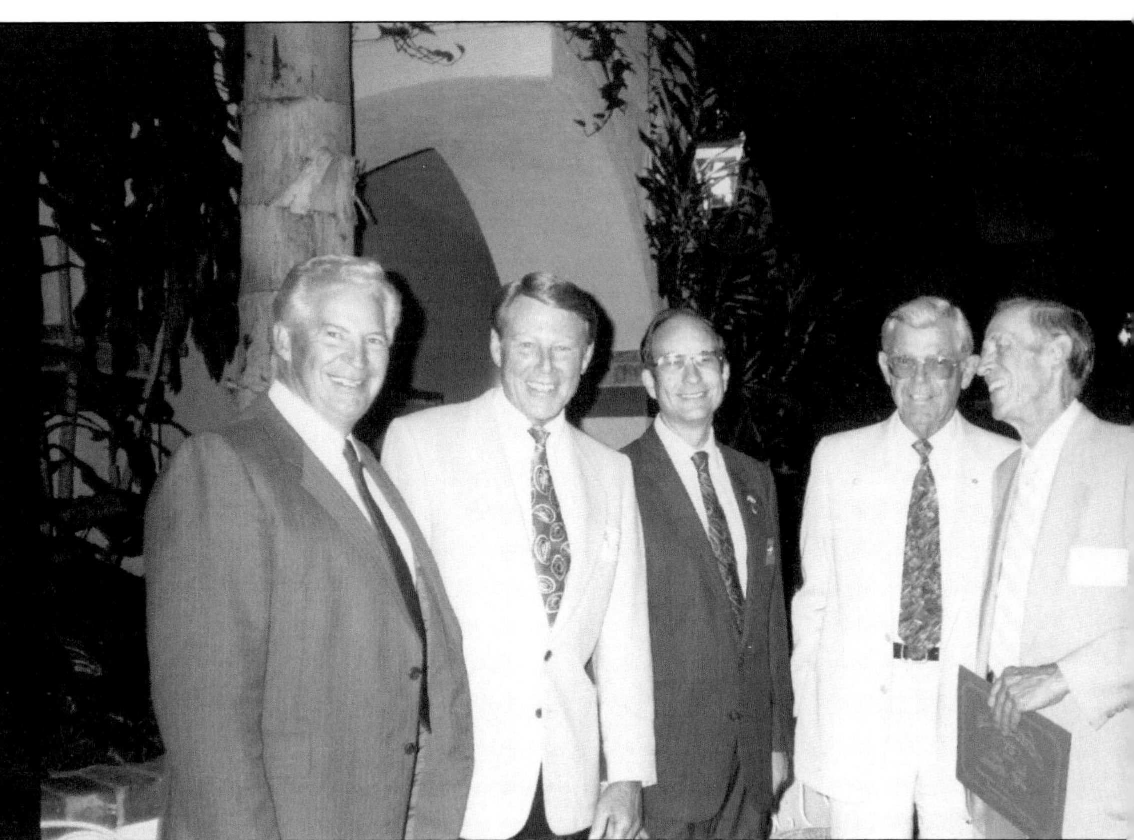

Former City Mayors, 1992. This very distinguished and elite group is made up of gentlemen who left their own legacies as mayors of El Segundo. From left to right are Gordon Stephens, Bill Bue, Carl Jacobson, Floyd Carr, and Richard Van Vranken, who was also a former president of the Rotary Club.

Six

Arriving at the City's Centennial 2000–2017

As the city heads into its centennial year in 2017, residents, workers, and even others who visit the town often can easily see the historical markers of a proud and rich heritage. The 1920s-style high school campus on Main Street is a common site for movie location sets, as are the original brick buildings from the same era along Richmond Street, including the Old Town Music Hall. Other familiar structures that have remained an integral part of historic downtown are the 1936 Lafayette Building at Grand Avenue and Main Street, the 1911 Hamburg Apartments or Showboat on Concord Street, and the Woman's Club on Mariposa Avenue, which was an elementary schoolhouse from the 1930s. Essentially, the attraction of living and working in El Segundo must be attributed to the small-town atmosphere with a strong sense of community values and participation.

In looking towards the future, there are many technology-based companies, space and defense system corporations, and a host of other Fortune 500 business leaders ensuring that El Segundo keeps pace with the dynamic changes in the world around it while also maintaining a strong and stable economic presence in the South Bay. Financial support by the local businesses, excellent schools, and the high level of safety services practiced within its borders by its own city police and fire departments are vital elements for sustaining this unique environment. For a finer quality of life, a variety of leisure activities are provided by top-notch programs from the recreation and parks and library departments. Finally, continued redevelopment and infrastructure improvements by the planning, building and public works departments demonstrate an ability to retain existing businesses and attract many new ones to town on the near horizon. All these partnerships, business and civic alike, make up a strongly committed team that strives for the best in keeping El Segundo a great city. Recently, this group effort has been more than justified a second time by winning the distinguished Annual Eddy Award title of "Most Business-Friendly City in Los Angeles County."

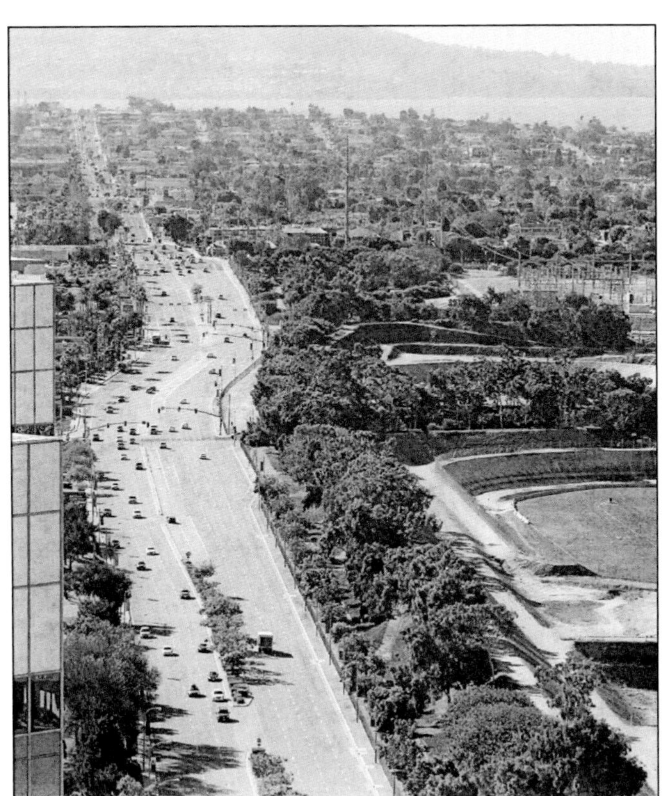

Southwest Sepulveda Boulevard, November 2015. This is one of several aerial views taken from the rooftop of 222 Sepulveda Boulevard Corporate Towers on a clear fall day. On the right, at the northwestern tip of town, is the border of Chevron Products Company up to Rosecrans Avenue. On the left side along the Sepulveda corridor are the El Segundo Golf Course, El Segundo Plaza, and Manhattan Beach Village. In the background are the other beach cities of Hermosa Beach and Redondo Beach and a view of the Palos Verdes peninsula.

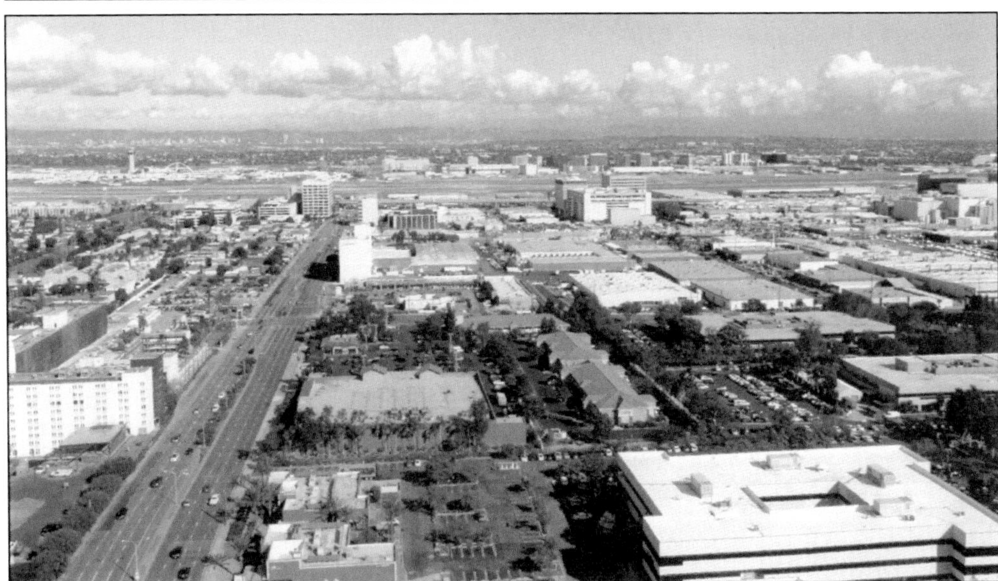

Northwest Sepulveda Boulevard, November 2015. This aerial view taken facing the opposite direction shows major businesses in El Segundo along the northeastern section. A reconstructed Hacienda Hotel will be converted to two hotels, Aloft and Fairfield Inn, pictured in the left foreground. The massive complexes of the aerospace giants Raytheon and Boeing can be seen stretching across the west end of the 105 Freeway and before the runways at Los Angeles International Airport in the right background.

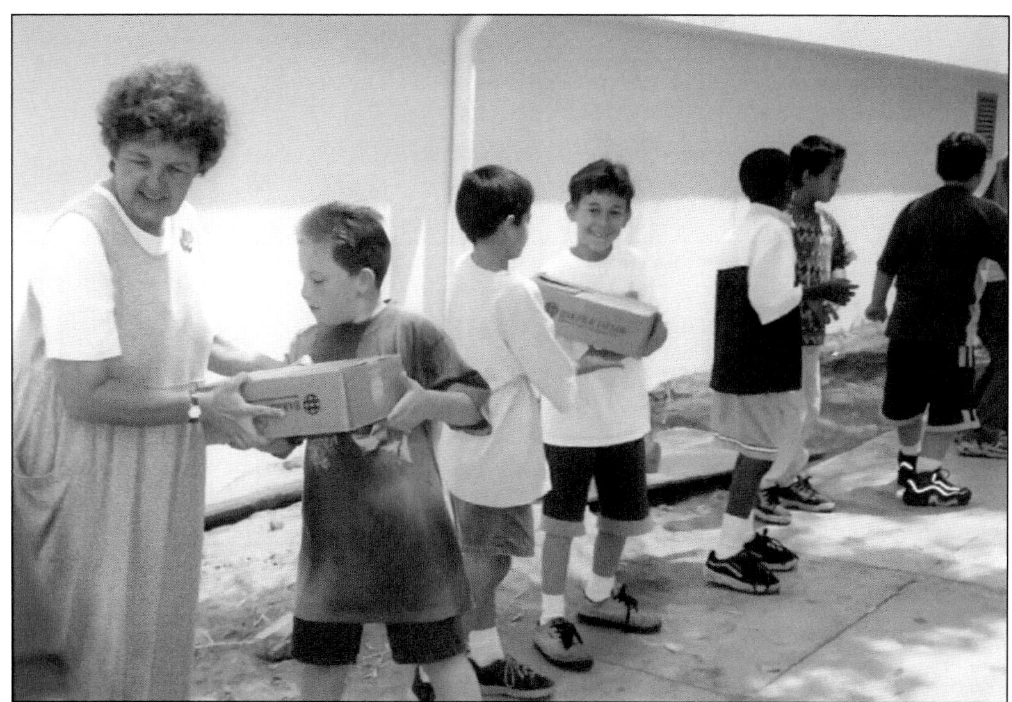

Bucks for Books Campaign, June 14, 2000. The newly renovated Richmond Street Elementary School Library needed a core collection of books and materials. Together, the Friends of the El Segundo Public Library and the El Segundo Unified School District's PTA raised enough donations to place new books in the school library for kindergarten through fifth grade. A human chain of teachers, students, and staff transferred over 200 boxes of new books that were processed and stored at the main public library across Richmond Street to the school library shelves. Pictured is teacher Nancy Trachtenberg along with some strong student helpers.

Campus El Segundo Athletic Fields, 2007. Located at 2201 East Mariposa Avenue, the Campus El Segundo Athletic Fields are operated by the city's recreation and parks department. Primarily used for soccer, lacrosse, and football, the park consists of two 100-by-65-yard synthetic turf multipurpose fields with a snack bar and restrooms.

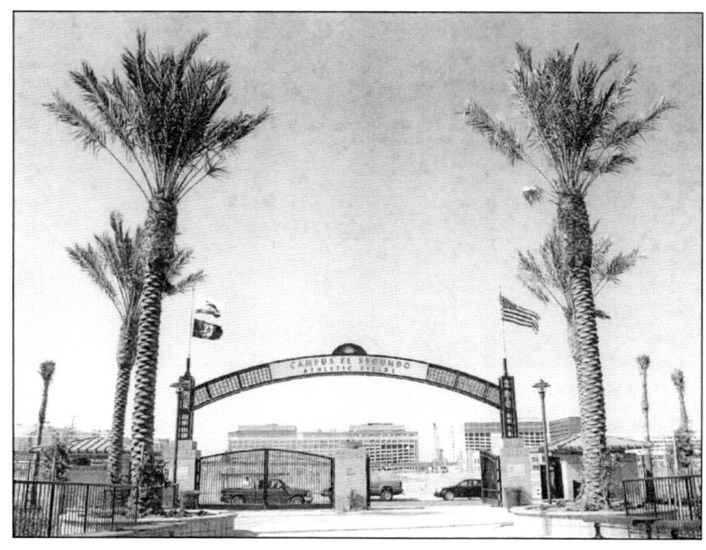

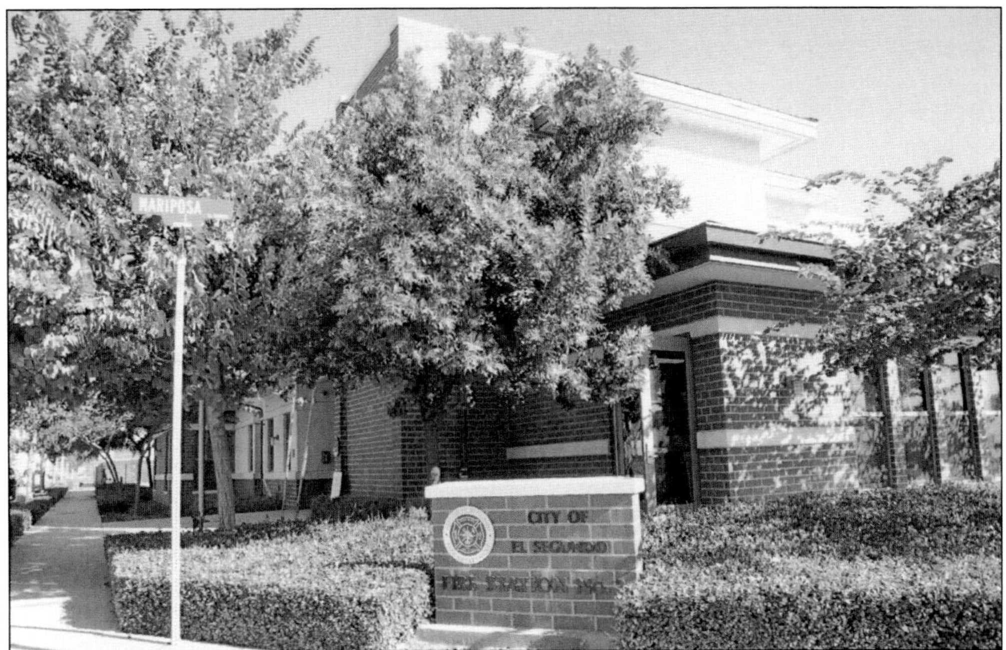

El Segundo Fire Station No. 2, 2009. A new, 14,000-square-foot, two-story fire station was completed and dedicated on December 16, 2009, to serve the emergency needs of the city's structures east of Sepulveda Boulevard. Fire Station No. 2 achieved the state-of-the-art building status of LEED Platinum. The first level includes the administration area, kitchen, dining room, training room, workout room, and three apparatus bays. The second story is where the dorm rooms house up to 10 staff members.

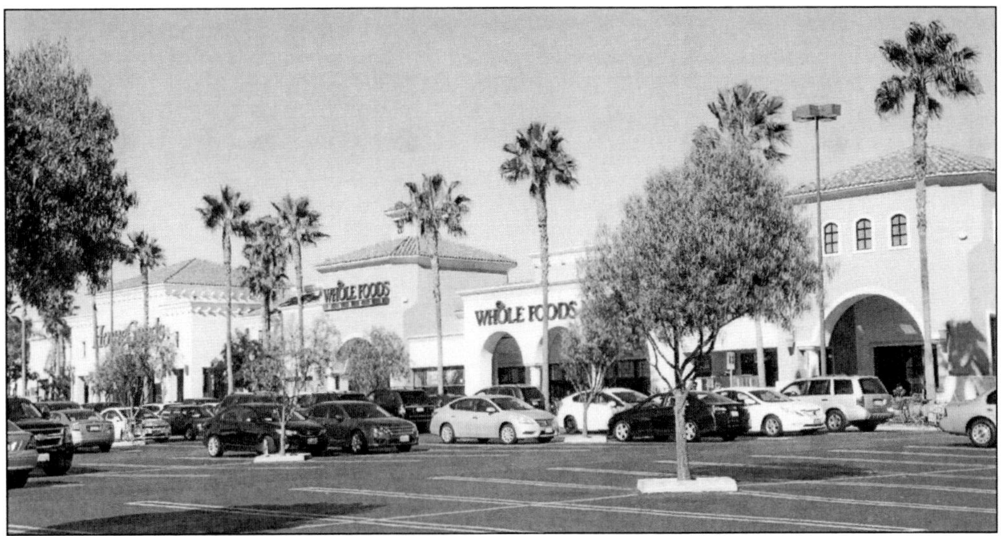

Plaza El Segundo, 2006. Plaza El Segundo was the first phase of a 107-acre retail project that greatly changed the northeast corner of Sepulveda Boulevard and Rosecrans Avenue, one of the last underdeveloped sites in the city. The land was previously owned by Allied Signal and other industrial companies that warranted cleanup of the soil and groundwater before development began. The initial tenants include Whole Foods, Best Buy, Dick's Sporting Goods, Cost Plus, PetSmart, Salt Creek Grill, Sur La Table, Lululemon, and more.

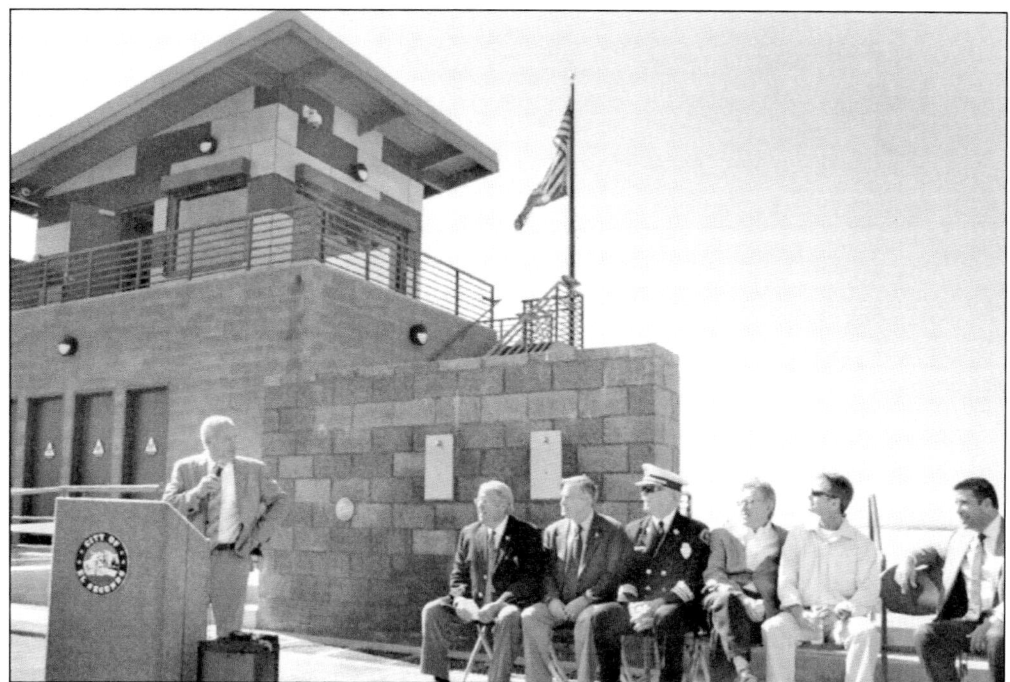

El Segundo Lifeguard Tower Dedication, August 29, 2013. In 2009, the Los Angeles County Board of Supervisors set aside $1.7 million for a lifeguard station and restrooms at El Segundo Beach, located between Playa Del Rey and the north end of Manhattan Beach's El Porto area. The facility is a combination bathroom and lifeguard station, with a two-story tower atop a vehicle and storage garage for the Junior Lifeguard Program equipment. Pictured are, from left to right, El Segundo city manager Greg Carpenter, county supervisor Don Knabe, former mayor Bill Fisher, Los Angeles County assistant fire chief Barry Nugent, Chevron representative Rod Spackman, former councilman Jim Boulgarides, and an unidentified representative.

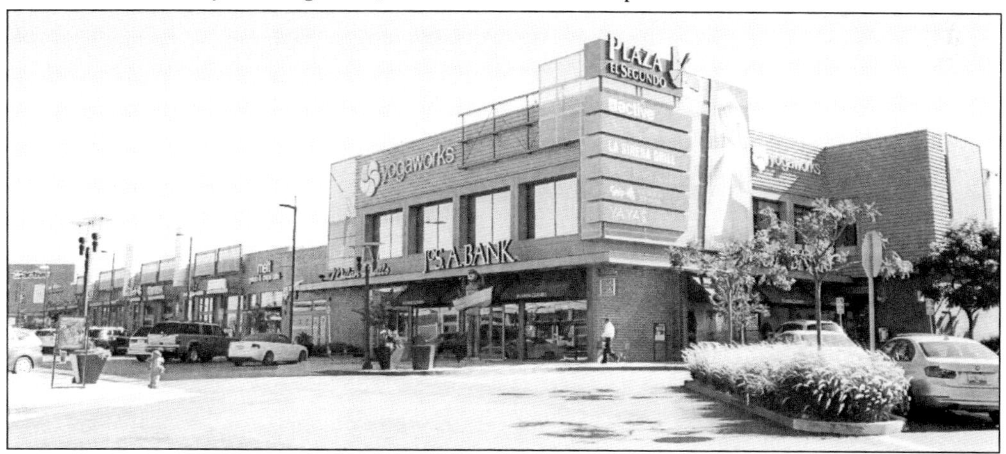

The Edge, Plaza El Segundo, 2010. The Edge was the second phase of the Plaza El Segundo development, located off of Allied Way. With approximately 21 boutique stores and eateries that are smaller than those at the Plaza El Segundo next door, it invites an outdoor strolling and shopping experience. It opened a couple of years after the Plaza El Segundo. Some of the retail establishments include Yoga Works, Jos. A. Bank, Wondertree Kids, Legacy Dance Academy, La Sirena Grill and Cantina, and California Fish Grill.

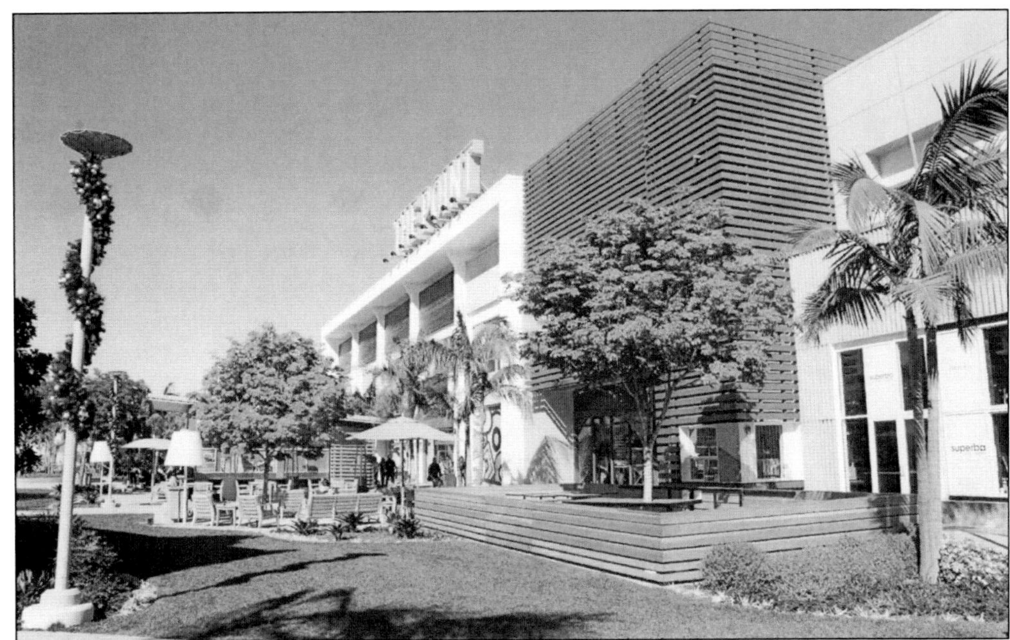

THE POINT, 2015. The final phase of the Rosecrans Avenue and Sepulveda Boulevard development is called the Point and opened in the summer of 2015, offering an expansive outdoor plaza with a fire pit, fountains and live music. The larger anchor stores and restaurants are Lucky Brand, True Food Kitchen, North Italia, Athleta, and Prana.

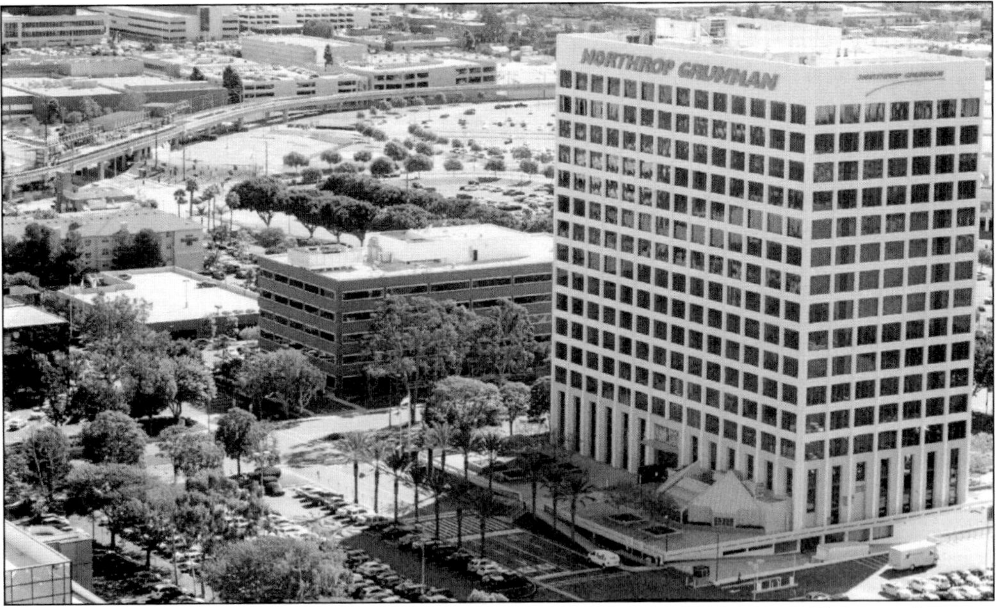

NORTHROP GRUMMAN, 2015. With a long-standing aerospace presence in El Segundo since the 1930s, starting with a partnership with Douglas Aircraft, present-day Northrop Grumman still commands a major corporate office complex at 1 Northrop Grumman Avenue, as well as many other locations throughout the South Bay. The company is ranked as a Fortune 500 firm headquartered in West Falls Church, Virginia, and its website currently lists offices in all 50 states and 21 countries; it employs 16,000 workers.

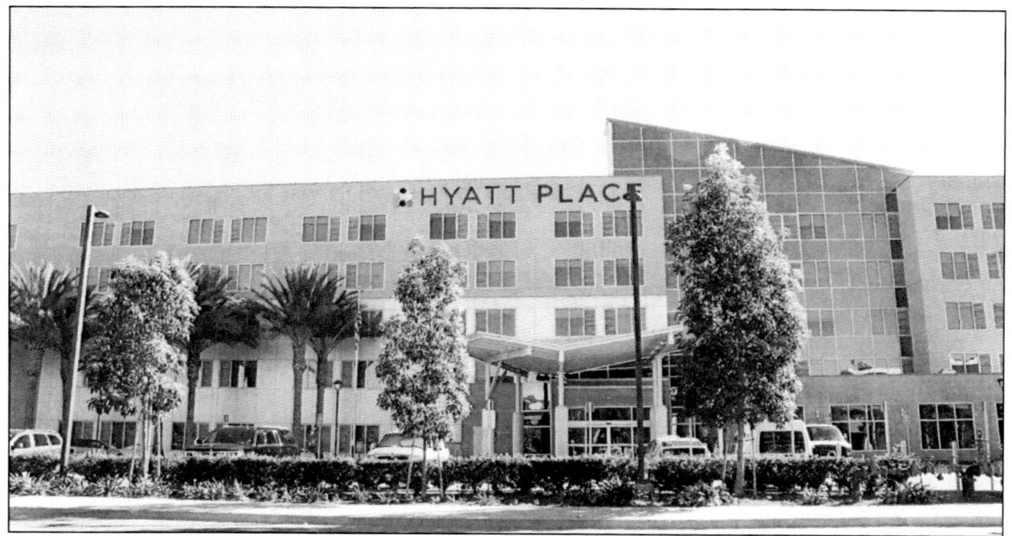

Hyatt Place, 2014. One of the newest hotels catering to business clientele is the Hyatt Place LAX El Segundo, located at 750 North Nash Street. With 143 rooms, a business center, outdoor pool, restaurant, 24-hour fitness center, and two large meeting rooms, the hotel provides easy access to local retail shops and recreational activities, and it connects guests to the Los Angeles International Airport with a free shuttle.

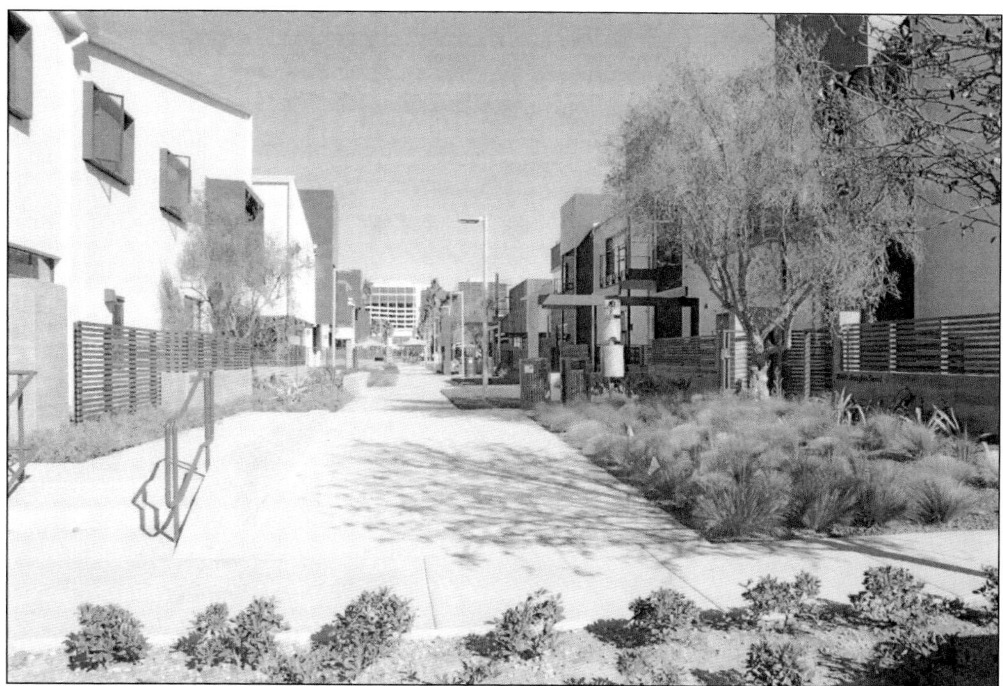

Elevon at Campus El Segundo, 2015. The $100 million, 210,000-square-foot complex developed by Continental Development Corporation and Mar Ventures is one of the largest commercial office projects to break ground in the last decade. Located at 710 North Nash Street, it is slated to bring an additional 100–200 full-time employees to the city. The Los Angeles Lakers will also have a new training facility constructed at this site, with a completion date of January 2017.

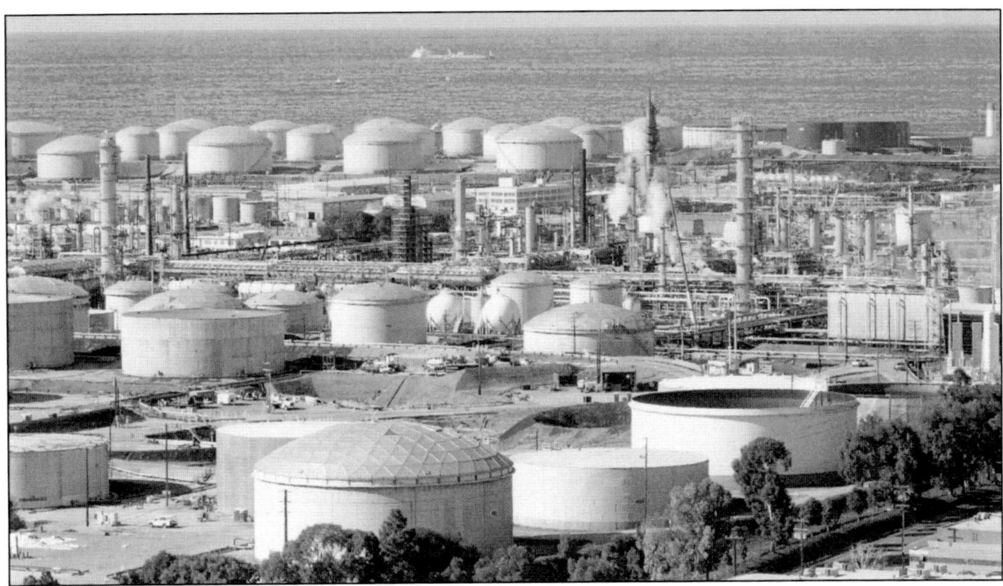

Chevron Products Company, 2015. In 2011, the Chevron El Segundo Refinery celebrated its 100th anniversary in the city. The company has employed multiple generations of families who have lived in the area for decades, and it supports strong community ties that have lasted over a century. In this view looking west, the refinery stretches from Sepulveda Boulevard to the Pacific Ocean. Its current website states that the local refinery is the "largest producing oil refinery on the west coast processing more than 274,000 barrels of transportation fuel per day."

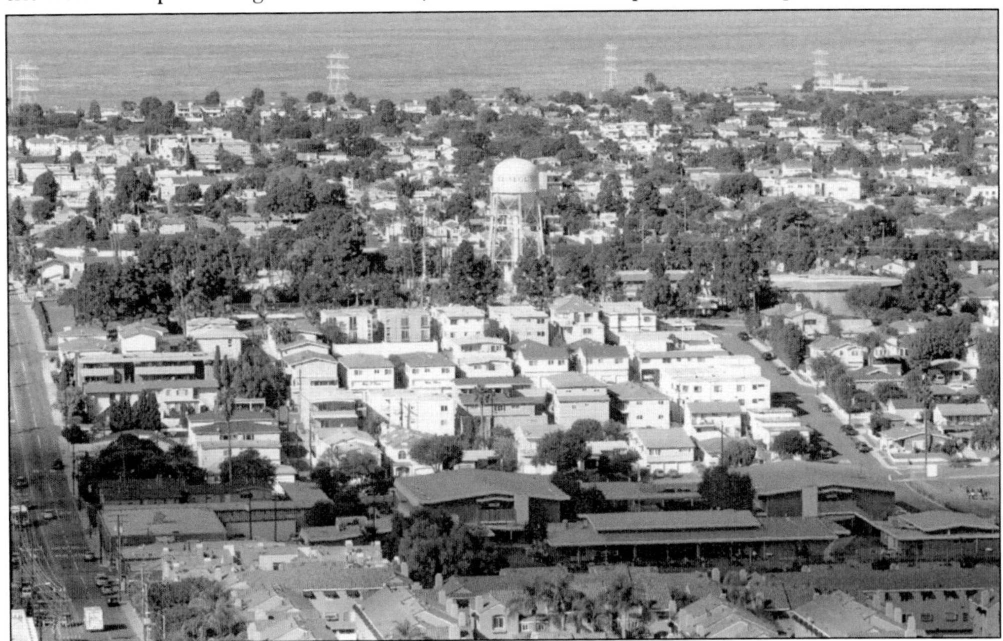

Aerial of El Segundo, November 2015. Today, the city of El Segundo has a residential population of 16,654 and a daytime employee base of 70,000 workers in small and large businesses distributed along the west and east sides of Sepulveda Boulevard. According to the 2010 census, there are 7,310 households, with a median age of 39.2 years, and 46.4 percent have bachelor's degrees or higher.

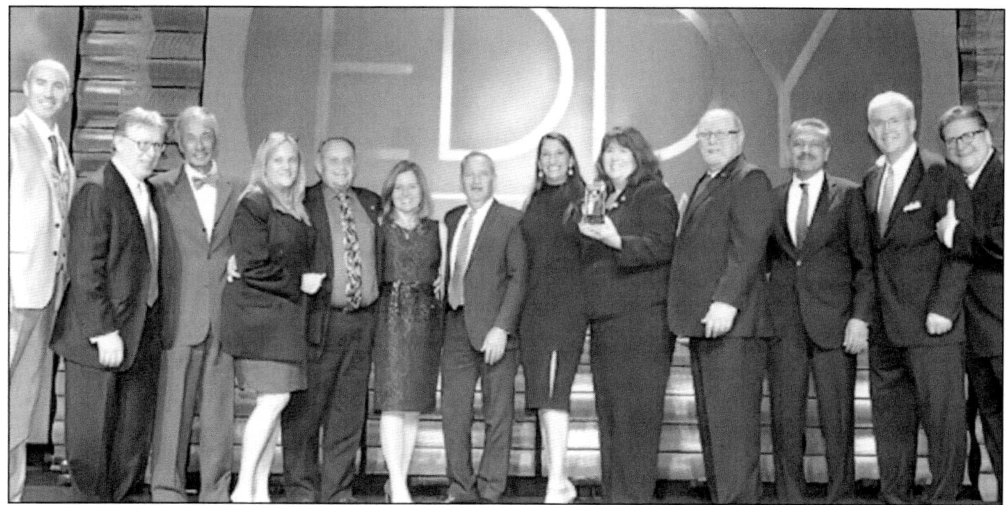

"Most Business-Friendly City in Los Angeles County," November 12, 2015. Pictured from left to right are Steve Napolitano, Rod Spackman, Al Keahi, Marsha Hansen, Councilman Dave Atkinson, Barbara Voss, city manager Greg Carpenter, Councilman Marie Fellhauer, Mayor Suzanne Fuentes, Deane Leavenworth, Praful Kulkami, Bill Allen, and Bob Hertzberg. New business developments on the horizon include a state-of-the-art golf course redevelopment project by Top Golf Corporation; a 2.1-million-square-foot South Campus project by Raytheon; Hampton Inn and a Cambria Hotel project; an EVA Airways Campus; and a new Lakers training facility at 199 North Continental Boulevard.

Bibliography

Chevron El Segundo Refinery. *Chevron El Segundo Refinery: Energizing California for 100 Years.* El Segundo, CA, 2011.

El Segundo Chamber of Commerce. *2015 Community and Business Directory.* El Segundo, CA: Atlantic West Publishers, Inc., 2015.

Hunter, Eileen C. *El Segundo Seventy-Five Years: A Pictorial History of El Segundo, California.* El Segundo, CA: H2 Limited, Publishers, 1991.

Mulcahy, Robert. *The Douglas Aircraft Plant That Became Los Angeles Air Force Base.* El Segundo, CA: Space and Missile Systems Center, Los Angeles Air Force Base, 2012.

Standard Oil Company of California. *1879–1979: One Hundred Years Helping to Create the Future.* San Francisco: Pisani Carlisle Graphics, 1979.

"Technology at Work." *Boeing Frontiers* (May 2015): Front Cover Photograph.

White, Gerald T. *Formative Years in the Far West: A History of Standard Oil Company of California and Predecessors Through 1919.* New York: Appleton-Century-Crofts, 1962.

Consistent with our mission to preserve history on a local level, this book was printed in South Carolina on American-made paper and manufactured entirely in the United States. Products carrying the accredited Forest Stewardship Council (FSC) label are printed on 100 percent FSC-certified paper.

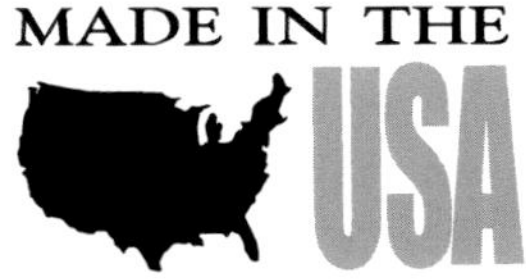